FORTY-ONE FALSE STARTS

JANET MALCOLM

FORTY-ONE FALSE STARTS

Essays on Artists and Writers

Farrar, Straus and Giroux   New York

Farrar, Straus and Giroux
18 West 18th Street, New York 10011

The essays in this volume originally appeared in the following publications: *The New York Review of Books*: "Salinger's Cigarettes," "Capitalist Pastorale," "The Genius of the Glass House," "Good Pictures," "Edward Weston's Women," "Nudes Without Desire," "The Not Returning Part of It," "Thoughts on Autobiography from an Abandoned Autobiography"; *The New York Times Book Review*: "The Woman Who Hated Women"; *The New Yorker*: "Forty-one False Starts," "Depth of Field," "A House of One's Own," "A Girl of the Zeitgeist," "Advanced Placement," "William Shawn," "Joseph Mitchell."

The Library of Congress has cataloged the hardcover edition as follows:
Malcolm, Janet.
    Forty-one false starts : essays on artists and writers / Janet
Malcolm. — 1st ed.
        p.   cm.
    ISBN 978-0-374-15769-2 (hardcover)
    1. Authors.   2. Artists.   3. Authorship.   I. Title.

PN453 .M35 2013
808.02—dc23
                                                    2012034570

Paperback ISBN: 978-0-374-53458-5

Farrar, Straus and Giroux books may be purchased for educational, business, or promotional use. For information on bulk purchases, please contact the Macmillan Corporate and Premium Sales Department at 1-800-221-7945, extension 5442, or write to specialmarkets@macmillan.com.

Designed by Jonathan D. Lippincott

www.fsgbooks.com
www.twitter.com/fsgbooks • www.facebook.com/fsgbooks

To the memory of Gardner

CONTENTS

INTRODUCTION

by Ian Frazier

Janet Malcolm is a wild writer. A first-time reader of her work might not expect this, given the carefully described domestic scenes where many of her journalistic dramas begin. Early in her career she wrote a column for *The New Yorker* called About the House, which discussed the beauty of simplicity, among other related subjects, and sharpened her eye for interiors. If you go back today and read those columns in light of her later pieces they somehow seem also to shimmer with a rich and possibly sinister foreshadowing. A lot of journalism is a bedtime story you are sleepily hearing for the hundredth time, but with a piece by Janet Malcolm you never know where things will lead. I have read pieces in which I watch her make a swerve, and I straighten up in my chair and gasp and try to correct her errant and scary course with body English, as if I were sitting at a hotel window watching a car drive calmly up an off-ramp. The chance of being taken completely by surprise keeps you alert through everything she writes. That she is smarter than almost everybody goes without saying; plus, I know of no other nonfiction writer who can be more hair-raisingly fun to read.

Once I interviewed Ms. Malcolm onstage at the New Yorker Festival. The large audience was full of people who knew her work well, as I could tell by the texture of their listening quiet. During the questions period someone asked about the first sentence of her book *The Journalist and the Murderer*, a work that examines the relationship between Jeffrey MacDonald, a man convicted of a terrible crime, and

Joe McGinniss, the writer who befriended MacDonald and wrote a book about him. The sentence is, "Every journalist who is not too stupid or too full of himself to notice what is going on knows that what he does is morally indefensible." (And by the way, this is a rare example of a Malcolm piece in which the wild ride starts at the first word.) I had figured a question about the sentence was likely to come up, because it is probably the most widely known sentence she ever wrote, and one of the most discussed in all modern nonfiction. The questioner said he disagreed with it and he asked her to explain it.

Honestly, the sentence had freaked me out, too, when I read it the first time. Back then I had reacted to it with indignation. Later I realized how subtle it was, and that it had a real point. To the questioner at the event Ms. Malcolm replied that the sentence could be taken as a premise, a proposal for debate. What had brought me up short about the statement originally was that it could be proposed at all. I guess I had assumed that as a writer I was exempt from moral scrutiny. But to write is to judge, if only implicitly, and a judge is also getting something out of the transaction, and can be judged himself, and may actually be doing something indefensible. The interesting question that *The Journalist and the Murderer* posed was whether a writer has any obligation to a subject whose crime puts him outside the world of decent people. Is it okay for a writer to betray someone the writer is writing about, when that someone is a depraved murderer? The interesting conclusion turns out to be that it is not.

Moral questions of such weight set many of Ms. Malcolm's plots in motion and get people careening around and crashing into one another and implicate the reader and sometimes the writer, too. Throughout her work she follows, quietly and unassumingly, what she has called "the spectre of wrongdoing." The pursuit takes her through domestic and social and cultural arrangements of all kinds, willy-nilly, as if she were one of those outdoor enthusiasts who follow lines of latitude or longitude guided by handheld GPS and regardless of what is in their way.

This collection, Ms. Malcolm's first since *The Purloined Clinic: Selected Writings* (1992), brings together a wide range of pieces that display her unique skills. To cite just one: she is the best describer of mess and chaos working today. In fact, I can't think of a better one ever. Her patience for confusion and her due deliberation in sorting it out are—I don't know—Augustinian? (I'm thinking of a section in *The Confessions of St. Augustine* where he parses the doctrinal errors of the Manicheans.) Ms. Malcolm can descend into mind-numbing chaos and depict its elements severally and collectively and bring order to it as if she were swooping in and out on one of those grand old-time dolly shots in the movies. A good big mess activates her powers to the full. In this book a fine example is her elucidation of the controversy around the installation of Richard Serra's sculpture *Tilted Arc* in the plaza of a federal office building in lower Manhattan some years ago. When she takes on something complicated and messy like that I always want a front-row seat.

Ms. Malcolm's quick and precise sketching of interiors and related domestic details—note her double and triple takes as she tries to register the art-designed neutral immaculateness of the studio of David Salle—is another reliable pleasure of this collection, as is the focus she brings to writing about people who happen to be a bit nuts. Perhaps because her father was a psychiatrist she has a fondness for nuts, and they turn up throughout her work; examples here are her picture of Julia Margaret Cameron, the Victorian-era photographer, and of Gene (Geneva) Stratton-Porter, author of *A Girl of the Limberlost*, who wrote sweet-natured popular novels extolling material comforts a hundred years ago and who also as a side interest worked out intricate and awful theories of racial purity.

One of Ms. Malcolm's recurring themes examines the hazards of portraiture. Being so careful and self-aware and circumspect with her own human subjects, she waxes irate at the large number of writers who aren't. Anyone planning to write a biography should first read Janet Malcolm to get an idea of how the process usually goes wrong. When she notes that "biographical research leads to a kind of insufferable familiarity," she defines the one-way relationship between the mute, helpless, dead biographee and the all-too-alive biographer. Simply, and sensibly, Ms. Malcolm favors hewing to the subject's own words and surviving documents; as she points out, biography "(like its progenitor, history) functions as a kind of processing plant where experience is converted into information the way fresh produce is converted into canned vegetables. But, like canned vegetables, biographical narratives are so far removed from their source—so altered from the plant with soil clinging to its roots that is a letter or a diary entry—that they carry little conviction."

When I interviewed Ms. Malcolm at the festival she had just published her piece about Thomas Struth, one of the most successful art photographers in the world ("Depth of Field"). Much of the piece is about Struth's photographing Queen Elizabeth and Prince Philip for an exhibition celebrating her sixty years as queen. Everybody loves Struth, and Ms. Malcolm's portrait of a portraitist came up against the rather unfamiliar problem (for her) of a subject who is brilliant, widely liked, and completely nice.

A questioner at the festival event asked her about a small part of the piece in which Struth mentions some influential teachers of his who emphasized connections across art forms, like "the Paris photographs of Atget as the visualization of Marcel Proust." In the piece Ms. Malcolm had not let this go by, but asked Struth how Atget's photographs relate to Proust. It turns out that for Struth they don't, really, because he had never read Proust. No big deal, everybody says fancy-sounding stuff like that from time to time—it's a sort of background noise for cultured people. Ms. Malcolm's questioner asked why she chose to include this minor exchange, which made Struth look slightly ridiculous and seemed unfair. She stood by it as an important part of her picture. And it is—at the level of fabulousness where Struth operates there's a risk of everything becoming so wonderful and nice that meaninglessness sets in. Not leaving out the Atget-Proust conversation gave a final optical adjustment to the image of herself as well as of him and added her maker's mark to the piece.

Although Ms. Malcolm writes nonfiction, most of these pieces are devoted to other art forms—painting, photography, fiction—as well as to editing, an aspect of writing that she considers an art in itself. This breadth shows the size of her ambition. For a work of nonfiction to be really good it must compete in the "open" category;

that is, it can't justify itself merely by fulfilling its important journalistic task of informing the reader; it has to aspire to be art, whatever that is and however one aspires to it. In the title essay, Ms.
Malcolm takes her lead from the accumulative style of David Salle's
paintings, a body of work that strikes her as "unprecedented, like a
new drug or a new crime." Salle's art "refuses to narrate"; he says he
is "bored by plot." His painting is informed by absences, by what is
left out or scratched out; she chooses a similarly nervous and impatient approach to describing him and his work, progressing by repetition, revision, erasure, and stopping whenever she feels she is
heading into an area that might be sort of dead. The style makes for
an exhilarating and new form of reporting, where part of the plot
becomes whether this way of describing someone will succeed, and
the resolution is that it does.

Will Rogers's famous advice, "Never miss a good chance to shut
up," goes unheeded nowadays, when most of us express ourselves
aplenty. Against that trend, Ms. Malcolm is a writer of eloquent omis-
sion. Tolerant of enormous boredom while pursuing her research,
she has a dread of inflicting any particle of it on the reader. Deadness, dullness, the "autistic" and monotonous quality of memory—
all are out there, waiting to sap the life out of art. Taken together,
the pieces collected here comprise a how-to for avoiding anything
that is, as Salinger's Glass family might say, "fishy." Ms. Malcolm
watches for fishiness and finds it in unexpected places, even a little bit
in Salinger himself, whose Glass stories she faults (rightly, I think)
for condescension in his sentimental paean to "the Fat Lady." She
suggests he would've done well to bail out of that particular para-
graph a few lines earlier. Her pieces detail an aesthetic arrayed
resolutely against what she calls "the pretentiousness, intellectual
shallowness, moral murkiness, and aesthetic limpness that come
naturally to the pen."

Personally, I like to lapse into pretentiousness and intellectual
shallowness once in a while. I find them occasionally relaxing, like
the journalistic bedtime stories I mentioned above. Or rather, I in-
dulge such failings when they're my own, but in other people they
drive me crazy. Reading these pieces in search of a one-word anti-
dote to bogus art—maybe a bogus search in itself, but I am a fix-it

type of person; I couldn't resist—I came across a possible candidate in "Good Pictures," the essay about Diane Arbus and her photographs. While struggling with the tough job of photographing a wealthy Manhattan family, Arbus was able to get a good picture of only one family member, the eleven-year-old daughter, who, Ms. Malcolm says, went along with Arbus's "project of defamiliarization." The word does not appear in my dictionary, but it should. (In fact, it is a concept of Russian formalist literary theory dating from 1925.) Defamiliarization, as I imagine it, is what every artist strives for. You take what people think they see or know and make them see it or know it afresh. Defamiliarization is what Julia Margaret Cameron does when she roughly musses the hair of children she is about to photograph so they won't look the way Victorian children usually do. Defamiliarization provides the magic charm when Edith Wharton deprives her best fiction of predictable contemporary background, and it's Irving Penn's goal when he subjects his photographs of nudes to darkroom ordeals that render them flat and abstract and almost unrecognizable, and it's in Ms. Malcolm's own scrupulous self-awareness, when she sometimes steps back and describes a misgiving she has about the work in progress, so that the reader may revisualize the scene and understand its artificiality.

When a good jolt of defamiliarization knocks the rust off your perceptions, you don't forget. Usually the result is delight. Of the many places in this collection where I saw something anew and got a kick out of it, I refer the reader to Ms. Malcolm's description of Ingrid Sischy, editor of *Artforum* magazine, chopping tomatoes. Going about the task in "the most inefficient manner imaginable," Ms. Sischy proceeds to fill a bowl painstakingly with tiny pieces; obviously she has never been taught a better approach, but she's undiscouraged by any inexperience. Ms. Malcolm concludes, "She is less afraid than anyone I have ever met of expending energy unnecessarily." I have cut tomatoes in just that way and seen other unskilled people do it, but until I read that description I'd observed it only out of the corner of my eye. It's not the kind of activity a reporter usually records; I laughed when this piece made me notice it straight on for the first time.

Journalism that succeeds as art usually does not appear to be art in its presentation. The surface appearance of a work of journalism is humbler, more routine, more daily, as per the etymology of the word "journalism." Such works do not announce themselves as belonging to any capitalized arts category, like Sculpture or Painting or the Novel or the Dance. When a work of journalism is also art its surface is almost like a red herring. A jury-rigged term such as "faux ordinary" might describe it. Through forty years of writing nonfiction Ms. Malcolm has kept in mind a higher purpose of artistic and moral rigor, and it has been thrillingly productive of art. In "A House of One's Own," her essay about the lives and aesthetics of Bloomsbury, she says its members exhibited "the values by which Chekhov's good characters are ruled: patient, habitual work and sensible, calm behavior." This is how she herself lives and writes. Her work has put her among the masters of modern nonfiction, like Joseph Mitchell, A. J. Liebling, Truman Capote, and John McPhee. Over and over she has demonstrated that nonfiction—a book of reporting, an article in a magazine, something we see every day—can rise to the highest level of literature.

FORTY-ONE FALSE STARTS

FORTY-ONE FALSE STARTS

1994

1

There are places in New York where the city's anarchic, unaccommodating spirit, its fundamental, irrepressible aimlessness and heedlessness have found especially firm footholds. Certain transfers between subway lines, passageways of almost transcendent sordidness; certain sites of torn-down buildings where parking lots have silently sprung up like fungi; certain intersections created by illogical confluences of streets—these express with particular force the city's penchant for the provisional and its resistance to permanence, order, closure. To get to the painter David Salle's studio, walking west on White Street, you have to traverse one of these disquieting intersections—that of White and Church Streets and an interloping Sixth Avenue—which has created an unpleasantly wide expanse of street to cross, interrupted by a wedge-shaped island on which a commercial plant nursery has taken up forlorn and edgy residence, surrounding itself with a high wire fence and keeping truculently irregular hours. Other businesses that have arisen around the intersection—the seamy Baby Doll Lounge, with its sign offering GO-GO GIRLS; the elegant Ristorante Arquà; the nameless grocery and Lotto center; the dour Kinney parking lot—have a similar atmosphere of insularity and transience. Nothing connects with anything else, and everything looks as if it might disappear overnight. The corner feels like a no man's land and—if one happens to be thinking about David Salle—looks like one of his paintings.

Salle's studio, on the second floor of a five-story loft building, is a long room lit with bright, cold overhead light. It is not a beautiful studio. Like the streets outside, it gives no quarter to the visitor in search of the picturesque. It doesn't even have a chair for the visitor to sit in, unless you count a backless, half-broken metal swivel chair Salle will offer with a murmur of inattentive apology. Upstairs, in his living quarters, it is another story. But down here everything has to do with work and with being alone.

A disorderly profusion of printed pictorial matter covers the surfaces of tables in the middle of the room: art books, art journals, catalogs, brochures mingle with loose illustrations, photographs, odd pictures ripped from magazines. Scanning these complicated surfaces, the visitor feels something of the sense of rebuff he feels when looking at Salle's paintings, a sense that this is all somehow none of one's business. Here lie the sources of Salle's postmodern art of "borrowed" or "quoted" images—the reproductions of famous old and modern paintings, the advertisements, the comics, the photographs of nude or half-undressed women, the fabric and furniture designs that he copies and puts into his paintings—but one's impulse, as when coming into a room of Salle's paintings, is to politely look away. Salle's hermeticism, the private, almost secretive nature of his interests and tastes and intentions, is a signature of his work. Glancing at the papers he has made no effort to conceal gives one the odd feeling of having broken into a locked desk drawer.

On the walls of the studio are five or six canvases, on which Salle works simultaneously. In the winter of 1992, when I began visiting him in his studio, he was completing a group of paintings for a show in Paris in April. The paintings had a dense, turgid character. Silk-screen excerpts from Indian architectural ornaments, chair designs, and photographic images of a woman wrapped in cloth were overlaid with drawings of some of the forms in Duchamp's *The Bride Stripped Bare by Her Bachelors, Even*, rendered in slashing, ungainly brushstrokes, together with images of coils of rope, pieces of fruit, and eyes. Salle's earlier work had been marked by a kind of spaciousness, sometimes an emptiness, such as surrealist works are prone to. But here everything was condensed, impacted, mired. The paintings were like an ugly mood. Salle himself, a slight, handsome man with shoulder-length hair, which he wears tied back, like a matador, was feeling bloody-minded. He was going to be forty the following September. He had broken up with his girlfriend, the choreographer and dancer Karole Armitage. His moment was passing. Younger painters were receiving attention. He was being passed over. But he was also being attacked. He was not looking forward to the Paris show. He hated Paris, with its "heavily subsidized aestheticism." He disliked his French dealer . . .

2

In a 1991 interview with the screenwriter Becky Johnston, during a discussion of what Johnston impatiently called "this whole Neo-Expressionist Zeitgeist Postmodernist What-ever-you-want-to-call-it Movement" and its habit of "constantly looking backward and reworking or recontextualizing art history," the painter David Salle said, with disarming frankness, "You mustn't underestimate the extent to which all this was a process of educating ourselves. Our generation was pathetically educated, just pathetic beyond imagination. I was better educated than many. Julian"—the painter Julian Schnabel—"was totally uneducated. But I wasn't much better, frankly. We had to educate ourselves in a hundred different ways. Because if you had been hanging around the Conceptual artists, all you learned was the Frankfurt School. It was as if nothing existed before or after. So part of it was the pledge of self-education—you know, going to Venice, looking at great paintings, looking at great architecture, looking at great furniture—and having very early the opportunity to kind of buy stuff. That's a form of self-education. It's not just about acquisition. It was a tremendous explosion of information and knowledge."

To kind of buy stuff. What is the difference between buying stuff and kind of buying it? Is "kind of buying" buying with a bad conscience, buying with the ghost of the Frankfurt School grimly looking over your shoulder and smiting its forehead as it sees the money actually leave your hand? This ghost, or some relative of it, has hung over all the artists who, like Salle, made an enormous amount of money in the eighties, when they were still in their twenties or barely in their thirties. In the common perception, there is something unseemly about young people getting rich. Getting rich is supposed to be the reward for hard work, preferably arriving when you are too old to enjoy it. And the spectacle of young millionaires who made their bundle not from business or crime but from avant-garde art is particularly offensive. The avant-garde is supposed to be the conscience of the culture, not its id.

3

All during my encounter with the artist David Salle—he and I met for interviews in his studio, on White Street, over a period of two years—I was acutely conscious of his money. Even when I got to know him and like him, I couldn't dispel the disapproving, lefty, puritanical feeling that would somehow be triggered each time we met, whether it was by the sight of the assistant at a sort of hair-salon receptionist's station outside the studio door; or by the expensive furniture of a fifties corporate style in the upstairs loft where he lives; or by the mineral water he would bring out during our talks and pour into white paper cups, which promptly lost their take-out-counter humbleness and assumed the hauteur of the objects in the design collection of the Museum of Modern Art.

Salle was one of the fortunate art stars of the eighties—young men and women plucked from semi-poverty and transformed into millionaires by genies disguised as art dealers. The idea of a rich avant-garde has never sat well with members of my generation. Serious artists, as we know them or like to think of them, are people who get by but do not have a lot of money. They live with second or third wives or husbands and with children from the various marriages, and they go to Cape Cod in the summer. Their apartments are filled with faded Persian carpets and cat-clawed sofas and beautiful and odd objects bought before anyone else saw their beauty. Salle's loft was designed by an architect. Everything in it is sleek, cold, expensive, unused. A slight sense of quotation marks hovers in the air, but it is very slight—it may not even be there—and it doesn't dispel the atmosphere of dead-serious connoisseurship by which the room is dominated.

4

During one of my visits to the studio of the artist David Salle, he told me that he never revises. Every brushstroke is irrevocable. He doesn't correct or repaint, ever. He works under the dire conditions of performance. Everything counts, nothing may be taken back, everything must always go relentlessly forward, and a mistake may be fatal. One day, he showed me a sort of murdered painting. He had worked on it a little too long, taken a misstep, killed it.

5

The artist David Salle and I are sitting at a round table in my apartment. He is a slight, handsome man of thirty-nine, with dark shoulder-length hair worn tightly sleeked back and bound with a rubber band, accentuating his appearance of quickness and lightness, of being sort of streamlined. He wears elegant, beautifully polished shoes and speaks in a low, cultivated voice. His accent has no trace of the Midwest, where he grew up, the son of second-generation Russian Jewish parents. It has no affectation, either. He is agreeable, ironic, a little detached. "I can't remember what we talked about last time," he says. "I have no memory. I remember making the usual artist's complaints about critics, and then saying, 'Well, that's terribly boring, we don't want to be stuck talking about that'—and then talking about that. I had a kind of bad feeling afterward. I felt inadequate."

6

The artist David Salle and I met for the first time in the fall of 1991. A few months earlier, we had spoken on the telephone about a mystifying proposal of his: that I write the text for a book of reproductions of his paintings, to be published by Rizzoli. When I told him there must be some mistake, that I was not an art historian or an art critic and had but the smallest acquaintance with his work, he said no, there wasn't a mistake. He was deliberately looking for someone outside the art world, for an "interesting writer" who would write an unconventional text. As he talked, I found myself reluctant to say no to him then and there, even though I knew I would eventually have to refuse. Something about the man made me say I would think about it. He then said that to acquaint me with his work and with himself, he would send some relevant writings. A few days later, a stylish package arrived, preceded by a telephone call from an assistant at Salle's studio to arrange the details of the delivery. It contained three or four exhibition catalogs, several critical articles, and various published interviews, together with a long interview that was still in typescript but was bound in a hard black cover. It was by the screenwriter Becky Johnston, who, I later learned, was an "interesting writer" Salle had previously approached to do the Rizzoli book. She had done the interview in preparation for the text but had never written it.

7

David Salle's art has an appearance of mysterious, almost preternatural originality, and yet nothing in it is new; everything has had a previous life elsewhere—in master paintings, advertising art, comics, photographs. Other artists have played the game of appropriation or quotation that Salle plays—Duchamp, Schwitters, Ernst, Picabia, Rauschenberg, Warhol, Johns—but none with such reckless inventiveness. Salle's canvases are like bad parodies of the Freudian unconscious. They are full of images that don't belong together: a woman taking off her clothes, the Spanish Armada, a kitschy fabric design, an eye.

8

David Salle is recognized as the leading American postmodernist painter. He is the most authoritative exemplar of the movement, which has made a kind of mockery of art history, treating the canon of world art as if it were a gigantic dog-eared catalog crammed with tempting buys and equipped with a helpful twenty-four-hour-a-day 800 number. Salle's selections from the catalog have a brilliant perversity. Nothing has an obvious connection to anything else, and everything glints with irony and a sort of icy melancholy. His jarring juxtapositions of incongruous images and styles point up with special sharpness the paradox on which their art of appropriated matter is poised: its mysterious, almost preternatural appearance of *originality.* After one looks at a painting by Salle, works of normal signature-style art—paintings done in a single style with an intelligible thematic—begin to seem pale and meager, kind of played out. Paintings like Salle's—the unabashed products of, if not vandalism, a sort of cold-eyed consumerism—are entirely free of any "anxiety of influence." For all their borrowings, they seem unprecedented, like a new drug or a new crime. They are rootless, fatherless and motherless.

9

The artist David Salle has given so many interviews, has been the subject of so many articles, has become so widely inscribed as an emblematic figure of the eighties art world that it is no longer possible to do a portrait of him simply from life. The heavy shadow of prior encounters with journalists and critics falls over each fresh encounter. Every writer has come too late; no writer escapes the sense of Bloomian belatedness that the figure of Salle evokes. One cannot behave as if one had just met him, and Salle himself behaves like the curator of a sort of museum of himself, helpfully guiding visitors through the exhibition rooms and steering them toward the relevant literature. At the Gagosian Gallery on Madison Avenue, where he exhibits, there is a two-and-a-half-foot-long file drawer devoted exclusively to published writings about Salle's art and person.

My own encounter with Salle was most heavily shadowed by the interviews he had given two writers, Peter Schjeldahl and Becky Johnston. Reading their dialogues with him was like listening to conversations between brilliant characters in a hastily written but inspired play of advanced ideas and intense, slightly mysterious relationships.

10

The specter of wrongdoing hovers more luridly over visual art than over literature or music. The forger, the pornographer, and the fraud

are stock figures in the allegory that constitutes the popular conception of the art world as a place of exciting evil and cunning. The
artist David Salle has the distinction of being associated with all
three crimes. His paintings are filled with "borrowed" images (twice
he has settled out of court with irked owners); often contain drawings of naked or half-undressed women standing or lying in inde-
cent, if not especially arousing, positions; and have an appearance of
messy disjunction that could be dismissed (and has been dismissed
by Hilton Kramer, Robert Hughes, and Arthur Danto) as inepti-
tude palming itself off as advanced art. Most critics, however, have
without hesitation accepted Salle's work as advanced art, and some
of them—Peter Schjeldahl, Sanford Schwartz, Michael Brenson,
Robert Rosenblum, Lisa Liebmann, for example—have celebrated
its transgressive quality and placed his paintings among the works
that most authoritatively express our time and are apt to become its
permanent monuments.

11

Unlike David Salle's enigmatic, difficult art, his life is the banal
story of a boy who grew up in Wichita, Kansas, in a poorish Jewish
family, took art lessons throughout his childhood, went to art
school in California, came to New York, and became rich and famous overnight.

12

During an interview with the artist David Salle, published in 1987,
the critic and poet Peter Schjeldahl said to him:

> I've noticed, looking at your work attentively for six years or
> so, a repeating phenomenon, that of going away from seeing
> your things extremely stimulated and with vivid memories,
> and thought processes that seem to continue on their own,
> but eventually they get attenuated and fall apart, leaving a
> rather sour residue. If I haven't seen something by you for
> a while, I can start to think that I'm overliking it . . . Then,

when I see something new, something good by you, there is an immediate freshening, an immediate dropping away of that mood of depression.

I recognize in Schjeldahl's feelings about Salle's work an echo of my own feelings about Salle the man. When I haven't seen him for several weeks or months, I begin to sour on him, to think I'm over-liking him. Then I see him again, and I experience Schjeldahl's "immediate freshening." As I write about him now—I haven't seen him for a month—I feel the return of antagonism, the sense of sourness. Like the harsh marks Salle makes over the softer images he first applies to his canvas, they threaten to efface the benign, admiring feelings of the interviews.

13

It is rare to read anything about the artist David Salle in which some allusion isn't made to the question of whether his work is pornographic and whether his depictions of women are humiliating and degrading. Images of women with panties down around their ankles who are pulling blouses over their heads, or women standing bent over with outthrust naked buttocks, or women lying naked on tables with their legs spread recur in Salle's paintings and have become a kind of signature of his work. The images are monochrome—they are copied from black-and-white photographs—and the pudenda are usually so heavily shaded as to foreclose prurience. To anyone who has seen any of the unambiguously dirty pictures of art history—Courbet's *The Origin of the World*, say, or Balthus's *The Guitar Lesson*—the idea of Salle as a pornographer is laughable. However, the poses of Salle's women are unsettling. Someone has stage directed them—someone with a very cold eye and with definite and perhaps unpleasant ideas, someone who could well be taking photographs for a girlie magazine, maybe a German girlie magazine. As it happens, some of Salle's images of women are, in fact, derived from the files of an American girlie magazine called *Stag*, for which he briefly worked in the art department (the magazine was on the verge of folding when he left, and he helped himself to cartons of

photographs, mostly of women but also of car and airplane crashes);
others are copied from photographs he took himself of hired models.

14

In a review of a show of David Salle's paintings, drawings, and wa-
tercolors at the Menil Collection, in Houston, in 1988, Elizabeth
McBride wrote, "He indulges himself in degrading, depersonaliz-
ing, fetishistic images of women which constitute . . . a form of ob-
scenity . . . Paintings such as these are a way of giving permission for
degrading actions. This work has all the cold beauty and the im-
morally functional power of a Nazi insignia." Of the same show
Susan Chadwick wrote, "Salle's work . . . is even more mean-
spirited, more contemptuous, and more profoundly misogynist than
I had realized . . . That brings us to the difficult question concerning art that is socially bad. Art that presents a message which is
in some way wrong, bad, evil, corrupting, immoral, inhumane, destructive, or sick. What can be done about negative artists? I cringe
when I see parents bringing their young children through this show
at the Menil on weekends."

15

In the winter of 1992, I began a series of interviews with the artist
David Salle. They were like sittings for a portrait with a very practiced sitter. Salle has given many—dozens of—interviews. He is a
kind of interview addict. But he is remarkably free of the soul-
sickness that afflicts so many celebrities, who grow overly interested
in the persona bestowed on them by journalism. Salle cultivates the
public persona, but with the detachment of someone working in
someone else's garden. He gives good value—journalists come away
satisfied—but he does not give himself away. He never forgets, and
never lets the interviewer forget, that his real self and his real life are
simply not on offer. What is on offer is a construct, a character who
has evolved and is still evolving from Salle's ongoing encounters
with writers. For Salle (who has experimented with sculpture, video,
and film) the interview is another medium in which to (playfully)

work. It has its careerist dimension, but he also does it for the sport. He once told me that he never makes any preparatory drawings for or revises anything in his paintings. Every stroke of the brush is irrevocable; nothing can be changed or retracted. A few false moves and the painting is ruined, unsalvageable. The same sense of tense improvisation pervades Salle's answers to interviewers' questions. He looks ahead to the way his words will read in print and chooses them with a kind of fearful carefulness. He also once told me of how he often gets lost as he paints: "I have to get lost so I can invent some way out." In his interviews, similarly, moments of at-a-lossness become the fulcrum for flights of verbal invention. Sometimes it almost seems as if he were provoking the interviewer to put him on the spot, so that he can display his ingenuity in getting off it.

16

During recent talks I had with the painter David Salle, who was one of the brightest art stars of the eighties, he would tell me— sometimes in actual words, sometimes by implication—that the subject of his declining reputation in the art world was of no real interest to him. That this was not where his real life lay, but was just something to talk about with an interviewer.

17

Writers have traditionally come to painters' ateliers in search of aesthetic succor. To the writer, the painter is a fortunate alter ego, an embodiment of the sensuality and exteriority that he has abjured to pursue his invisible, odorless calling. The writer comes to the places where traces of making can actually be seen and smelled and touched expecting to be inspired and enabled, possibly even cured. While I was interviewing the artist David Salle, I was coincidentally writing a book that was giving me trouble, and although I cannot pin it down exactly (and would not want to), in his studio something clarifying and bracing did filter down to my enterprise. He was a good influence. But he was also a dauntingly productive artist, and one day, as I walked into the studio and caught a glimpse of his new work, I blurted out my envious feelings. In the month since we last met, he had produced four large, complex new paintings, which hung on the walls in galling aplomb—while I had written maybe ten pages I wasn't sure I would keep. To my surprise, instead of uttering a modest disclaimer or reassuring words about the difference between writing and painting, Salle flushed and became defensive. He spoke as if I were accusing him, rather than myself, of artistic insufficiency; it appears that his productivity is a sensitive subject. His detractors point to his large output as another sign of his lightweightness. "They hold it up as further evidence that the work is glib and superficial," Salle said.

"If work comes easily, it is suspect."

"But it *doesn't* come easily. I find it extremely difficult. I feel like I'm beating my head against a brick wall, to use an image my father would use. When I work, I feel that I'm doing everything wrong. I feel that it can't be this hard for other people. I feel that everyone else has figured out a way to do it that allows him an effortless, charmed ride through life, while I have to stay in this horrible pit of a room, suffering. That's how it feels to me. And yet I know that's not the way it appears to others. Once, at an opening, an English critic came up to me and asked me how long I had worked on the five or six paintings I was showing. I told her, and she said, 'Oh, so fast! You work so fast!' She was a representative of the new, politically correct, antipleasure school of art people. I could easily visualize her as a dominatrix. There was some weird sexual energy there, unexpressed. I immediately became defensive."

"I just realized something," I said. "Everyone who writes or paints or performs is defensive about everything. I'm defensive about not working fast *enough*."

In a comradely spirit, Salle showed me a painting that had failed. It was a painting he had dwelled on a little too long, had taken a fatal misstep with, and had spoiled. I was shocked when I saw it. I had seen it in its youth and bloom a few months earlier; it had shown a ballet couple in a stylized pose radiantly smiling at each other, a mordant parody of a certain kind of dance photography popular in the 1950s. (Its source was a photograph in a fifties French dance magazine.) Now the man's face was obliterated. It looked as if someone had angrily thrown a can of gray paint at it. "It's a reject, a failed painting. It's going to be cut up," Salle said, as if speaking of a lamed horse that was going to be taken out and shot.

"It was so fine when I saw it first."

"It wasn't fine. It never worked. It's so bad. It's so much worse than I remembered. It's one of the worst things I've done in years. The image of the couple is so abrasive, so aggressive. I tried to undercut it by painting out the man's face. It was even more obnoxious than hers. But when I did that, I was on a course of destruction."

18

The painter David Salle, like his art, which refuses to narrate even though it is full of images, declines to tell a story about himself, even though he makes himself endlessly available for interviews and talks as articulately as any subject has ever talked. Salle has spoken with a kind of rueful sympathy of the people who look at his art of fragmentary, incongruous images and say it is too complicated, too much trouble to figure out, and turn away. He, of all people, should know what they are feeling, since his work, and perhaps his life as well, is about turning away. Nothing is ever resolved by Salle, nothing adds up, nothing goes anywhere, everything stops and peters out.

19

On an afternoon in April 1992, the painter David Salle and I sat on a pristine yellow 1950s corporate-style sofa in his loft, on White Street, looking at a large horizontal painting that was hanging there, a work he had kept from a group of what he calls "the tapestry paintings," done between 1988 and 1991. The painting made me smile. It showed a group of figures from old art—the men in doublets and the women in gowns and wearing feathers in their hair—arranged around a gaming table, the scene obviously derived from one of de La Tour's tense dramas of dupery: and yet not de La Tour exactly, but a sardonic pastiche of sixteenth- and seventeenth-century Dutch and Italian genre styles. In the gesture for which Salle is known, he had superimposed on the scene incongruous-seeming fragments: two dark monochrome images of bare-breasted women holding wooden anatomy dolls, a sketchily rendered drawing of a Giacometti sculpture, a drawing of a grimacing face, and a sort of abstract expressionist rectangle of gray paint with drips and splatters obliterating a man's leg. As if participating in the joke of their trans-plantation from baroque to postmodernist art, the costumed men and women had set their faces in comically rigid, exaggerated ex-pressions. When I asked Salle what paintings he had in mind when he made his pastiche, he gave me an answer that surprised me—and then didn't surprise me. One of the conditions of Salle's art is that nothing in it be original; everything must come from previously made work, so even a pastiche would have to be a pastiche done by someone else. In this case, it was an anonymous Russian tapestry maker whose work Salle had found reproduced in a magazine and had copied onto his canvas. The tapestry paintings, perhaps more richly and vividly than any of Salle's other groups of work, illustrate the paradox on which his art is poised—that an appearance of orig-inality may be achieved through dumb copying of the work of oth-ers. Salle has been accused of all kinds of bad things by his detractors (Hilton Kramer, Robert Hughes, and Arthur Danto, the most prominent of the critics who hate his work, have all said that he can't draw), but no one has ever accused him—no one can accuse him—of being derivative. His work has always looked like new art and, as time goes on and his technique and certain of his recurrent images have grown familiar, like art by David Salle. The tapestry paintings—there are more than ten of them—were a culmination. They have an energy, an invention, a kind of gorgeousness, and an atmosphere of success, of having pulled something off against heavy odds, that set them apart from Salle's other works. It is no wonder that he wanted to keep a memento of his achievement.

But now the achievement only seemed to fuel Salle's bitterness, his sense of himself as "someone who is no longer current," who is "irrelevant after having been relevant." He looked away from the painting and said, "The younger artists want to kill you off. They want to get rid of you. You're in their way. I haven't been the artist who is on young artists' minds for a long time. It has been six or seven years since I was the artist who was on young artists' minds.

That's how fast it moves. The artists young artists have on their minds are people I've barely heard of. I'm sure there are young artists who think I'm dead." I laughed, and he joined me. Then, his bitterness returning, Salle said, "I feel like I've just gotten started, marshaled my forces, done the research, and learned enough about painting do something interesting. What I do used to matter to others—for reasons that may not have had anything to do with its merit. But now, when I feel I have something to say, no one wants to hear it. There has always been antagonism to my work, but the sense of irritation and annoyance has stepped up. 'What, *you're* still around?'"

20

In an interview with the screenwriter Becky Johnston, in 1991, the artist David Salle, during a discussion of his childhood, in Wichita, Kansas, gave this answer to a question about his mother:

> You know, I don't really remember her very well. I just remember that she had a lovely gray skirt and a pink blouse with French cuffs and she had her monogram embroidered on the skirt in pink thread. She worked in the dress store [where Salle's father worked as a buyer, window dresser, and advertising-layout man]—she was a saleswoman on the floor—and she dressed very chicly. I remember her then—which was when I was about six—and then I remember her ten or fifteen years later, when she worked at night as a cashier in the accounting department of the J.C. Penney store, and she was completely and utterly changed: she wore brown or beige double-knit pants suits. And I honestly don't remember what happened to her in between. I have no images of her in between. In my mind, she just went from being this very chic, very lovely, kind of slightly elevated person, to being this horrible drudge.

In an interview with me, in 1992, Salle returned to this memory and told me how upset his mother had been when she read a version of it in an essay by Henry Geldzahler, which appeared in the catalog of Salle's photographs of naked or partly naked women posed in strange positions. "I had been hesitant to send the catalog to my mother because of the imagery," Salle told me. "It never occurred to me that something in the *text*, which is innocuous, would upset her. But when she called me up she was in tears."

21

In the introduction to a book-length interview with the artist David Salle, published in 1987 by Random House, the critic and poet Peter Schjeldahl writes, "My first reaction to meeting this twenty-seven-year-old phenom was, I'm afraid, a trifle smug. Simply, he was so transparently, wildly ambitious—even by the standards of his generation, whose common style of impatient self-assurance I had begun to recognize—that I almost laughed at him."

22

When I was interviewing the artist David Salle, an acutely intelligent, reserved, and depressed man, he would tell me about other interviews he was giving, and once, he showed me a transcript of a conversation with Barbaralee Diamonstein (it was to appear in a book of interviews with artists and art-world figures published by Rizzoli) that was marked by a special confrontational quality and an extraordinary air of liveliness. It was as if the interview had provoked the artist out of his usual state of skeptical melancholy and propelled him into a younger, less complex, more manic version of himself.

There is a passage, for example, in which Diamonstein confronts Salle with a piece of charged personal history. "From what I have read, you worked as a layout man at what was referred to as a porn magazine. Is that true?" Salle says yes. "How much did it affect your sensibility? I think you should address the issue and get rid of it one way or another," Diamonstein sternly says. Salle, disconcerted, lamely points out that actually he wasn't a layout man but a pasteup person at the porn magazine. Still floundering, he irrelevantly adds that he and the other young men in the art department were "pretty stoned most of the time." Diamonstein continues to push Salle on the question of what the experience of working at a men's magazine

called *Stag* meant to him. "So, did this affect your sensibility by either informing you, giving you a skill? Repelling you, amusing you?
Finding it absurd, interesting—how did you react? How did you
ever get there in the first place?"

Salle begins to see a way out of the impasse. "A friend of mine
worked there," he says. "It was just a job on one level, but 'absurd/
interesting' describes it pretty well. Nobody there took it very seriously. It wasn't *shameful*—people who worked there didn't tell their
families they did something else. At least, I don't think so. I just
remembered there was one guy who worked there because his father
worked there—they were both sitting there all day airbrushing tits
and ass. Like father, like son, I guess."

Diamonstein meets this with an inspiration of her own. "You
could have had a job at *Good Housekeeping*, too," she points out.

"Well, I only worked there for about six months," a momentarily
crushed Salle retorts. Then he finds his tone again: "There has been
so much made of it. Even though I had no money, I quit as soon as
I could. You know, this assumption of *causality* assigned to the
artist's life like plot points in a play is really nutty. Do people think
I learned about tits and ass working on *Stag* magazine? Do I seem
that pathetic?"

23

In an essay published in *The Village Voice* in 1982, the critic Peter
Schjeldahl wrote of his initial reaction to the work of David Salle, who
was to become "my personal favorite among current younger artists":

When I first encountered Salle's work, two or three years
ago, its vertiginous mix of blatancy ("storytelling" pictures)
and elusiveness (the "story" was impossible to figure out)
made me a little sick. I was also rattled by the frequent use of
pornographically posed female nudes. It now seems to me
hardly conceivable that in his determined excavation of the
culture's most charged pictorial matter, Salle would not have
availed himself of these ritualized vehicles of male fantasy. But
it made me so nervous that I rather comically felt a surge of
relief when in last year's show Salle presented a male nude.

What may have been even more shocking was Salle's cavalierly offhand exploitation of classically modernist pictorial devices, those sacred signs. He was using them like cheap tools, without even the upside-down respect accorded by satirical irony (as in Lichtenstein). I itched to dislike this stuff.

Then it started to get me. It was like a welling, congested, sentimental weepiness without an object, as emotions triggered by images of, say, a depressed-looking girl smoking in bed and some unspecific tragedy in a crowded street sought cathartic resolution in vain. It was an abstracted sensation of dislocation, yearning, and loss that started resonating with my sense of what both art and life are like here in the late twentieth century. Suddenly Salle's harsh artifice seemed heroic, an earnest of authenticity—without ceasing to seem perverse, against the grain.

24

One day, the artist David Salle and I talked about Thomas Bernhard's novel *The Loser*.

"I'm a third of the way through it," I said, "and at first I was excited by it, but now I'm a little bored. I may not finish it."

"It's so beautiful and pessimistic," Salle said.

"Yes, but it doesn't hold your interest the way a nineteenth-century novel does. I'm never bored when I'm reading George Eliot or Tolstoy."

"I am," Salle said.

I looked at him with surprise. "And you're *not* bored when you're reading Bernhard?"

"I'm bored by plot," Salle said. "I'm bored when it's all written out, when there isn't any shorthand."

25

In the fall of 1991, I attended a book party for the writer Harold Brodkey given by the painter David Salle in his loft, in Tribeca. The first thing I saw on walking into the room was Brodkey and Norman Mailer in conversation. As I approached, I heard them jovially talking about the horrible reviews each had just received, like bad boys comparing their poor marks. The party took place early in my acquaintance with Salle, and this fragment of conversation was a sort of overture to talks I had with him about his own sense of himself as a bad boy of art and about his inability to stop picking at the sore of his own bad reviews. He is an artist who believes in the autonomy of art, who sees the universe of art as an alternative to the universe of life, and who despises art that has a social agenda. But he is also someone who is drawn to the world of popular criticism, to the bazaar where paintings and books and performances are crudely and carelessly rated, like horses or slaves, and who wants to be one of the Chosen even as he disdains the choosers; in other words, he is like everybody else. Only the most pathologically pure-hearted writers, artists, and performers are indifferent to how their work is received and judged. But some hang more attentively than others on the words of the judges. During my talks with Salle, he kept returning to the subject of his reception, like an unhappy moth helplessly singeing itself on a lightbulb. "I don't know why I keep talking about this," he would say. "This isn't what is on my mind. I don't care that much. I spend a disproportionate amount of time complaining to you about how I am perceived. Every time we finish one of these talks, I have a pang of regret. I feel that all I do is complain about how badly I'm treated, and this is so much not what I want to be talking about. But for some reason I keep talking about it."

26

David Salle is one of the best-received and best-rewarded artists who came to prominence in the 1980s, but he is not one of the happiest. He is a tense, discontented man, with a highly developed sense of irony.

27

In several of David Salle's paintings, a mysterious dark-haired woman appears, raising a half-filled glass to her lips. Her eyes are closed, and she holds the glass in both hands with such gravity and absorption that one can only think she is taking poison or drinking a love potion. She is rendered in stark black and white and wears a period costume—a dress with a sort of Renaissance aspect. The woman disturbs and excites us, the way people in dreams do whom we know we know but can never quite identify. David Salle himself has some of the enigmatic vividness of the drinking woman. After many interviews with him, I feel that I only *almost* know him, and that what I write about him will have the vague, vaporous quality that our most indelible dreams take on when we put them into words.

28

One of the leitmotifs of a series of conversations I had in 1992 and 1993 with the painter David Salle was his unhappiness over the current reception of his work. "I don't think anyone has written a whole essay saying my work is passé," he said. "It's more a line here and there. It's part of the general phenomenon called eighties bashing. The critics who have been negative all along, like Robert Hughes and Hilton Kramer, have simply stepped up their negativity. The virulence of the negativity has grown enormously in the past couple of years. The reviews by Hughes and Kramer of my '91 show were weirdly, personally insulting. The two of them were always negative, but now it was as if they smelled blood and were moving in for the kill."

I told Salle I would like to read those reviews, and a few days later his assistant sent them to me. Salle had not exaggerated. Hughes and Kramer seemed beside themselves with dislike and derision; their reviews had an almost hysterical edge. "The exhibition of new paintings by David Salle at the Gagosian Gallery . . . has one tiny merit," Hughes wrote in *Time* on April 29, 1991. "It reminds you how lousy and overpromoted so much 'hot' 'innovative' American art in the 1980's was. If Julian Schnabel is Exhibit A in our national wax museum of recent duds, David Salle is certainly Exhibit B." He went on:

> Yet is there a duller or more formula-ridden artist in America than Salle in 1991 as he approaches the Big Four-Oh? . . . Drawing, as anyone who has seen a few Salles knows, is not

what the artist does. He never learned how to do it, and probably never will. He is incapable of making an interesting mark . . . Thus his pictures enable critics to kvetch soulfully about the dissociation of signs and meanings, and to praise what all good little deconstructors would call their "refusal of authoritarian closure," meaning, roughly, that they don't mean anything in particular. It's as though those who bet on him can't bear to face the possibility that his work was vacuous to begin with . . . The Gagosian Gallery . . . has even hired a guard to stand at the entrance to the room in which Salle's six new paintings are displayed, presumably in case some collector from the bottom of the waiting list is seized by the impulse to grab one of those tallowy objects from the wall and make a run for it. Ten minutes into the show, your heart goes out to that guard. Eight hours a day, five days a week, of this!

Kramer had wrung his hands in *The New York Observer* of April 15:

About some art exhibitions nowadays, we hardly know whether to laugh or cry. Their pretensions, not to mention the atmosphere of piety surrounding them, are undeniably laughable. Yet their artistic realization is at once so barren and so smug—and offers so few of the satisfactions we look to art to bring us—that the sense of comedy they elicit turns, almost before we know it, to feelings of grief and depression . . .

Consider the David Salle exhibition that is currently occupying the lush precincts of the Gagosian Gallery . . .

In the 80's, a taste for the raunchy and outrageous functioned in the fashionable art world very much the way junk bonds functioned in the financial markets, and it was no accident that the artists who produced art of this sort often found their most enthusiastic patrons among the collectors who were the principal beneficiaries of such junk-bond enterprises. These collectors often knew very little about the art that had been created in the past—in the days, that is, before they made their first fortunes. For such collectors, art history began the day they first walked into Leo Castelli's or Mary Boone's. In that world, the Old Masters were Jasper Johns and Andy Warhol, and artists like David Salle who had been nominated to succeed were guaranteed a sensational success.

The hostility and snobbery of both Hughes and Kramer toward the collectors of Salle's work is worthy of note. This kind of insult of the consumer has no equivalent in book or theater or movie reviewing. That is probably because the book/play/film reviewer has some fellow feeling with the buyers of books and theater and film tickets, whereas the art reviewer usually has no idea what it is like to buy a costly painting or sculpture. He is, per financial force, a mere spectator in the tulipomaniacal drama of the contemporary art market, and he tends to regard the small group of people rich enough to be players as if they were an alien species, quite impervious to his abuse. As for the collectors, they repay the critics for their insults by ignoring their judgments: they go right on buying—or, at any rate, they don't immediately stop buying—the work of artists who get bad reviews. Eventually the critical consensus (the judgments of museum curators form a part of it) is reflected in the market, and in time collectors bow to its will, but at the moment they were not bowing to Hughes's and Kramer's opinions and were continuing to trade in Salles. Salle smarted under the attacks but continued to make money.

29

I once asked the artist David Salle if he had read an article in *The New Republic* by Jed Perl (who also frequently writes for Hilton Kramer's *The New Criterion*) about how the wrong artists are celebrated and how the really good artists are obscure. The article was entitled "The Art Nobody Knows," with the subhead "Where Is the Best American Art to Be Found? Not in the So-called Art World." It articulated the antagonism of an older generation toward the art stars of the eighties, and complained of the neglect suffered by a group of serious artists, who had been quietly working and, over the years, "making the incremental developments that are what art is all about." The world of these artists, Perl said, was "the real art world," as opposed to the world of Salle and Schnabel and Cindy Sherman. Perl held up two artists—the sculptor Barbara Goodstein and the painter Stanley Lewis, whose work "is rarely seen by anybody beyond a small circle of admirers"—as examples of the neglected "real artist." "What happens to an artist whose development receives so little public recognition?" he asked. "Can artists keep on doing their damnedest when the wide world doesn't give a damn?"

Salle said that he had not read the article and that it sounded interesting. "I have always wanted to know what Jed Perl likes," he said. "Maybe he's right. Maybe these *are* the good artists." He asked me to send him the article, and I did so. The next time we met, he greeted me with it in his hand and an amused look on his face. "What a pity they illustrated it," he said. "Without the illustrations, you might think Perl was onto something. But when you see the work you just have to laugh. It's so *small.*"

30

I used to visit the artist David Salle in his studio and try to learn the secret of art from him. What was he doing in his enigmatic, allusive, aggressive art? What does any artist do when he produces an artwork? What are the properties and qualities of authentic art, as opposed to ersatz art? Salle is a contemplative and well-spoken man, and he talked easily and fluently about his work and about art in general, but everything he said only seemed to restate my question. One day, he made a comment on the difference between collages done by amateurs and collages done by artists, which caused my ears to prick up. It occurred to me that a negative example—an example of something that wasn't art—could perhaps be instructive. Accordingly, on my next visit with Salle I took with me three collages I had once made for my own pleasure. At the time, Salle was himself making collages, in preparation for a series of paintings featuring images of consumer products of the fifties. He was going to copy his collages in oil paint on large canvases, but they already looked like works of art. "Why are your collages art and mine not?" I asked him.

Salle propped up my collages and regarded them closely. At last he said, "There's nothing that says your collages aren't art. They're art if you declare them to be so."

"Yes, that's the Duchamp dictum. But I don't declare them to be so. Don't you remember the distinction you drew between collages made by amateurs and collages made by artists?"

"I was speaking generally," Salle said.

I realized that he was being delicate, that he didn't want to voice his true opinion of my collages. I assured him that I hadn't brought the collages to be praised, that I had no investment in them, that I had brought them only in order to engage him in a discussion. "Please say anything that occurs to you."

"Stuff occurs to me, but I don't want to say it. I might sound mean-spirited."

Eventually Salle conquered enough of his reluctance to make a few mild criticisms of the composition of my collages, and to say that his own collages were composed along simple principles that any art school freshman would recognize. Looking back on the incident, I see that Salle had also seen what any first-year student of psychology would have seen—that for all my protests to the contrary, I *had* brought them to be praised. Every amateur harbors the fantasy that his work is only waiting to be discovered; a second fantasy—that the established contemporary artists must (also) be frauds—is a necessary corollary.

31

I once visited the artist David Salle in his studio, on White Street, when he was making preparatory collages for a series of paintings based on consumer products, and he told me that he had noticed himself being obsessively drawn to two images: watches and shoes. They had seemed meaningful to him—he had been cutting pictures of watches and shoes out of newspapers and magazines—but he didn't know why. The meaning of the watches remained obscure, he said, but a few days earlier he had cracked the code of shoes.

"The shoe as presented in the selling position isn't the thing. The thing is underneath the shoe. *It's the idea of being stepped on.*" Salle's sense of himself as being stepped on—by people who are jealous of him, by people who feel superior to him, by people who don't like his sexual politics, by people who find his work too much trouble to decipher—has become a signature of his public persona.

32

There is a kind of man who is always touchingly and irritatingly mentioning his wife—touchingly because one is moved by the depth of his affection, and irritatingly because one feels put down by the paragon who inspires it. During the two years I interviewed the artist David Salle, he was always mentioning the dancer and choreographer Karole Armitage, with whom he had lived for seven years. Although Salle and Armitage had separated a few months before our talks began, he would speak about her as if he were still under her spell. They had met in 1983 and had become a famous couple. She had been a lead dancer in the Merce Cunningham company and had then formed her own avant-garde company. Her choreography was a kind of version in dance of what Salle was doing in painting: an unsettling yoking of incongruous elements. (The fusion of classical ballet with punk rock music was Armitage's initial postmodernist gesture.) That Salle should become her collaborator—painting sets and designing costumes for her ballets—seemed almost inevitable. The first product of the Armitage-Salle collaboration was a ballet called *The Mollino Room*, performed at the Metropolitan Opera House in May 1986, which had been commissioned by American Ballet Theater and in which Baryshnikov himself danced. In an article entitled "The Punk Princess and the Postmodern Prince," published in *Art in America*, Jill Johnston wonderfully wrote of the premiere, "It attracted a capacity audience of art world luminaries and suburban bankers or whoever they were in their tuxedos and jewels and wild satisfied looks of feeling they were at just the right place that opening evening in Manhattan." As events proved, however, the bankers were in the wrong place. The ballet got terrible reviews, as did Armitage's subsequent ballets *The Tarnished*

Angels and *The Elizabethan Phrasing of the Late Albert Ayler*, both staged at the Brooklyn Academy in 1987. "Little talent, much pretension. Any other comment might seem superfluous," the *Times* dance critic Anna Kisselgoff wrote of Armitage on the latter occasion.

"The dance world is controlled by one person, Anna Kisselgoff," Salle told me bitterly. "She controls it internationally as well as locally. A good review from Anna will get you a season in France, and a bad review will cancel it. Karole was literally run out of town by Anna. She can't work in New York anymore." Armitage now lives and works in Los Angeles and abroad.

Salle and Armitage have remained close friends; they talk frequently on the telephone and meet whenever she comes to New York. Salle speaks of her with a kind of reverence for the rigor and extremity of her avant-gardism. She and her dancers represent to him the purest form of artistic impudence and intransigence. "During the seven years I was with Karole, I lived a different life from that of any artists I know," he told me. "I lived her life. She would probably tell you she lived mine. At any rate, during those years I was more involved with her work than with my own. Her work was about being on the edge, performed by people who enjoyed being on the edge, for an audience who wanted to be on the edge. Her life was much more urgent and alive and crisis oriented. The performing arts are like that. When I was with Karole, artists seemed boring to me—staid and self-satisfied. Solid, like rocks in a stream. Very few people had her inquisitiveness and restlessness, her need for stimulation in the deepest sense. When I was with Karole, artists seemed almost bovine to me, domestic, house oriented, safe."

Salle and I were talking in his sleek, cold, obsessively ordered loft on White Street, furnished with 1950s corporate-style sofas and chairs, and I asked him if Armitage had helped furnish the place.

"No," he said. "I wasn't with her when I bought the loft. She moved in a few years later. I came to see this place through her eyes. Through her eyes it was intimidating and alienating. There was no place for her in it."

"Was there an area that she took possession of, that became her own domain?"

"No, not really. Because there was no way to divide it. She had a desk—sort of where that painting is. There was a country house in upstate New York. I bought it because she liked it. It was an old house, and she had a romantic feeling about it. But we never had time to go there."

33

In a long interview with the artist David Salle by the screenwriter Becky Johnston, there is a passage about the painting tradition of the female nude in Western art and about Salle's sense of himself as not belonging to that tradition. "It would be interesting," Johnston says, "to try to point out what is different about your nude women from the parade of nude women which has gone by."

"Well, we both agree there's a difference," Salle says. "It feels like a complete break."

"Absolutely. But I want to know what you think that break is."

Salle struggles to answer and gives up. "I'm not getting anywhere. I know it's different, but I don't know why. I don't know how to express it in words. What do you think?"

Johnston says shrewdly, "I think the difference between the nude woman in your paintings and those in others is that *she's not a woman*. She's a representative of something else. She's a stand-in for your view. I don't think that's true of most of the women in art. And I don't think it's a sexual obsession with women which motivates your use of the nude, as it does, say, Picasso's. It's much deeper, more personal and subjective. That's my opinion."

Salle doesn't protest, and Johnston goes on to ask him, "If you had to describe it—and I know this is asking you to generalize, but feel free to do so widely—what's 'feminine' to you?"

Salle stops to consider. "I have the feeling that if I were to start talking about what I think is feminine, I would list all the qualities I can think of."

34

David Salle is a slight, handsome man of forty-one who wears his dark shoulder-length hair pulled back and bound with a rubber band, though sometimes he will absently pull on the rubber band and let the hair fall around his thin, not always cleanly shaven face.

In 1992 and 1993, I would visit him at his studio, and we would talk about his work and life. I did not find what he said about his work interesting (I have never found anything any artist has said about his work interesting), but when he talked about his life—especially about his life as an unsettling presence in the art world and his chronic feeling of being misunderstood—that was something else. Then his words took on the specificity, vividness, and force that had drained out of them when he talked about art. But even so, I felt dissatisfied with the portrait of the artist that was emerging for me—it seemed too static—and one day I said to him, "I keep thinking there should be some action."

"Action?"

"Yes. Something should happen. There has been some action—I've been to your studio and to your loft and to your drawing show and to the dinner afterward—but I want more."

"We'll think of something," Salle said.

"What if I watched you paint?"

"We could try it, though I think it would be pretty boring, like being around a film set. A lot of waiting around." Salle then recalled artists he had seen on TV as a child, who painted and talked to the audience. "My friend Eric Fischl tells me there's a whole raft of them on TV now—wildly entertaining, creepy guys who paint and talk a blue streak. Fischl is an expert on TV painters. He says there's a guy on TV who is the fastest painter in the world. It's a funny thing to think about. Painting, like theater, is about illusion, and I think it might be shocking to you to see how undramatic the process is through which the illusions are created."

"We could go to a museum together."

Salle said he had already done that with a journalist—Gerald Marzorati for an article in *ARTnews*. "We went to the Met. I was badly hungover, and it only magnified the pathetic limitations of what I had to say about other art. We were looking at these Rembrandts, and I didn't have anything to say about them. It came down to 'They sure are good.'"

I never watched Salle paint (his talk about the TV artists somehow took care of that), but I did go to a museum with him once—to the Met, to see the Lucian Freud show. I had had a rather cumbersome journalistic idea. Robert Hughes, who had written scathingly about Salle, had called Freud "the best realist painter alive," and I imagined doing a set piece in which Salle would make acidic comments on a favorite of Hughes's as a sort of indirect revenge. I called up Salle and put the idea to him. Salle said he'd be glad to go to the Freud show, but couldn't oblige me with my set piece, since he didn't hate Freud's work—he admired it and had even "quoted" from it in his own work. At the show, Salle moved through the rooms very quickly. He could tell at a glance what he wanted to look at and what he didn't, and mostly he didn't. He strode past paintings, only occasionally pausing to stand before one. He lingered appreciatively before a small nude owned by a film actor—"Ah, the Steve Martin," he said when he spotted it—and a large painting of Freud's family and friends in his studio, flanked by a studio sink and a massive scented geranium with many dead leaves. What Salle said about the paintings that captured his interest was technical in character; he spoke of strategies of composition and of the depositing of paint on canvas. Of the well-known painting of Freud's mother lying down, Salle said, "It has the same palette as *Whistler's Mother*—a ravishing palette." In the last rooms of the show, where the provocative large paintings of the overweight performance artist Leigh Bowery were hanging, Salle permitted himself a negative comment. "That's completely unremarkable," he said of *Naked Man, Back View*, a huge painting of a seated, naked Bowery. He added, "Freud is adored for being 'bad'—by the same people who hate my work because I'm 'bad.'"

I recalled a conversation I'd once had with Salle about Francis Bacon. Salle had been speaking about his own work, about his images of women—"They're all kind of dire, they have a dire cast," he said—and I had asked him, speaking of dire, whether Bacon had been an influence. "You're not the first person to ask me that," Salle said. "Several people have observed that to me. Bacon is actually not an artist I'm interested in, but lately I've been thinking about him a lot in attempting to defend myself against certain criticisms. If you turned these criticisms around and leveled them against Bacon, it would be absurd. And it's purely because his work is homosexual and mine is heterosexual. The same attitudes transposed are incorrect."

"Why are dire images done by a homosexual more correct than those done by a heterosexual?"

"Because in art politics, to be homosexual is, a priori, more correct than to be heterosexual. Because to be an artist is to be an outsider, and to be a gay artist is to be a double outsider. That's the correct condition. If you're a straight artist, it's not clear that your outsiderness is legitimate. I know this is totally absurd. But the fact is that in our culture it does fall primarily to gays and blacks to make something interesting. Almost everything from straight white culture is less interesting, and has been for a long time."

35

After the opening of a show of David Salle's drawings at the uptown Gagosian Gallery in March 1992, a celebratory dinner was held at a suavely elegant restaurant in the East Seventies, and as the evening proceeded I was struck by the charm and gaiety of the occasion. The ritual celebrations of artistic achievement—the book parties, the opening-night parties, the artists' dinners—give outward form to, and briefly make real, the writer's or performer's or painter's fantasy that he is living in a world that wishes him well and wants to reward him for his work. For a few hours, the person who has recently emerged from the "horrible pit," as Salle once called it, of his creative struggles is lulled into forgetting that the world is indifferent to him and intent only on its own pleasures. Occasionally the world is pleased to applaud and reward an artist, but more often than not it will carelessly pass him by. And what the world gives, it delights in taking away: the applauded and rewarded artist does not remain so; the world likes to reverse itself. What gives the book party or the opening-night party or the artist's dinner its peculiar feverish glitter is the lightly buried consciousness of the probable bad fate that awaits the artist's offering.

Since shows of painters' drawings are considered relatively minor affairs, the dinner was a small one (for about twenty people) and had a more relaxed and less complicated atmosphere than a full-scale show would have elicited. The restaurant was a very expensive and a very good one; we ordered carefully and ate seriously. Salle, who was wearing a kind of sailor's blouse, sat quietly and calmly and watchfully, like a boy at a birthday party. I retain an image of Sabine Rewald, a curator at the Metropolitan, who looks like a Vermeer, lifting a spoonful of pink sorbet to her mouth and smiling happily. My table partners—Robert Pincus-Witten, an art critic and emeritus professor of art history who is now a director at Gagosian, and Raymond Foye, another director, who also publishes tiny books of exotica, such as the poems of Francis Picabia—were masters of the art of intimate, complicit table talk. Our host, Larry Gagosian, was absent. He was out of town; the opening was evidently not important enough for him to fly in for.

Two years later, the opening, at the Gagosian downtown gallery, of a Salle show of eight large *Early Product Paintings* based on images in 1950s advertising, was something else again. This was a high-stakes show—each painting was priced at around a hundred thousand dollars—and an entire restaurant had been hired for the artist's dinner. Things were no longer simple. Things were very complicated. The restaurant, filled with artists, writers, performers, filmmakers, collectors, critics, gallery owners, hangers-on, hummed with a sense of intrigue and with the threat of something not coming off. Gagosian, a tall, dark-skinned, gray-haired man in his late forties, with a deadpan manner, walked through the room casting looks here and there, like Rick in *Casablanca* checking the house. Pincus-Witten and Foye, again on duty, skimmed about on anxious, obscure errands. Salle (playing the Paul Henreid role?) wore a dark jacket over a tieless white shirt and jeans, and was only slightly more reserved, detached, and watchful than usual. I left before the Vichy police came. The image I retain from the occasion, like Sabine Rewald's pink sorbet from the previous one (though it comes from the opening proper), is the sight of a tall, thin man in a gray suit who stood in the center of the gallery and stood out from everyone else because of the aura of distinction that surrounded him. He had a face with clever, European features, but it was his bearing that was so remarkable. He carried himself like a nobleman; you expected to look down and see a pair of greyhounds at his feet. Throughout the opening he had his arm around a young black man with an elaborate tribal hairdo. He was the painter

Francesco Clemente, another of Gagosian's hundred-thousand-dollars-a-picture artists, and another of the painters who came to prominence during the 1980s. Unlike Salle, however, he had not seen his star fall.

During a series of talks I had with Salle over a two-year period, he was always careful to say nothing bad about fellow painters—even his comments on Julian Schnabel, with whom he had had a public falling-out, were restrained. But I gathered from a few things he let drop about Clemente's charmed life in art that it was a bitter reminder of everything his own wasn't. "What I've been circling around trying to find a way to ask," Salle once told me, "is the simple question: How is it that some people are basically taken seriously and other are basically not taken seriously?" In spite of the money he makes from his art, in spite of the praise sometimes bordering on reverence he has received from advanced critics (Peter Schjeldahl, Sanford Schwartz, Lisa Liebmann, Robert Rosenblum, Michael Brenson, for example), Salle feels that admission into the highest rank of contemporary painting has been denied him, that he will always be placed among the second-stringers, that he will never be considered one of the big sluggers.

36

The artist David Salle, in a 1990 catalog of his prints called the *Canfield Hatfield* series (A. J. Liebling wrote about Hatfield in *The Honest Rainmaker*), wrote,

> Professor Canfield Hatfield was a supposedly real-life character who figured prominently in racetrack operations and betting schemes of all types in this country in the first part of the twentieth century. Among the Professor's many activities to promote belief in a higher system of control over seemingly random events were his exploits as a paid maker of rain for drought-stricken communities in the West—a high-wager kind of job and by extension a useful metaphor for the relationship between risk, hope, and fraud that enter into any art-making or rain-making situation.

37

The lax genre of personality journalism would not seem to be the most congenial medium for a man of David Salle's sharp, odd mind and cool, irritable temperament. And yet this forty-one-year-old painter has possibly given more interviews than any other contemporary artist. Although the published results have, more often than not, disappointed him, they have not deterred him from further fraternization with the press; when I was interviewing him, in 1992 and 1993, he would regularly mention other interviews he was giving. One of them—an interview with Eileen Daspin, of the magazine *W*—turned out badly. Salle lost his subject's wager that the interviewer's sympathetic stance wasn't a complete sham, and had to endure the vexation of reading a piece about himself that shimmered with hostility and turned his words against him. "It can't be easy being David Salle in the 1990's," Daspin wrote in the October 1993 issue. "He is definitely out. Like fern bars and quiche. A condition that's a little hard to take after having been one of the genius artist boy wonders of the Eighties." This was the style and tone of the article. Salle himself sounded petulant and egotistical. ("I was completely ignored by the same people at the beginning of my career who then celebrated me and who are now happy to ignore me.")

A month or so later, Salle told me of his feelings about the article. "I read it very, very quickly, in disgust, and threw the magazine in the trash. I had been ambushed. I should have known better. I have no one to blame but myself. She gave off plenty of signals that should have raised alarms. It led to my saying interesting things—except I said them to the wrong person."

"It interests me that you always take responsibility for the interview—that if you don't like it, you blame yourself rather than the interviewer."

"Oh, I can blame her," Salle said. "I didn't do it single-handed. She did it. She kept saying 'What does it feel like to be a has-been? Don't you feel bad being put in the position of a has-been?' and I kept saying—with a misguided sense of pedagogical mission—'Well, you have to understand that this has a context and a history and a trajectory.' I was talking about the tyranny of the left. But it came out with her saying merely how angry and unhappy I was about being a has-been. All the pains I took to explain the context had gone for nothing."

"She made you sound like a very aggressive and unpleasant person."

"Maybe I am. I was trying out the thesis that the art world lionizes bullies. In any case, I'm reaching the point where I'm resigned to being misinterpreted. Instead of seeing this as a bad fate that befell me through no fault of my own, I now see it as a natural state of affairs for an artist. I almost don't see how it can be otherwise."

"Then why do you give all these interviews?"

Salle thought for a moment. "It's a lazy person's form of writing. It's like writing without having to write. It's a form in which one can make something, and I like to make things."

I remembered something Salle had once made that had failed, like the *W* interview, and that he had destroyed in disgust, as he had destroyed his copy of the magazine. It was a painting of two ballet dancers.

38

The artist David Salle—as if speaking of another person—once talked to me about his impatience. "I have a way of making people feel that they don't have my attention, that I have lost interest and turned away. People I'm close to have complained about it."

"And then?"

"I get even more impatient."

"Is it that your thoughts wander?"

"I start thinking that my life is going to be over soon. It's that simple. I don't have that much time left. I felt this way when I was twenty."

Salle had recently turned forty. He had noticed—without drawing the almost too obvious inference—that he was cutting images of watches out of newspapers and magazines. One day, after arriving a little late for an appointment with me, he apologized and then told me that he used to be obsessively punctual. "I had to train myself not to arrive exactly on the dot. It was absurd and unseemly to be so punctual. It was particularly unseemly for an artist to be so punctual."

I asked Salle what his punctuality had been about.

"I think it had to do with focusing so much on people's expectations of me. But it was also because I myself hate to wait. For all my, I'm sure, bottomless inconsiderateness of other people, I'm always empathizing with the other person. I empathize with the torturer. I find it very easy to empathize with Robert Hughes when he writes of his aversion to my work. I feel I know exactly what he's thinking and why. It's a kind of arrogance, I know, but I feel sorry for him. He doesn't know any better. I had to learn to be late and I had to learn to be cruel, to exude hostility. But it's not really my nature. I do it badly because it's not who I am."

39

Toward the end of a long series of interviews with the artist David Salle, I received this letter from him:

> After the many hours of trying to step outside of myself in order to talk about who or what I am, I feel that the only thing that really matters in art and in life is to go against the tidal wave of literalism and literal-mindedness—to insist on and *live* the life of the imagination. A painting has to be the experience, instead of pointing to it. I want to have and to give *access to feeling*. That is the riskiest and only important way to connect art to the world—to make it alive. Everything else is just current events.
>
> Most of our conversations, I think, were about how this idea has a special frequency which is easily drowned out by the din of the moment. That is, we talked, or I talked, mostly about its being "drowned out." But the important thing is not really the "underdogness" of it—but just the feeling itself.

40

To write about the painter David Salle is to be forced into a kind of parody of his melancholy art of fragments, quotations, absences—an art that refuses to be any one thing or to find any one thing more interesting, beautiful, or sobering than another.

41

One day, toward the end of a conversation I was having with the painter David Salle in his studio, on White Street, he looked at me and said, "Has this ever happened to you? Have you ever thought that your real life hasn't begun yet?"

"I think I know what you mean."

"You know—soon. Soon you'll start your real life."

DEPTH OF FIELD

2011

Last April, the German photographer Thomas Struth went to Windsor Castle and took a picture of the Queen of England and the Duke of Edinburgh for the National Portrait Gallery in London. This is not the kind of photography Struth usually does. He is one of today's most advanced and acclaimed art photographers, whose monumental color photographs hang in museums throughout the world, and whose interests do not extend to taking inoffensive pictures of famous people. But when he got the call from the National Portrait Gallery in January, he found himself saying yes. The occasion was an exhibition of paintings and photographs of Elizabeth II done in the sixty years of her reign, which the Diamond Jubilee of 2012 will celebrate. Struth's photograph would be the final portrait in the exhibition.

"When the National Portrait Gallery called and said that in their eyes I was the best person to do the portrait, I was quite shocked," Struth told me. "My immediate reaction was 'What can I possibly do that's not only affirmative but would include a message from me? Would I be able to say something new about people like this?'"

Struth and I were eating lunch in a Berlin hotel restaurant; it was a month after the sitting, and I had come to Germany to interview him and watch him at work. He is a tall, bearded man of fifty-six, with large pale eyes and an exceptionally likable persona. He radiates decency and straightforwardness. He is kind and calm and modest. He is the kid in the class everyone wants to sit next to.

Struth went on to tell me of his elaborate preparations for the portrait of Elizabeth and Philip. He studied old photographs and found most of them wanting. He saw the technical mistakes, "what should not happen"—notably their distracting backgrounds. He visited Buckingham Palace and decided it was too cluttered. When the gilded green, red, and white drawing rooms at Windsor Castle were offered, he selected the green room (the white room was "too tired" and the red room "too much") and spent a day there making test shots. "While I was there, I said, 'I want to see the dresser'—the woman who is in charge of the Queen's wardrobe. Because the second thing I noticed when I looked at the past photographs of the Queen was that many of the dresses she wears are very unfortunate. She has quite big boobs, and she often wears something that goes up to the neck, and then there is this stretch of fabric under the face that makes it look small." (I smiled to myself at Struth's coarse reference to the royal bosom—a rare lapse in his excellent English.) The day before the sitting, Struth continued, "the dresser came in with twenty dresses. She was a very nice woman, and we had an immediate chemistry. I felt that she saw me. Later, she told the Queen that I was okay—that I was a nice guy. I selected the dress, a pale-blue brocade with garlands, a bit shiny, and it matched nicely against the dark green."

I asked if the Queen accepted his choice and he said yes. He did not choose the Duke's costume, except to ask for a white shirt. At the sitting, the Duke wore a dark suit and a blue tie. "He was perfect," Struth said.

In further preparation, Struth read a biography of Elizabeth, and "I felt sympathy. They were my parents' generation. She was exactly my mother's age, and Philip was born in 1921, two years after my father was born." He added, "I said okay to the commission for reasons I cannot name, but I thought, I'm going to have sympathy for these people."

The paradoxicality of Struth's association of Elizabeth and Philip with his parents—his mother was in the Hitlerjugend and his father served in the Wehrmacht from 1937 to 1945—could not have been lost on him and was surely implicit in the "reasons I cannot name." Like many, if not most Germans of his generation, Struth has been haunted by the Nazi past, and speaks of the Holocaust as a major influence on his life and work. "If you want to know what formed me," he said in our first interview, "this is the big thing: the culture of guilt that I was born into and that surrounded me in my childhood." He told me that he learned about the Holocaust early in his life, though he doesn't know exactly when—"I feel as if I always knew about it"—and was tormented by the question of his parents' complicity. His father liked to tell stories about his bad war. He had fought in France and then in Russia, where he was severely wounded twice, and survived "almost as if by a miracle." These stories "irritated" the young Thomas. "Whenever my father talked about the war, he told only his personal story. He never said something like 'Oh, my God, when I came out of it and realized what we had done, I felt so sorry!' That would have been the natural thing to say. But he never said it. I don't know what he believed." Struth went on to speak, in a somewhat amorphous way, of his work as a form of the *Vergangenheitsbewältigung* ("coming to terms with the past") by which Germany's best spirits remain gripped. Will his portrait of the monarch who was on the right side of history ("the last living connection to an episode—the island race standing up to Hitler—that has become the foundation story, almost the creation myth, of modern Britain," as Jonathan Freedland recently characterized Elizabeth II in *The New York Review of Books*) bring his project of expiation to a remarkable kind of culmination?

If so, it will not be visible in the portrait itself. Struth's work does not reflect the culture of guilt he speaks of. Unlike, for example, the gritty, dread-inducing paintings of Anselm Kiefer, whose thoughts never seem far from Auschwitz, Struth's photographs evoke nothing bad. They have a lightness of spirit, you could almost say a sunniness, that is not present in the work of the other major practitioners of the new oversize color photography—Andreas Gursky, Candida Höfer, Jeff Wall, Thomas Ruff among them. Struth is the Sunday child of the lot. His huge photographs—city streets, people looking at paintings in museums, industrial landscapes, factories, laboratories, rain forests, and family groups—are as pleasing as his persona; they seem to be an extension of it. Michael Fried, in his tautly argued book *Why Photography Matters as Art as Never Before* (2008), pauses to remark, with apparent (uncharacteristic) irrelevance—but evident intuitive understanding of the force of Struth's radiance— "A striking fact about Struth's public career is the almost universally enthusiastic response that his work has received." An early enthusiast, Peter Schjeldahl, wrote in the Swiss art journal *Parkett* in 1997, "It is time to say that Struth's pictures regularly take my breath away. I find it hard to look at them steadily for any length of time, so intense is their effect on my emotions." In the catalog of a 2003 Struth retrospective at the Metropolitan Museum in New York, Maria Morris Hambourg and Douglas Eklund testified to "a remarkable feeling" they experienced while looking at Struth's photograph of two women standing before Gustave Caillebotte's *Paris, Street; Rainy Day*, "of stepping into one's own skin again, while alienation from others and from history—the curse of the modern—is dissolved in the image." Today there is no diminution of the enthusiasm; if anything, it is growing, and sane critics are continuing to lose it under Struth's mesmerizing spell.

The morning after the lunch in Berlin, Struth and I drove to a factory outside Dresden, operated by a company called Solar-World, where he would spend the day photographing. He had been there a few weeks earlier to ascertain whether he would find a subject, and he did. We were greeted by an agreeable young woman named Susanne Herrmann, the plant's public relations manager, who took us to a changing room where we put on white jumpsuits, white plastic hairnets, and white booties over our shoes so that we would bring no contaminating dust particles into the plant. Dan Hirsch, Struth's new assistant, who had driven in from Düsseldorf with Struth's equipment—numerous cameras, tripods, and film— had already arrived. ("I desired somebody like this for a long time," Struth said of Hirsch, a twenty-eight-year-old Israeli, who had written to Struth and to Candida Höfer a few months earlier, offering his services; he had heard back only from Struth, who interviewed him and hired him on the spot. "Everything he said seemed very honest and made sense.")

We entered a large room filled with machinery that made a great din and nowhere disclosed the function that its beautiful forms followed. I immediately saw why Struth wanted to photograph here. Everywhere you looked, a fetching ensemble of industrial parts appeared—like a found object—to tempt the eye even as it baffled the mind. While Struth and Hirsch set up a large view camera in front of one of these ready-mades and took preparatory pictures with a digital camera, I was given a tour of the factory by Ulrike Just—another agreeable employee, with the title of quality manager—and learned what all the activity and complexity was about: inert little tiles, about six inches square, called wafers, were being converted into vital solar panels. The wafers were sent from place to place on the floor to undergo endless chemical alterations, washings, and inspections—all done by machinery. The occasional person we came across on the factory floor was tending to a machine, like a nurse. Watching the machines work was amazing: it seemed as if the merest of functions required the most violent exercise of machinery. A certain inspection of the wafers, for example, was done by a machine that fairly jumped up and down with excitement. The single human intervention—a final inspection by specially trained eyes and hands—would one day cease; inevitably, machines that could do this work would be invented.

Struth was laboring as mightily as the machines to take his pictures. He had covered his head and shoulders with a gray photographer's cloth, and every shot seemed to cost him great effort. He would emerge from under the cloth looking beaten down and depleted. His assistant did things to assist, but Struth continued to look as if he were undergoing a shattering ordeal. He moved to another place on the factory floor, and the exertions continued. At around two, he reluctantly stopped, and he and Hirsch and I and Susanne Herrmann drove to a restaurant where the founder of Solar-World, Frank Asbeck, was giving us lunch. A long table in a shady courtyard had been set with nine places. The party was filled out by four executives from the factory, dressed in dark suits, who filed in together and talked only to one another. Lunch was delicious, featuring the white asparagus then in season and being served everywhere in Germany. Asbeck, who was fat and exuberant, more Bacchic than Apollonian, told an amusing story about his previous work, something about being fired before he was hired to run a trout farm because he had written an article about the antibiotics that were being secretly given to the trout. The conversation turned to green subjects, and I quoted Michael Pollan's mantra: "Eat food. Not too much. Mostly plants." Asbeck laughed and said, "I guess I don't do the not too much part." As he spoke, he patted himself fondly, like one of the large, rich men of the past who took pleasure in their fatness.

After lunch, we returned to the factory and Struth went back to his strenuous labors under the photographer's cloth, with Hirsch hovering nearby, performing his assisting functions when Struth signaled for them. He worked through the afternoon and into the evening hours. The time set for us to drive to Dresden for the night went by, but he showed no signs of quitting. Ulrike Just was staying after hours—she had been told to stay as long as Struth wanted to work. I tried to busy myself by taking pictures with my Instamatic camera. Finally, I rather crossly left for Dresden in a taxi.

Of course, my crossness was unjustified. I had wanted to see a master photographer at work and had just had the chance to do so. Struth's invisible cloth of obliviousness was as necessary to his art making as the actual cloth he worked under. To enter the state of absorption in which art is made requires reserves of boorishness that not every exquisitely courteous person can summon but that the true artist unhesitatingly draws on.

The next day, Struth, his courtliness restored, and I walked around Dresden and talked about his project of taking photographs at industrial and scientific workplaces. I asked him if he felt he was making some sort of "statement" about society with these photographs.

"I think yes," he said, but he added, "Some of the pictures don't show what I was thinking. For instance, when I went to Cape Canaveral as a tourist, I was struck with the sense of the space program as an instrument of power. When, as a state, you demonstrate that you are able to do that, it contributes to cultural dominance. I hadn't realized this before. But when I went there to photograph I saw that it is something you cannot put into a photograph."

"Do you feel you need to put large meanings into your work?" I asked.

"Well, it's part of my thinking. It's something that stimulates me. To have a narrative is an incentive. If it was only about composition and light and beautiful pictures, I could just photograph flowers."

"Forget the flowers," I said. "Let's stay in the factory. Because there were very beautiful forms there. Wouldn't that be enough for you? If you just found beautiful compositions there and made beautiful photographic abstractions. You want to do more than that?"

"Yes."

"I'm trying to elicit from you what the more is."

"The more is a desire to melt, like to—how can I say it?—be an antenna for a part of our contemporary life and to give this energy, put that into parts of this narrative of visual, of sort of symbolic visual expression . . ." Struth struggled, and gave up.

I asked him if the fact that SolarWorld's activity had to do with solar energy was part of his interest in photographing there.

He said that it was, and added, "My own personal energy account is very bad, because I fly so often and drive, and can't claim that I'm a good sustainable-energy person. But I've almost always voted for the Green Party, and since it was founded, I always thought these subjects were important and are a fascinating challenge for the world."

"How will your pictures show that what is being produced at SolarWorld is good for mankind?"

"Just by the title."

"So photographs don't speak."

"The picture itself is powerless to show."

That afternoon, we flew to Düsseldorf, where Struth has lived and worked for most of his life. He recently moved his living quarters to Berlin and was about to move his studio there as well. But Düsseldorf has been the center of his artistic life since he entered its Kunstakademie, in 1973, and studied first with the painter Gerhard Richter and then with the photographers Hilla and Bernd Becher. He entered the academy as a student of painting. The paintings he has preserved from this period show a penchant for surrealist creepiness—they depict looming landscapes and sinister people and are painted in a precise, Magritte-like style. After two and a half years, Richter proposed that Struth go and study with the Bechers. Struth had started photographing as an aid to his painting. He would photograph people on the street, who became the haunted figures in his paintings, as well as the streets themselves, in early-morning de Chirico emptiness. His paintings became more realistic, and cost him more effort, and, as they did so, he had an epiphany. "I realized, this takes too long," he said over lunch in a Düsseldorf café. "And that I'm not interested in the painting process. I'm interested in making pictures. And if I'm not interested in spending time accurately rendering the shadows in the coat and getting the color of the hat right and stuff like that, I realized—"

"You realized that someone else or, rather, something else—a camera—could do this for you?" I cut in, imagining the eureka moment.

"Yes. After I started taking photographs from which I would make my paintings, I realized that the photograph already does it. The photograph already shows what I want to show. So why make a painting that takes me five months to finish and then it looks like a photograph?"

"That's what the photo-realists did," I said.

"Yes, but that's naive. I remember when I first saw those paintings, I thought, That's not very interesting. They are only trying to show they can paint. That's not art."

Struth, of course, was mischaracterizing the photo-realist project— which was not to display painterly skills but to cast a cold eye on the psychopathology of mid-twentieth-century American life. The huge paintings of Airstream campers and gooey pies on luncheonette counters brought the details of the color photographs they were based on to an arresting, sometimes almost comical degree of visibility. These paintings were about scale—in much the way that the oversize photographs of Struth, Gursky, Wall, Höfer, et al. are—and in this sense they anticipated the new photography, though they were evidently not a conscious influence on the new photographers.

Recalling his student days, Struth spoke of the atmosphere of seriousness that permeated the academy: "When I came there, it was a shock to realize that I had to regard art as a serious activity and de-velop a serious artistic practice. Painting and drawing was no lon-ger my hobby, a private activity that I enjoyed. It was something that had categories. Artists were people who took positions and represented certain social and political attitudes. It was an intense experience to realize this. There was very intense judgment by the students—who is doing something interesting and who is an idiot painting lemons as if he were living in the time of Manet and Cézanne."

In a 1976 student exhibition at the academy, Struth showed forty-nine of the black-and-white photographs he had taken of empty Düsseldorf streets from a frontal perspective leading to a vanishing point, and the success of the series led to a scholarship in New York, where he did the work for which he was first known—black-and-white photographs of empty New York streets, again taken head-on. The assumption that these single-minded works were inspired by the Bechers' über-single-minded photographs of industrial struc-tures turns out to be wrong. As it happens, when Struth took his Düsseldorf pictures, he had not yet seen the Bechers' photographs—another example of the zeitgeist's uncanny ways.

The Bechers are cult figures, known in the photography world for their "typologies" of water towers, gas tanks, workers' houses, winding towers, and blast furnaces, among other forms of the indus-trial vernacular. In the late fifties, they began going around Ger-many, and then around the world, taking the same frontal portrait of each example of the type of structure under study, and arranging the portraits in grids of nine or twelve or fifteen, to bring out the individual variations. They did this for fifty years, never deviating from their austere formula: all the photographs were taken at the same aboveground-level height and under overcast skies (to elimi-nate shadows), as if they were specimens for a scientific monograph.

Struth is reserved about the Bechers' photographs, though he respects what he sees as the ideological backbone of their enterprise. "When Bernd and Hilla made this contract with themselves in the 1950s to catalog these kind of objects, German photography was all abstract subjectivism," he said. "People didn't want to look at real-ity, because what you saw in Germany in the fifties was destruction and the Holocaust. It was all a terrible reality, so precise looking was not a widespread impulse." The Bechers' precise looking was a model of ethical rigor. But Struth believes that "eventually their meaning in the history of art will be linked more with their teaching and the influence it had than with their work."

I asked Struth about the influence on him of the Bechers' pedagogy.

"Their big pedagogical influence was that they introduced me and others to the history of photography and to its great figures. They were fantastic teachers, and they were fantastic teachers in the way that they demonstrated the complexity of connections. It was an outstanding thing that when you met with Bernd and Hilla, they didn't talk about photography alone. They talked about movies, journalism, literature—stuff that was very comprehensive and complex. For example, a typical thing Bernd would say was, 'You have to understand the Paris photographs of Atget as the visualization of Marcel Proust.'"

I said, "I don't get it. What does Atget have to do with Proust?"

"It's a similar time span. What Bernd meant was that when you read Proust, that's what the backdrop is. That's the theater."

"Did you read Proust while you were studying with the Bechers?"

"No, no. I didn't."

"Have you read Proust since?"

"No."

"So what was the point for you of connecting Atget with Proust?"

Struth laughed. "Maybe it's a bad example," he said.

"It's a terrible example," I said. We both laughed.

Struth went on to contrast the beloved, *haimish* Bechers, whose classes were often held at their house or in a Chinese restaurant, with the "much more difficult to deal with" Gerhard Richter: "Gerhard was very ironic. I never had the feeling that he is someone who speaks naturally or openly. He was friendly, but you never knew what he really meant. It was very coded language and coded behavior."

Struth's characterization of Richter did not surprise me. I had seen the portrait of him and his wife and two children that Struth took for *The New York Times Magazine* in 2002, on the occasion of a Richter retrospective at the Museum of Modern Art in New York.

It is a beautifully composed picture of four people whose bodies are rigid with tension and whose staring faces illustrate different ways of looking hostile. White lilies in a glass vase and a picture of a skull on the wall reinforce the photograph's primal unease.

I was surprised to hear that Richter and his wife liked the picture.

"It's a very sad and disturbing picture," I said.

"Okay," Struth said.

"They do not look like a happy family."

"Well, that's not the issue."

"That almost *is* the issue of the picture."

Struth conceded that "they don't look relaxed and happy," and added, "He's not an easy person, that's for sure. He's a very particular person."

As we were leaving the café, Struth said, "I feel bad about Proust and Atget." Struth is a sophisticated and practiced subject of interviews. He had recognized the Proust-Atget moment as the journalistic equivalent of one of the "decisive moments" when what the photographer sees in the viewfinder jumps out and says, "This is going to be a photograph." I made reassuring noises, but I knew and he knew that my picture was already on the way to the darkroom of journalistic opportunism.

During our conversation in the café, Struth received a phone call from the Grieger printing lab telling him that the first test prints of his portrait of the Queen and the Duke were ready for his inspection. Grieger is considered the supreme printing lab for large-scale photography and is the place where many of its practitioners go to have their prints made. At Grieger, we were met by Dagmar Miethke, Struth's "special person" there, on whose eye and taste he depends for the finish of his photographs. Miethke, an easy and friendly woman of around fifty, pinned the print to the white wall, and the three of us silently regarded it.

My first impression was of a vaguely familiar elderly couple posing for a formal portrait in a corner of the palatial Minneapolis hotel ballroom where their fiftieth wedding anniversary is being celebrated.

The pair were seated on an ornate settee, and my attention was drawn to the woman's sturdy legs in beige stockings, the right knee uncovered where the skirt of her pale-blue silk dress had hitched up a bit as she settled her ample figure into the settee; and to her feet, in patent leather pumps planted firmly on the fancy hotel carpet. Her white hair was carefully coiffed, in a sort of pompadour in front and fluffy curls on the sides, and her lipsticked mouth was set in an expression of quiet determination. The man—a retired airline pilot?— was smaller, thinner, recessive. They were sitting a little apart, not touching, looking straight ahead. Gradually, the royal couple came into focus as such, and the photograph assumed its own identity as a work by Struth, the plethora of its details somehow tamed to serve a composition of satisfying serenity and readability.

Struth broke the silence and said that the picture was too yellow, and for the next half hour color adjustments were made on test strips until he was satisfied that the print had reached the degree of coolness he wanted. Then the issue of size arose. The print we were looking at was big, around sixty-three by seventy-nine inches, and he asked that a larger print be made. When this was produced, he regarded the two prints side by side for a long while. It seemed to me that the smaller print was more flattering to the Queen—the larger print made *her* look larger, almost gross. Struth finally asked that the smaller print be taken away so that he could study the larger print without distraction, and he finally decided on it. Further color adjustments were made on the big print—the Queen's hands were made less red, the background was darkened, to noticeably good effect—and Struth was satisfied.

Struth had positioned the settee—upholstered in green silk brocade, with curved gilded arms and legs—at a slant, so that the Queen was more prominent and lit with a kind of white glow, while the Duke receded into the shadows. The Duke is still handsome at ninety, his military bearing intact, but in the double portrait, next to the Queen's amplitude, he looked a bit shrunken.

Struth said of the sitting, "When we walked in"—he was accompanied by Hirsch and another assistant, named Carolina Müller— "they were not particularly friendly. No smiles. I was very nervous. I took a few shots and realized I hadn't adjusted the shutter opening. Then I saw that the pillow behind the Queen was not in a good position—exactly the kind of mistake I didn't want to make—so I said to her, 'Excuse me, can you lean forward?' and I just fixed the pillow behind her back. Then I made three or four more shots. And one of those shots was it. I knew it was it."

At his studio, Struth showed me the contact sheets of the sitting. There were the pictures with the badly positioned pillow behind the Queen. In another reject, the Duke had both hands on his thighs, rather than one hand strategically placed—as Struth instructed him to place it—on the seat of the sofa. Another showed the Queen looking majestic, the way she looks on money. In others, her mouth was slightly and awkwardly open, or her hands were folded on her lap in what Struth called a "defensive" position. The selected picture was indeed the right one.

Struth said he believed that his preparations impressed the royal couple and contributed to the success of the portrait: "They saw we took the task seriously." He spoke again of the bad photographs of the Queen and the Duke that he had studied, this time in terms of "the mistakes that make them look like almost comic impersonators of their functions rather than like real people. You would be shocked by how many terrible photographs there are of them. It's clear that the best pictures of Elizabeth and Philip are by Lord Snowdon, because he was a family member. Elizabeth looks happiest in Snowdon's photographs." He added, "I think what matters is that when the circumstances are prepared well and the people sit and look into the camera, there is always a chance of truth."

In fact, there is more than a chance. Photography is a medium of inescapable truthfulness. The camera doesn't know how to lie. The most mindless snapshot tells the truth of what the camera's eye saw at the moment the shutter clicked. Only the person being photographed can assume the lying appearance of "naturalness" that the portrait photographer seeks and tries to elicit with his repertoire of blandishments. But this appearance is not enough to give the portrait the look of art. For that, the preparations that Struth talked of—the fussing with pillows and the tilting of sofas and, most crucially, the selection of site—are necessary. The portraits of August Sander, who may be the greatest portrait photographer in the history of the medium, are a great object lesson in the significance of settings in the art of the photographic portrait. His settings are not incidental backgrounds for the figures whose souls he seems to have captured with his camera; they are intrinsic to the viewer's sense that such a capture has taken place. And so it was with Struth's portrait of Elizabeth and Philip.

In one of our talks, Struth told me that when he was in high school, he belonged to a little band of classmates—four boys and four girls—who spent all their time together and were determined not to be like their parents, whose recoil from the catastrophe of the war had taken the form of ultra-conventional behavior and a devotion to what was "safe and clean." Later, as I was leafing through a book of Struth's photographs, this phrase came floating to mind, for there is a sense in which it describes the world of Struth's huge, handsome pictures, from which the dangerous and dirty is conspicuously absent. *Dallas Parking Lot* (2001), for example, a magnificent composition of cool grays and icy blues and warm browns that Struth extracted from the ugly mess of the construction boom in Dallas, shows a rooftop parking lot in early-morning near emptiness and after-rain freshness, over which pristine glass high-rise buildings hover like benign guardians of the sleeping city's security. As it happened, this picture was not included in a retrospective of Struth's work in Düsseldorf (these days, there seems to be a Struth exhibition opening somewhere at every moment), to which he accompanied me on my last day in Germany, but in which many other representations of Struth's safe and clean world were on view.

His monumental (fifty-seven by seventy-four inches) portrait of the eight members of the Ayvar family in Lima is a rare encounter with poverty. That the family is poor may be inferred from the room in which they sit—a piece of plasterboard with cracks in it appears behind the group; the foreground shows part of a patterned velvet sofa over which a sheet has been thrown to hide something torn or ruined; a dark, muddy linoleum covers the floor; a small, cheap religious print hangs high on the wall. Clearly the spareness of the room is an object not of advanced taste, but of want, of not having the things that advanced taste keeps at bay. The family members—a tiny dark-haired mother, a gray-haired father, and six children, ranging in age from a seven- or eight-year-old boy to a grown son and daughter—sit at a small table facing the photographer. A current of sympathy runs between the subjects and the photographer that brings to mind the sympathy that flowed between Walker Evans and the sharecropper family he photographed in Dust Bowl Alabama in the 1930s. But with this difference: Evans's black-and-white photographs are heavyhearted pictures. They show the hopelessness of the struggle of the people they dignify and beautify. The smell of poverty wafts out of them. If any smell wafts out of the photograph of the Ayvars, it is that of laundry detergent. The father's crisply ironed short-sleeved dress shirt, the children's neat white and pastel-colored T-shirts, decorated with cartoons, and, most conspicuously, the bleached white cloth draped over the table, every stitch of whose green-and-red cross-stitched border is made visible, you could almost say celebrated, by the oversize print's magnification— all this creates a gestalt that is far removed from that of the rueful Evans's homage to the dirt-poor. As with all of Struth's photographs, it is hard to say what "statement" it makes, but its note is characteristically cheering, even elating. The dazzling white cross-stitched tablecloth (to which the eye is drawn as if to a central figure) emblematizes the work's optimism, like that of an Easter Sunday service—or an encounter with a friendly photographer.

As Struth and I were looking at another big picture, and he was pointing out something in its foreground, a museum guard suddenly materialized and told him that he was standing too close and should step back behind a line on the floor. Struth did not say, "I took that picture," but obediently stepped back behind the line. A little further into our tour of the show, the guard—a small woman of Japanese origin, now informed of Struth's identity—reappeared and profusely apologized for her blunder. Struth good-humoredly reassured her, but she could not stop apologizing and finally withdrew, walking backward with her hands held in supplication and her head bobbing up and down in little Japanese bows.

The picture we had been standing in front of showed a semi-submersible oil rig in a shipyard on Geoje Island in South Korea—a huge red thing, a colossus on four legs on a platform afloat near the shore, taut cables anchoring it to the concrete pavement onshore, on which piles of miscellaneous building materials are strewn. The photograph (110 by 138 inches) magisterially represents what can be called the new optics of the new photography, which sees the world as no human eye does. When you look at these photographs, it is as if you were looking through strange new bifocals that focus on things at a distance at the same moment that they focus on things close up. Everything is equally sharp. Struth's photograph of Notre Dame is another striking example of this phenomenon. Every detail of the facade is rendered in razor sharpness, as are the clothes and knapsacks of the dwarfed tourists in the plaza in front of it. Reproductions of these photographs in books give only a hint of their breathtaking strangeness. One needs to see them full size to marvel at them.

After the museum, Struth took me to his studio, which was in the process of being dismantled. It was a very long room on the second floor of a former printing plant, filled with desks and computers, sofas and bookcases, a drum set, and a narrow mattress on the floor neatly covered with blankets, where, after giving up his Düsseldorf apartment, Struth would sleep when in town. Windows facing the street lined one long wall, and a line of black file boxes sat on the floor along the wall opposite. These files, which relate to the business end of Struth's enterprise, were being reorganized before being shipped to Berlin; Struth wanted them to be in order before the move. Much of Struth's work these days is running his business. His art has made him rich, and his dealings with the people who have made him (and themselves) so occupy a good portion of his time (and of the studio's functions). He is on the phone a lot: someone is always calling him about some business particular; he seems to be under pressure.

It wasn't always like this, he told me, and cited two events that changed his life from that of a carefree rich artist to that of one who feels he has to hustle to remain one. The first was the renovation, in 2005, for a hundred and fifty thousand euros, of the Düsseldorf studio. The second was his marriage, in 2007, to Tara Bray Smith, a young American writer who gracefully accepted living in Düsseldorf for two and a half years and then proposed the move to Berlin—which Struth was happy to make. "The time was over. I was so used to Düsseldorf—it seemed good to move somewhere else." Good but not cheap.

"Before I did the renovation of the studio and before I got married, I had one assistant, not three, I needed very little money, my apartment was very inexpensive," Struth said. "I made much more money than I needed—and I paid a fifty percent tax to the German state. Then I did the renovation, I met Tara, we moved to Berlin, I rented a studio there that was six thousand euros a month, I hired two more assistants, Tara said she would love to have a small place in New York, and I thought, Okay, it makes sense, and we found one, though a bigger place than I thought. All of a sudden my expenses exploded, and I felt much more pressure to sell." I asked Struth what his photographs sell for, and he replied that at Marian Goodman, in New York, it is around a hundred and fifty thousand dollars. The gallery takes fifty percent, and the state takes fifty percent of Struth's share. Goodman sold thirty-five pictures in his last show, in 2010, but in Berlin only ten pictures sold that year. "There's never certainty," he said. At the same time, "I'm not worried. There's always something." For example: a commission from a billionaire (who wishes to go unnamed) to photograph his family, which Struth might not have accepted when he was flush and photographing only people he knew and liked.

At the studio, Struth leafed through the catalog of the Metropolitan Museum exhibition to illustrate another seminal event. This was the taking of a photograph entitled *The Restorers at San Lorenzo Maggiore*, on the last day of a three-month stay in Naples, in 1988. In Naples, Struth experienced the famous effect that the South has on industrious Northerners. "I discovered I was just very happy there. I fell in love twice. I thought, I'm not only the strict German; I have some joyful capacity in me that wasn't unearthed until now." The picture—a lovely composition in muted ocher and umber colors of four people posed in front of a long row of the large old religious paintings on which they have been working in a high-ceilinged

room in a former abbey—was the first photograph Struth saw reason to print big. It was also the work that opened the door to the
project for which he is perhaps best known: his museum pictures.
These show what we see when we walk into a museum gallery:
people looking at paintings. We only secondarily see the pictures
themselves.

For about a decade Struth ingeniously played with this conceit.
In some of the museum photographs, the relationship between
disturbing subject matter—such as that of *The Raft of the Medusa*—
and unperturbed viewers was the point, or part of it. In others,
spatial relationships were explored, such as in the photograph
entitled *Galleria dell'Accademia I*, a work showing Veronese's *Feast
in the House of Levi*, whose depth perspective supports the momentary illusion that the visitors in shorts and jeans standing before it
are about to enter its bustling scene. Yet another concept was to focus solely on museum visitors, photographing them from the point
of view of the work they were gazing at. In one series, Struth shows
tourists at the Galleria dell'Accademia in Florence gazing up at
Michelangelo's *David* and in another at The Hermitage, looking at
a da Vinci *Madonna and Child*. These "audience" pictures are in-
termittently amusing but, to my mind, a bit trite. We have seen
pictures of unself-consciously gaping tourists before. I am also unable to appreciate the series called *Paradise*, large, straightforward
pictures of jungles and forests. ("His jungles look like the potted
plants in a dentist's office," the critic Lee Siegel wrote in 2003, putting his finger on it.)

Struth's photographs taken in factories, laboratories, and nuclear
power plants, on the other hand, look like nothing one has ever
seen before. These glimpses into what the critic Benjamin Buchloh
calls "the technological sublime" were on view at Marian Goodman
last year and constitute some of Struth's most powerful images.
While at SolarWorld with Struth, I had these images in mind. The
feeling of not understanding what one is seeing, of not knowing the
functions of madly tangled wires and tubes and cables and mysterious flanges and pulleys and levers, is brilliantly conveyed by these
huge pictures of places few of us have ventured into and on whose
products many of us depend. Predictably, the places are not satanic

mills, but belong to the world of Struth's benign photographic vision. They reassure even as they baffle. They tell us that the people who are absent from the pictures are back there somewhere and that they know what it all means and know what they are doing.

On our way out of the Düsseldorf studio, Struth paused to play a twenty-second riff on the drums, relics of the days when he played in a rock band. We drove to my hotel for dinner, where Struth—after ascertaining that he wouldn't be acting like a rude guest—joined me in mocking the pretentious food served in mercifully stingy portions. (Everywhere else I ate in Germany, the food was elegant and delicious.) Back in New York, I have been corresponding with Struth by e-mail. In August, he sent me digital images of four of the pictures he had taken at SolarWorld. They were both surprising—while at the factory I hadn't "seen" any of these images myself—and of a piece with the incomparable Marion Goodman photographs. I wrote to ask if he or Hirsch could also send me the snapshots that, after the formal sitting, Hirsch had taken of the Queen and the Duke looking at a picture of Struth's dog, Gabby, which Struth had thought to pack when making his meticulous preparations. Hirsch promptly sent three of them. They are wonderful. My favorite shows Elizabeth beautifully smiling at the picture of the dog that Struth and Philip hold toward her as they broadly grin at each other over her head. In another e-mail Struth wrote that he had heard from the curator of the exhibition at the National Portrait Gallery that Philip "was clearly touched by the portrait, and asked, 'How did he do that?' " I wrote back and asked about the Queen's reaction, and the answer was that it was unknown. In a recent e-mail Struth wrote, "Still have not given up to find out what the Queen thinks. I tried to get in touch with the dresser, but I heard they are all in Scotland right now." He added, "Not that that is at the top of my agenda."

A HOUSE OF ONE'S OWN

1995

> If one is to try to record one's life truthfully, one must aim at get-
> ting into the record of it something of the disorderly discontinuity
> which makes it so absurd, unpredictable, bearable.
> —Leonard Woolf, *The Journey Not the Arrival Matters*

The legend of Bloomsbury—the tale of how Virginia and Vanessa
Stephen emerged from a grim, patriarchal Victorian background
to become the pivotal figures in a luminous group of advanced and
free-spirited writers and artists—takes its plot from the myth of
modernism. Legend and myth alike trace a movement from darkness to light, turgid ugliness to plain beauty, tired realism to vital
abstraction, social backwardness to social progress. Virginia Woolf
chronicles her own and her sister's coming-of-age in the early years
of this century much as Nikolaus Pevsner celebrated the liberating
simplifications of modern design in his once influential but now perhaps somewhat outdated classic *Pioneers of the Modern Movement:
From William Morris to Walter Gropius* (1936). As Pevsner shuddered
over the "coarseness and vulgar overcrowding" of a carpet shown in
the Great Exhibition of 1851 in London ("We are forced to step
over bulging scrolls and into large, unpleasantly realistic flowers . . .
And this barbarism was by no means limited to England. The other
nations exhibiting were equally rich in atrocities"), so Virginia, in her
memoir "Old Bloomsbury" (1922), recoiled from the suffocating

closeness of her childhood home, at 22 Hyde Park Gate in Kensing-ton—a tall, narrow, begloomed house of small, irregular rooms crammed with heavy Victorian furniture, where "eleven people aged between eight and sixty lived, and were waited upon by seven servants, while various old women and lame men did odd jobs with rakes and pails by day." And, as Pevsner turned with relief to the spare, *sachlich* designs of the twentieth-century pioneers, so Virginia exulted in the airy and spacious house on Gordon Square, in Bloomsbury, where she and Vanessa and their brothers, Thoby and Adrian, went to live by themselves in 1904, after the death of their father. (Vanessa was twenty-five, Thoby was twenty-four, Virginia was twenty-two, and Adrian was twenty-one.) "We decorated our walls with washes of plain distemper," Virginia wrote, and, "We were full of experiments and reforms . . . We were going to paint; to write; to have coffee after dinner instead of tea at nine o'clock. Everything was going to be new; everything was going to be different. Every-thing was on trial."

Nine years earlier, when Virginia was thirteen, her mother, Julia Stephen, had died, suddenly and unexpectedly, of rheumatic fever, at the age of forty-nine, and two years after that Stella Duckworth, one of Julia's three children from a previous marriage, who had be-come the angel of the house in Julia's place, died of peritonitis, at the age of twenty-eight. These deaths only darkened the darkness, coarsened the atrocious figures in the carpet. Leslie Stephen, the eminent Victorian writer and editor, tyrannized the household with his Victorian widower's hysterical helplessness, and George Duck-worth, Stella's brainless brother, couldn't keep his hands off Vanessa and Virginia while affecting to comfort them. Virginia's strength was unequal to the pressure of "all these emotions and complica-tions." A few weeks after Leslie's death, she fell seriously ill. "I had lain in bed at the Dickinsons' house at Welwyn"—Violet Dickinson was then her best friend—"thinking that the birds were singing Greek choruses and that King Edward was using the foulest possi-ble language among Ozzie Dickinson's azaleas," Virginia wrote of this descent into madness, the second in the series (the first fol-lowed her mother's death) by which her life was plagued and even-tually cut short. When she recovered—the antipsychotics of the time were bed rest, overfeeding, and boredom—her old home was gone and the new was in place. It was on Vanessa's sturdier shoulders that the weight of life at Hyde Park Gate had fallen after Stella's death (her siblings called her the Saint when they wanted to enrage her), and it was she who engineered the move to Gordon Square, selecting the neighborhood (then an unfashionable one), finding the new house, renting the old one, and distributing, selling, and burning its accretions.

There is a photograph of Stella, Virginia, and Vanessa, taken in 1896, the year after Julia's death, in which a classically profiled Stella looks demurely downward; an ethereal Virginia, in half profile, gazes pensively, perhaps a little strangely, into the middle distance; and mild Vanessa stares straight into the camera, her features set in an expression of almost harsh resolve. Without Vanessa's determination—and by the time of Leslie Stephen's death she was already making good on her ambition to be an artist, having studied drawing and painting since her early teens—it is doubtful whether the flight of the orphans to Gordon Square would have taken place. Nor, more to the point, would there have been the Thursday evening parties that were, Virginia playfully wrote, "as far as I am concerned the germ from which sprang all that has since come to be called—in newspapers, in novels, in Germany, in France, I daresay, in Turkey and Timbuktu—by the name of Bloomsbury." A period of happiness had begun that, as Virginia described it, was like the giddy early months of freshman life at college. She and Vanessa had not, of course, gone to college—even girls from literary families like the Stephens did not go to college then—but Thoby had gone to Cambridge, and came home on vacations to tell his wide-eyed sisters of his remarkable friends: of the frail, ultracultivated Lytton Strachey, who once, as Virginia wrote, "burst into Thoby's rooms, cried out, 'Do you hear the music of the spheres?' and fell in a faint"; of an "astonishing fellow called Bell. He's a sort of mixture between Shelley and a sporting country squire"; of a "very silent and thin and odd" man named Saxon Sydney-Turner, who was "an absolute prodigy of learning" and "had the whole of Greek literature by heart." These and other Cambridge classmates became the Thursday-evening harbingers of Bloomsbury and the sisters' initiators into the pleasures of late-night conversation on abstract subjects (beauty, reality, the good) with men who do not want to marry you and to whom you are not attracted. Evidently, they were an unprepossessing lot. "I thought that I had never seen young men so dingy, so lacking in physical splendor as Thoby's friends," Virginia wrote in "Old Bloomsbury" (doubtless exaggerating their nerdishness for comic effect; she wrote the piece to be read aloud to a gathering of Bloomsbury friends that included several of the ill-favored friends themselves). But "it was precisely this lack of physical splendor, this shabbiness! that was in my eyes a proof of their superiority. More than that, it was, in some obscure way, reassuring, for it meant that things could go on like this, in abstract argument, without dressing for dinner, and never revert to the ways, which I had come to think so distasteful, at Hyde Park Gate." However, things could not go on like this; the period of happiness abruptly ended. Once again, as she writes in a later memoir, "A Sketch of the Past" (1939), "the lashes of the random unheeding, unthinking flail," which had "brutally and pointlessly" destroyed Julia and Stella, descended on the Stephen family. In the fall of 1906, on a trip to Greece with his siblings, Thoby Stephen contracted typhoid and, apparently because of medical bungling (his illness was at first diagnosed as malaria), died a month after his return to England, at the age of twenty-six.

In the annals of Bloomsbury, Thoby's death, though as brutal and pointless as Julia's and Stella's, has not been accorded the same tragic status. Rather, in fact, the annalists have treated it almost as a kind of death of convenience, like the death of a relative who leaves deserving legatees a bequest of such staggering size that his own disappearance from the scene goes almost unnoticed. What happened was this: The previous year, one of the dingy young men, Clive Bell—who was actually neither as dingy nor as intellectual as the rest—had broken ranks and proposed to Vanessa, and she had refused him. Four months before Thoby's death, he had proposed again, and had again been refused. But now, two days after Thoby's death, Vanessa accepted him, and two months later she married him. As Leslie Stephen's death had allowed the children to flee from the ogre's castle, so Thoby's death melted the ice princess's heart. After

Clive's first proposal, Vanessa had written to a friend, "It really seems to matter so very little to oneself what one does. I should be quite happy living with anyone whom I didn't dislike . . . if I could paint and lead the kind of life I like. Yet for some mysterious reason one has to refuse to do what someone else very much wants one to. It seems absurd. But absurd or not, I could no more marry him than I could fly." Yet now, in the kind of emotional tour de force usually achieved by love potions, Vanessa's feeling for Clive suddenly ignited, so that three weeks after the death of her brother she could write to another friend, "I as yet can hardly understand anything but the fact that I am happier than I ever thought people could be, and it goes on getting better every day."

Quentin Bell, Vanessa's son, writing of Thoby's death in his extraordinary biography of his aunt, *Virginia Woolf* (1972), pauses to "wonder what role this masterful and persuasive young man, together with his wife—for he would surely have married—would have played in the life of his sisters." Quentin then goes on to coolly enumerate the advantages that accrued to the sisters from their brother's death:

> I suspect that, if he had lived, he would have tended to strengthen rather than to weaken those barriers of speech and thought and custom which were soon to be overthrown amongst his friends. It was his death which began to work their destruction: Mr Sydney-Turner and Mr Strachey became Saxon and Lytton, they were at Gordon Square continually and in her distress Virginia wanted to see no one save them and Clive . . . It was then that Virginia discovered that these young men had not only brains but hearts, and that their sympathy was something different from the dreadful condolences of relations. As a result of Thoby's death Bloomsbury was refounded upon the solid base of deep mutual understanding; his death was also the proximate cause for Vanessa's marriage.

Since Quentin's own existence was precariously poised on this concatenation of events, he may be forgiven for his rather unfeeling

words about his unfortunate uncle. Whether Thoby's influence on
Bloomsbury would in fact have been as baneful as Quentin postu-
lates cannot be known, of course. But this much is clear: the never-
never-land household of the four happy orphans had to be broken up
(just as the netherworld of Hyde Park Gate had to be fled) if Bloomsbury was to attain the form by which we know it—a coterie of
friends gathered around the nucleus of two very peculiar marriages.

After their wedding and honeymoon, in the winter of 1907, Clive
and Vanessa took over 46 Gordon Square, and Virginia and Adrian
moved to a house in nearby Fitzroy Square. Four years later, on July
3, 1911, another of Thoby's astonishing Cambridge friends—a
"violent trembling misanthropic Jew" who "was as eccentric, as remarkable in his way as Bell and Strachey in theirs"—came to dine
with the Bells at Gordon Square; Virginia dropped in after dinner.
He was Leonard Woolf, just back from seven years in Ceylon with
the Civil Service, and he was stunned by the great changes, the
"profound revolution" that had taken place in Gordon Square
since he dined there last, in 1904. In *Sowing*, the first volume of
his five-volume autobiography—a work of Montaigne-like con-
templativeness and poise, published in the 1960s, and the overture
to the Bloomsbury revival—Leonard recalled his first meeting
with the Stephen sisters, in Thoby's rooms at Cambridge. They
were around twenty-one and eighteen, and "in white dresses and
large hats, with parasols in their hands, their beauty literally took
one's breath away, for suddenly seeing them one stopped aston-
ished, and everything, including one's breathing for one second,
also stopped as it does when in a picture gallery you suddenly
come face to face with a great Rembrandt or Velasquez." In 1911,
Vanessa's and Virginia's beauty was undiminished (though Leonard
pauses to remark—he writes at the age of eighty-one and has out-
lived his wife by twenty-one years and his sister-in-law by one—that
"Vanessa was, I think, usually more beautiful than Virginia. The
form of her features was more perfect, her eyes bigger and better,
her complexion more glowing"). But what "was so new and so exhilarating to me in the Gordon Square of July 1911 was the sense of

intimacy and complete freedom of thought and speech, much wider than in the Cambridge of seven years ago, and above all including women." To understand Leonard's exhilaration, to see his revolution in action, we must return to Virginia's "Old Bloomsbury" memoir and a famous passage in it:

> It was a spring evening [in 1908]. Vanessa and I were sitting in the drawing room. The drawing room had greatly changed its character since 1904. The Sargent-Furse age was over. The age of Augustus John was dawning. His "Pyramus" filled one entire wall. The Watts' portraits of my father and my mother were hung downstairs if they were hung at all. Clive had hidden all the match boxes because their blue and yellow swore with the prevailing color scheme. At any moment Clive might come in and he and I should begin to argue—amicably, impersonally at first; soon we should be hurling abuse at each other and pacing up and down the room. Vanessa sat silent and did something mysterious with her needle or her scissors. I talked, egotistically, excitedly, about my own affairs no doubt. Suddenly the door opened and the long and sinister figure of Mr Lytton Strachey stood on the threshold. He pointed his finger at a stain on Vanessa's white dress.
>
> "Semen?" he said.
>
> Can one really say it? I thought and we burst out laughing. With that one word all barriers of reticence and reserve went down. A flood of the sacred fluid seemed to overwhelm us. Sex permeated our conversation. The word bugger was never far from our lips. We discussed copulation with the same excitement and openness that we had discussed the nature of good. It is strange to think how reticent, how reserved we had been and for how long.

"This was an important moment in the history of the mores of Bloomsbury," Quentin writes in *Virginia Woolf*, and—getting a bit carried away—"perhaps in that of the British middle classes." By the time Leonard came home from Ceylon, the transformation of the innocent girls in white dresses into women from whose lips the word "bugger" (Bloomsbury's preferred term for a homosexual) was never far was complete. Indeed, in the case of Virginia such talk was no longer of much moment or interest. She was doing regular reviewing, working on her first novel, finding Adrian irritating as a housemate, and looking for a husband. The society of buggers had, in fact, become "intolerably boring" to her. "The society of buggers has many advantages—if you are a woman," she allowed. "It is simple, it is honest, it makes one feel, as I noted, in some respects at one's ease." But

it has this drawback—with buggers one cannot, as nurses say, show off. Something is always suppressed, held down. Yet this showing off, which is not copulating, necessarily, nor altogether being in love, is one of the great delights, one of the chief necessities of life. Only then does all effort cease; one ceases to be honest, one ceases to be clever. One fizzes up into some absurd delightful effervescence of soda water or champagne through which one sees the world tinged with all the colours of the rainbow.

The married Vanessa, on the other hand, continued to be drawn to queer society. "Did you have a pleasant afternoon buggering one or more of the young men we left for you?" she wrote to John Maynard Keynes in April 1914. (Keynes was another Cambridge bugger, who had joined the Bloomsbury circle around 1907.) "It must have been delicious," she went on. "I imagine you . . . with your bare limbs intertwined with him and all the ecstatic preliminaries of Sucking Sodomy—it sounds like the name of a station." Vanessa's connection with Duncan Grant, which began during the First World War—he became her life's companion, even while continuing relationships with a series of boyfriends—has been called tragic; Duncan's inability to reciprocate Vanessa's love because he simply wasn't interested in women has been regarded as one of the sad mischances of her life. But the letter she wrote to Maynard and others of its kind—which appear in Regina Marler's excellently edited and annotated *Selected Letters of Vanessa Bell* (1993)—give one a whiff of something in Vanessa that may have impelled her to deliberately choose a homosexual as the love of her life; they suggest that Duncan's homosexuality may have been the very pivot of her interest in him. In a letter to Duncan of January 1914, Vanessa, bemoaning the British public's resistance to postimpressionist painting, wrote, "I believe distortion is like Sodomy. People are simple blindly prejudiced against it because they think it abnormal." Vanessa herself seemed almost blindly prejudiced *for* the abnormal.

But we are getting ahead of our story. Let us return to the scene of the sisters sitting in the drawing room of 46 Gordon Square in the spring of 1908. We will never know how much of Virginia's account is truth and how much comic invention. ("I do not know if I invented it or not," she offhandedly remarks, by way of introducing the scene.) But one detail stands out in its probable authenticity: *Clive had hidden all the match boxes because their blue and yellow swore with the prevailing color scheme.* Here, we feel, Virginia was reporting accurately. And here, we have to acknowledge, Clive was doing something that, in its way, was quite as remarkable for a man of his background as talking dirty was for girls of Virginia and Vanessa's background. In his hard-core aestheticism, Clive was behaving as few Victorian men behaved. Clive came from a rich family that had made its money from mines in Wales and had built a hideous and pretentious mansion in Wiltshire, decorated with fake-Gothic ornament and animal trophies. Numerous sardonic descriptions of the place have come down to us from Vanessa, who would visit there as a dutiful daughter-in-law and write to Virginia of the "combination of new art and deer's hoofs." At Cambridge, Clive had written poetry and hung a Degas reproduction in his rooms but had not got into the Apostles, the secret discussion society that, in the Bloomsbury gospel according to Leonard, was decisive to Bloomsbury's intellectual and moral avant-gardism. Thoby had not got into the Apostles, either (nor, for that matter, had Leslie Stephen), but Lytton, Maynard, Saxon, Leonard, Morgan (Forster), and Roger (Fry) had.

Clive was the lightweight of Bloomsbury; today nobody reads his books on art, and his own friends patronized him. When he became engaged to Vanessa, Virginia considered him unworthy. "When I think of father and Thoby and then see that funny little creature twitching his pink skin and jerking out his little spasm of laughter I wonder what odd freak there is in Nessa's eyesight," she wrote to Violet Dickinson in December 1906. In *Virginia Woolf*, Quentin writes that Henry James's "views of the bridegroom were even more unfavourable than those of Virginia in her most hostile moods." (James was an old family friend of the Leslie Stephens.) Quentin then quotes this passage from a letter of February 17, 1907, that James wrote to Mrs. W. K. Clifford:

> However, I suppose she knows what she is about, and seemed very happy and eager and almost boisterously in love (in that house of all the Deaths, ah me!) and I took her an old silver box ("for hairpins"), and she spoke of having got "a beautiful Florentine teaset" from you. She was evidently happy in the latter, but I winced and ground my teeth when I heard of it. She and Clive are to keep the Bloomsbury house, and Virginia and Adrian to forage for some flat somewhere—Virginia having, by the way, grown quite elegantly and charmingly and almost "smartly" handsome. I liked being with them, but it was all strange and terrible (with the hungry *futurity* of youth;) and all I could mainly see was the *ghosts*, even Thoby and Stella, let alone dear old Leslie and beautiful, pale, tragic Julia—on all of whom these young backs were, and quite naturally, so gaily turned.

The passage is wonderful ("the hungry *futurity* of youth"!) but puzzling. Quentin has said that James's views of Clive were even more unfavorable than Virginia's, but James says nothing bad about him—he doesn't single him out from the other callously happy young people. When we read the whole of James's letter (it appears in volume IV of Leon Edel's edition of James's letters), our puzzlement dissolves. In the sentence immediately preceding this passage, James writes:

> And *apropos* of courage, above all, oh yes, I went to see Vanessa Stephen on the eve of her marriage (at the Registrar's) to the quite dreadful-looking little stoop-shouldered, long-haired,

third-rate Clive Bell—described as an "intimate friend" of poor, dear, clear, tall, shy, superior Thoby—even as a little sore-eyed poodle might be an intimate friend of a big mild mastiff.

In his Notes, Quentin thanks Edel for bringing the letter to his attention, but when it comes to the point, he can't avail himself of Edel's offering. Like Hamlet pulling back from killing Claudius, Quentin cannot commit the parricide of publishing James's terrible words. However, in leaving the trace, the clue to the uncommitted murder, he has afforded us a rare glimpse into the workshop where biographical narratives are manufactured.

In an earlier work, *Bloomsbury*, published in 1968, Quentin confesses to the sin of discretion. "I have omitted a good deal that I know and much more at which I can guess concerning the private lives of the people whom I shall discuss," he writes in his introduction, and loftily continues, "This is, primarily, a study in the history of ideas, and although the *moeurs* of Bloomsbury have to be considered and will in a general way be described, I am not required nor am I inclined to act as Clio's chambermaid, to sniff into commodes or under beds, to open love-letters or scrutinize diaries." But when he accepted the commission from Leonard of writing Virginia's life, Quentin—obviously aware that the biographer *is* Clio's chambermaid—bowed to biography's lowering imperatives. He wrote of what his mother and his aunt, respectively, called George Duckworth's "delinquencies" and "malefactions," and of Gerald Duckworth's as well: of how during Leslie Stephen's final illness George would come to Virginia's bedroom late at night and fling himself on her bed, "cuddling and kissing and otherwise embracing" her, and of how Gerald (according to an early memory of Virginia's) had stood her on a ledge and, to her lifelong shivering distress, had meddled with her privates. Quentin wrote of an unconsummated but serious (and to his mother seriously wounding) flirtation between Clive and Virginia, which developed during the spring of 1908, when Vanessa was in thrall to her first baby, Julian, and Clive and the still unmarried Virginia would take long walks together to get away from Julian's nappies and screams. (The fastidious Clive "hated mess—the pissing, puking and slobbering of little children distressed him very much, so did their noise," his son writes.) He wrote of Virginia and Leonard's sexual incompatibility. (Like Vanessa, Virginia had initially refused her husband-to-be and, even when she was on the verge of accepting him, had told him of her doubts about "the sexual side of it." She wrote in a letter of May 1912, "As I told you brutally the other day, I feel no physical attraction in you. There are moments—when you kissed me the other day was one—when I feel no more than a rock.") Quentin quoted a letter from Vanessa to Clive written a few months after the Woolfs' wedding:

> They seemed very happy, but are evidently both a little exercised in their minds on the subject of the Goat's coldness. [Virginia's family nickname was Goat.] Apparently she still gets no pleasure at all from the act, which I think is curious. They were very anxious to know when I first had an orgasm. I couldn't remember. Do you? But no doubt I sympathised with such things if I didn't have them from the time I was 2.

What makes Quentin's biography such a remarkable work—one of the few biographies that overcome the congenital handicaps of the genre—is the force of his personality and the authority of his voice. He is perhaps more a butler than a chambermaid; he is certainly an upper servant. He has been with the family for a great number of years, and he is fiercely, profoundly loyal to it; he knows who are its friends and who its enemies. More important, he knows its members very well. He has carefully studied each of them for years; he has slowly turned their characters over in his mind for years, knowing their idiosyncrasies and weaknesses. He has been privy to their quarrels—the quarrels by which family life is defined and braced—and he has chosen sides, has discriminated and judged. In making his judgments and discriminations, he has picked up certain habits of mind from the family—habits of mind for which the family is famous—together with a certain tone. "The people I admire most are those who are sensitive and want to create something or discover something, and do not see life in terms of power." This statement, though made by E. M. Forster, might have been made by Quentin (or Vanessa or Virginia or Leonard or Clive or Lytton); it expresses the Bloomsbury ethos and is inflected in the Bloomsbury tone. Forster wrote these words in the essay "What I Believe," in which he also unforgettably said, "If I had to choose between betraying my county and betraying my friend, I hope I should have the guts to betray my country," and held up "an aristocracy of the sensitive, the considerate and the plucky." Here is how Quentin administers justice to the despicable, power-abusing George Duckworth, who fondled Vanessa as well as Virginia, little thinking that he was earning himself a place in literary history as one of its lowest worms:

> In later years Virginia's and Vanessa's friends were a little astonished at the unkind mockery, the downright virulence with which the sisters referred to their half-brother. He seemed to be a slightly ridiculous, but on the whole an inoffensive old buffer, and so, in a sense, he was. His public face was amiable. But to his half-sisters he stood for something horrible and obscene, the final element of foulness in what was already an appalling situation. More than that, he came to pollute the most sacred of springs, to defile their very dreams. A first experience of loving or being loved may be enchanting, desolating, embarrassing or even boring; but it should not be disgusting. Eros came with a commotion of leathern wings, a figure of mawkish incestuous sexuality. Virginia felt that George had spoilt her life before it had fairly begun. Naturally shy in sexual matters, she was from this time terrified back into a posture of frozen and defensive panic.

When Quentin judges his family, when he feels that one of its members hasn't behaved well (George wasn't a true family member), he reproves her (or him) as a nineteenth-century novelist might reprove a heroine (or hero)—as Jane Austen reproves Emma, say, when Emma has been thoughtlessly cruel to Miss Bates. This is the tone Quentin adopts in writing of Virginia's flirtation with Clive. He writes with a kind of loving disapproval, he feels that the whole thing was wrong because it was hurtful, but he sympathizes—as Jane Austen sympathized—with the impulse to heedlessly amuse oneself. He also sympathizes with Virginia's feeling of being left out of her sister's life after Vanessa's marriage. "She was not in the least in love with Clive," Quentin writes, "in so far as she was in love with anyone she was in love with Vanessa . . . It was because she loved Vanessa so much that she had to injure her, to enter and in entering to break that charmed circle within which Vanessa and Clive were so happy and by way of which she was so cruelly excluded, and to have Vanessa for herself again by detaching the husband who, after all, was not worthy of her."

What makes Bloomsbury of such continuing interest to us—why we emit the obligatory groan when the word is uttered but then go out and buy the latest book about Virginia and Vanessa and Leonard and Clive and Lytton and Roger and the rest—is that these people are so alive. The legend of Bloomsbury has taken on the dense complexity of a sprawling nineteenth-century novel, and its characters have become as real to us as the characters in *Emma* and *Daniel Deronda* and *The Eustace Diamonds*. Other early-modernist writers and artists, whose talents were at least equal to the Bloomsbury talents (except Virginia's), recede from view, but the Bloomsbury writers and artists grow ever more biographically prominent. Were their lives really so fascinating, or is it simply because they wrote so well and so incessantly about themselves and one another that we find them so? Well, the latter, of course. No life is more interesting than any other life; everybody's life takes place in the same twenty-four hours of consciousness and sleep; we are all locked into our subjectivity, and who is to say that the thoughts of a person gazing into the vertiginous depths of a volcano in Sumatra are more objectively interesting than those of a person trying on a dress at Bloomingdale's? The remarkable collective achievement of the Bloomsbury writers and artists was that they placed in posterity's hands the documents necessary to engage posterity's feeble attention—the letters, memoirs, and journals that reveal inner life and compel the sort of helpless empathy that fiction compels.

Toward the end of "A Sketch of the Past," there is a beautiful and difficult passage about the tendency Virginia has noticed in herself to write about the past in scenes:

> I find that scene-making is my natural way of marking the past. A scene always comes to the top; arranged; representative. This confirms me in my instinctive notion—it is irrational; it will not stand argument—that we are sealed vessels afloat upon what it is convenient to call reality; at some moments, without a reason, without an effort, the sealing matter cracks; in floods reality; that is a scene—for they would not survive entire so many ruinous years unless they were made of something permanent; that is a proof of their "reality." Is this liability of mine to scene-receiving the origin of my writing impulse?

At this point, Virginia, like the reader, begins to sense some of the problems with the passage: the confusion between "scene-making" and "scene-receiving" (which is it?) and the wobbliness of the word "reality," which totters from "what it is convenient to call reality" to plain "reality" to " 'reality.' " "These are questions about reality, about scenes and their connection with writing to which I have no answer; nor time to put the question carefully," she writes, and adds, "Perhaps if I should revise and rewrite as I intend, I will make the question more exact; and worry out something by way of answer." Virginia died before she could revise and rewrite the passage, and students of autobiography and biography are still worrying about the subject of "reality" versus reality—the made versus the received. But there is no question that the hyper-reality of the famous scenes in the Bloomsbury legend, like those of classical fiction, derives from a common artistic tradition and from certain technologies of storytelling, by which the wrought is made to appear as if it were the received. We call the tradition realism; the technologies are unnameable.

Virginia wrote "A Sketch of the Past" in spurts, between April 1939 and November 1940, as a diversion from a project that was giving her trouble—her biography of Roger Fry, the critic and painter who had introduced postimpressionist art to England. After writing the passage about scenes, she put the "Sketch" aside for a month, and when she returned to it she felt constrained to add, "Scenes, I note, seldom illustrate my relationship with Vanessa; it had been too deep for 'scenes.' "

Virginia and Vanessa's relationship was deep indeed—perhaps the deepest of all the Bloomsbury relationships. But it was not, in fact, impervious to—"too deep for"—Virginia's scenic imagination. In a letter to Violet Dickinson, for example, she gives this picture of Vanessa a month before her marriage, as she observed her in Bath walking down the street arm in arm with Clive: "She had a gauze streamer, red as blood flying over her shoulder, a purple scarf, a shooting cap, tweed skirt and great brown boots. Then her hair swept across her forehead, and she was tawny and jubilant and lusty as a young God."

It is the implicit comparison between the watcher and the watched, between the fragile and wistful Virginia and the powerful and sexually magnetic Vanessa, that gives the scene its novelistic shimmer. In Virginia's vision of her sister—it gleams out of her letters and diaries—Vanessa is a Kate Coy or Charlotte Stant to her own Milly Theale or Maggie Verver; she has not only the physical magnificence of James's wonderful "bad" heroines, whose robust beauty and splendid bearing so pointedly contrast with the slouching delicacy of the "good" heroines, but also their double-edged single-mindedness. ("You are much simpler that I am," Virginia wrote to Vanessa in August 1909. "How do you manage to see only one thing at a time? Without any of those reflections that distract me so much and make people call me bad names? I suppose you are, as Lytton once said, the most complete human being of us all; and your simplicity is really that you take in much more than I do, who intensify atoms.") Although it was Virginia/Milly/Maggie who had wronged Vanessa/Kate/Charlotte in the Clive affair, Virginia never ceased to feel obscurely wronged by her sister; she perpetually compared herself to Vanessa and found herself wanting. In June 1929, when she and Leonard joined Vanessa and Duncan in the South of France, she wrote in her diary of buying furniture and crockery for her country house in England; although it gave her pleasure, it "set my dander up against Nessa's almost overpowering supremacy. My elder son is coming tomorrow; yes, & he is the most promising young man in King's; & has been speaking at the Apostles' dinner. All I can oppose that with is, And I made £2,000 out of Orlando & can bring Leonard here & buy a house if I want. To which she replies (in the same inaudible way) I am a failure as a painter compared with you, & can't do more than pay for my models. And so we go on; over the depths of our childhood."

In 1926, after going to a show of Vanessa's paintings, Virginia wrote to her sister, "I am amazed, a little alarmed (for as you have children, the fame by rights belongs to me) by your combinations of pure artistic vision and brilliance of imagination." Of course, it is the parenthetical remark that leaps out of the passage. The fame is a poor thing, a devalued second best to the children. Vanessa is always the alarmingly invulnerable big sister, even though Virginia is capable of condescending to her when she feels particularly provoked. "What you miss [in Clive] is inspiration of any kind," she complained to Violet Dickinson, adding, "But then old Nessa is no genius." Vanessa would have been the first to agree; extreme modesty about her intellectual, and even artistic, attainments was one of her outstanding traits—and perhaps only added to her insufferable superiority in the eyes of her sister. In a memoir called "Reminiscences," addressed to the yet unborn Julian, Virginia shows us Vanessa behaving in girlhood as she would throughout her life: "When she won the prize at her drawing school, she hardly knew, so shy was she, at the recognition of a secret, how to tell me, in order that I might repeat the news at home. 'They've given me the thing—I don't know why.' 'What thing?' 'O they say I've won it—the book—the prize you know.' "

When Vanessa married, it was not she but Virginia and Adrian who were expelled from Gordon Square and had to "forage for some flat somewhere." "Nessa & Clive live, as I think, much like great ladies in a French salon; they have all the wits & the poets; & Nessa sits among them like a Goddess," Virginia wrote at about the time she and Adrian gave a party at Fitzroy Square whose high point was a dog being sick on the carpet. When Virginia accepted Leonard, it may have been, as Quentin characterizes it, "the wisest decision of her life," but it did not sweep her up and elevate her to the domestic rank of her sister. Vanessa's household remained the principal residence of the Bloomsbury court, and Virginia's was always secondary, an annex. In view of the fact that the Woolf marriage was a strong and lasting one, and the Bell marriage fell apart after only a few years, it is curious that this was so. But it was so. There was always something a little forlorn and tentative about Virginia and Leonard's household. There were, of course, the bouts of mental illness that Virginia suffered and Leonard nursed her through, which could not but leave in the air of the house their residue of tension and fear. But there was also the fact that Vanessa was a born chatelaine and Virginia was not. Virginia couldn't buy a penwiper without enduring agonies of indecision. As a result, though it is Virginia's literary achievement that has given Bloomsbury its place in cultural history, it is Vanessa's house that has become Bloomsbury's shrine.

Charleston Farmhouse, in Sussex, which Vanessa began to rent in 1916 as a country retreat, and where she and Duncan and (sometimes) Clive lived together for extended periods, was restored in the 1980s and opened to the public. In twentieth-century art, Vanessa and Duncan occupy a minor niche, but their decorations within the farmhouse, painted on door panels, fireplaces, windows, walls, and furniture, convinced some of the keepers of the Bloomsbury flame that the place should be preserved after the death of the ménage's last surviving member—Duncan—in 1978. A trust was formed, money was raised, and the place is now a museum, complete with a gift shop, teas, lectures, a twice-yearly magazine, and a summer-study program. Without the decorations, it is doubtful whether the house would have been preserved. Because of them, the legend of Bloomsbury has a site: readers of the novel of Bloomsbury need no longer imagine; they can now actually enter the rooms where some of the most dramatic scenes took place, can look out the windows the characters looked out of, can tread on the carpets they trod on and stroll in the garden they strolled in. It is as if Mansfield Park itself had been opened up to us as an accompaniment to our reading of the novel.

I visited Charleston last December on an extremely cold, gray day and immediately felt its Chekhovian beauty and sadness. The place has been preserved in its worn and faded and stained actuality. It is an artist's house, a house where an eye has looked into every corner and hovered over every surface, considering what will please it to look at every day—an eye that had been educated by Paris ateliers and villas in the South of France and is not gladdened by English prettiness. But it is also a house of an Englishwoman (an Englishwoman who, on arriving at her rented house in St.-Tropez in 1921, wrote to Maynard Keynes in London to ask him to send a dozen packages of oatmeal, ten seven-pound tins of marmalade, four pounds of tea, and "some potted meat")—a house where sagging armchairs covered with drooping slipcovers of faded print fabric are tolerated, and where even a certain faint dirtiness is cultivated. In a letter to Roger Fry about a house belonging to the American painters Ethel Sands and Nan Hudson (who had commissioned Vanessa and Duncan to decorate its loggia), Vanessa mocked the "rarefaction" and "spotless order" of the place. "Nan makes muslin covers to receive the flies' excrements (I don't believe Nan and Ethel have any—they never go to the W.), everything has yards and yards of fresh muslin and lace and silk festooned on it and all seems to be washed and ironed in the night," she wrote, and sighed for "a breath from one's home dirt." Vanessa's houses were never rarefied or dainty, but neither were they artless congeries of possessions, which was what she coldly judged Ottoline Morrell's Garsington to be: "To me it seems simply a collection of objects she likes put together with enormous energy but not made into anything."

Making things—visual or literary—was Bloomsbury's dominating passion. It was also, in a paradoxical way, its link to the nineteenth-century past that it was at such pains to repudiate. In their compulsive work habits, the Bloomsbury modernists were behaving exactly as their Victorian parents and grandparents had behaved. There is a moment in Virginia's "Reminiscences" that goes by so fast we may not immediately grasp what it has let drop about the iron hold that the work ethic had on the nineteenth-century mind. Writing of the excesses of grief to which Leslie Stephen was driven by the sudden death of Julia—"There was something in the darkened rooms, the groans, the passionate lamentations that passed the normal limits of sorrow . . . He was like one who, by the failure of some stay, reels staggering blindly about the world, and fills it with his woe"—Virginia pauses to recall Stella's strenuous efforts to distract the grief-stricken widower: "All her diplomacy was needed to keep him occupied in some way, when his morning's work was over." *When his morning's work was over.* Sir Leslie may have been staggering blindly about the world, but the world would have had to come to an end before he missed a morning at his writing table. Even when he was dying of bowel cancer, he continued to produce startling quantities of prose daily. Leonard, in the fourth volume of his autobiography, spells out what for Virginia went without saying:

> We should have felt it to be not merely wrong, but unpleasant not to work every morning for seven days a week and for about eleven months a year. Every morning, therefore, at about 9:30 after breakfast each of us, as if moved by a law of unquestioned nature, went off and "worked" until lunch at 1. It is surprising how much one can produce in a year, whether of buns or books or pots or pictures, if one works hard and professionally for three and a half hours every day for 330 days. That was why, despite her disabilities, Virginia was able to produce so very much.

(In volume V, lest any reader suppose that Leonard and Virginia spent the rest of the day in effete pleasure, he points out that with reviewing, reading for reviewing, and, in Virginia's case, thinking about work in progress or future work—and in his own case, running the Hogarth Press and serving on political committees—they actually worked ten or twelve hours a day.)

At Charleston, from which other spirits have fled and can now be conjured only by letters and diaries, the spirit of industry remains a felt presence. If the place is Chekhovian—as perhaps all country houses situated in precariously unspoiled country, with walled gardens and fruit trees and not enough bathrooms, are—it is not of Chekhovian idleness and theatricality that it speaks but, rather, of the values by which Chekhov's good characters are ruled: patient, habitual work and sensible, calm behavior. (Chekhov was a kind of Bloomsburian himself.) Charleston is dominated by its workplace— its studios and studies and the bedrooms to which guests retired to write. The communal rooms were only two in number—the living room (called the garden room) and the dining room—and were modest in size. They were not the house's hearth. That title belonged to the huge ground-floor studio, where for many years Vanessa and Duncan painted side by side, every day. (In Vanessa's later years she worked in a new studio, in the attic; after her death, Duncan, who stayed on in the house, gradually made the downstairs studio his living quarters.)

The ubiquitous decorations only extend our sense of Charleston as a place of incessant, calm productivity. They give the house its unique appearance, but they do not impose upon it. They belong to the world of high art and design, the world of postimpressionist painting and early-modernist design, and yet, quite mysteriously, they are of a piece with the English farmhouse that contains them and with the English countryside that enters each room through large, old-fashioned windows. During my tour of the house, I was drawn to the windows as if by a tropism. Today, we come to the house to see the decorations and the paintings that Clive and Vanessa and Duncan collected as well as the ones that Vanessa and Duncan produced; but what Clive and Vanessa and Duncan looked at when they entered a room was the walled garden and a willow and the pond and the fields beyond, and as I looked out of the windows they had looked out of, I felt their presence even more strongly than I had when examining their handiwork and their possessions. I visited the house on a day when it was closed to the public, in the company of Christopher Naylor, then the director of the Charleston Trust, who was at least as well acquainted with the novel of Bloomsbury as I was, and who called its characters by their first names, as I have done here—biographical research leads to a kind of insufferable familiarity. After the tour—which rang with "Christophers" and "Janets" as well as with "Clives" and "Duncans" and "Maynards"—my guide tactfully withdrew to allow me to commune alone with the ghosts of the house and to take notes on the decorations. Taking notes proved impossible: after an hour in the unheated house I could no longer move my fingers.

The cold brought my thoughts to the winter of 1918–19, when Vanessa was in the house with Duncan and his boyfriend David Garnett—known as Bunny—and Julian and Quentin and her newborn baby by Duncan, Angelica. Much water had gone over the dam since Clive and Vanessa married and lived like great ladies in Gordon Square. Their marriage had effectively ended in 1914. Clive had reverted to his old ways of philandering; Vanessa had fallen in love with Roger Fry and had had an affair with him, which ended when she fell in love with Duncan. The war had brought Vanessa and Duncan and Bunny to Charleston. Duncan and Bunny, who were conscientious objectors, maintained their status by doing farmwork. Their first employment was restoring an old orchard, but when the military board required more seriously unpleasant farmwork Vanessa rented Charleston, so that Duncan and Bunny could work on the adjoining farm. Although Duncan was passionately in love with Bunny, he sometimes graciously consented to sleep with Vanessa when Bunny was away. Frances Spalding, in her biography of Vanessa, published in 1983, quoted a rather awful entry in Duncan's diary of 1918, written during a five-day absence of Bunny's:

> I copulated on Saturday with her with great satisfaction to myself physically. It is a convenient way, the females, of letting off one's spunk and comfortable. Also the pleasure it gives is reassuring. You don't get this dumb misunderstanding body of a person who isn't a bugger. That's one for you Bunny!

Thus Angelica. She was born on Christmas Day of 1918, and in her first weeks she almost joined Julia and Stella and Thoby as a casualty of disastrously incompetent doctoring; the intervention of a new doctor saved her life. (Five years later, Virginia, writing in her diary of another near miss—Angelica had been knocked down by a car in London—described the terrible scene in a hospital ward with

Vanessa and Duncan when it appeared certain that "death & tragedy had once more put down his paw, after letting us run a few paces." Angelica turned out to be unharmed: "It was only a joke this time.")

After his appearance at Angelica's cradleside, "the great cat" retreated, and Vanessa was allowed almost twenty more years of the happiness she had willed into being when she left Hyde Park Gate and painted the walls of 46 Gordon Square with distemper. "How much I admire this handling of life as if it were a thing one could throw about; this handling of circumstances," her sister wrote about her, and "How masterfully she controls her dozen lives; never in a muddle, or desperate or worried; never spending a pound or a thought needlessly; yet with it all free, careless, airy, indifferent."

The man Vanessa had chosen to be her life's partner is still a veiled character; our understanding of Duncan must await Frances Spalding's biography, now in preparation. He seems to have been extremely good-looking and charming and disarming, as well as eccentrically vague, and perhaps somewhat selfish. He was six years younger than Vanessa, but she deferred to him as an artist; she considered herself several steps behind him. (This judgment was reflected in their relative positions in the British art world at the time; today, there seems less of a gap between their achievements.) He was one of the Bloomsbury aristocrats (he was Lytton's cousin), as Bunny Garnett, for example, was not. Bunny went straight—or reverted to being straight—soon after Angelica's birth. Duncan transferred his affections to another man, and to others after him, but he permanently remained Vanessa's companion, and she gamely accepted the terms of his companionship. (From her letters to Duncan we may gather that these terms were rather hard ones, and that she *was* sometimes in a muddle and desperate and worried about how to maintain her equilibrium in the face of them.) Her relationship with Clive, meanwhile, was friendly and intimate, a sort of unsinister version of the relationship between the former lovers of *Les Liaisons Dangereuses.*

Vanessa's remarkable domestic arrangement seems almost an inevitability: What could be a better riposte to Victorian hypocrisy and dreariness than a husband who brought his mistresses around for amused inspection and a lover who was gay? By any standard, the Bell-Grant household was a strange one, and in the 1920s there were still plenty of people who could find it excitingly scandalous. One of them was Madge Vaughan, an old family friend, ten years older than Vanessa, who was the daughter of John Addington Symonds. (Symonds, as it happens, was one of the biggest closet queens of the Victorian age, a fact that came out only years after his and Madge's deaths.) In March 1920, Vanessa received a letter from Madge that made her, she said, "half amused and half furious." The letter was written from Charleston, where Madge, in Vanessa's absence, was staying briefly while deciding whether or not to rent the place for a long family holiday. "I love you & I am *faithful* to old friends," Madge wrote, and she went on:

> I have set my back against slander and chatter and fought your battles always through the years. But I love, with increasing passion, *Goodness, purity* and *homeliness & the hearts of little children are the holiest things I know on earth.* And a question gnaws at my poor heart here in this house.
>
> It came stabbing my heart that day when I saw Angelica. I would like to meet you as a woman friend face to face at some *quiet place* and to *talk it out.* I don't feel I *could* come and live here with Will and the children unless I had done this.

Vanessa replied to this piece of flowery piety in prose as crushingly simple and elegant as the black gown Anna Karenina wore to the fateful opening ball:

> Why on earth should my moral character have anything to do with the question of your taking Charleston or not? I suppose you don't always enquire into your landlord's characters. However take it or not as you like . . .
>
> As for the gossip about me, as to which of course I have not been left in ignorance, I must admit that it seems to me almost incredibly impertinent of you to ask me to satisfy your curiosity about it. I cannot conceive why you think it any business of yours. I am absolutely indifferent to anything the

world may say about me, my husband or my children. The
only people whose opinion can affect one, the working
classes, luckily have the sense for the most part to realise that
they can know nothing of one's private life and do not allow
their speculations about what one does to interfere with their
judgment as to what one is. The middle and upper classes are
not so sensible. It does not matter as they have no power over
one's life.

In her reply, poor Madge put her foot in it even further by saying
she had not wanted to pry, oh, no—"I am too saddened by contact
with mean, sometimes cruel & inquisitive minds to entertain any
sort of mere idle 'curiosity' myself "—but had only written from the
Purest of Motives, *"out of a sort of passionate longing to help those I
love."*

Vanessa, roused to even greater heights of weary contempt, replied:

You say you offered me help, but surely that is not a true account of your motives, for had I shown any slightest sign of
wishing for help or needing it? And did not you wish to talk
to me really so that you might know what sort of person I was
to whose house you proposed to take your children?

That at any rate was the reason you seemed to give me for
writing.

Nor was there even the excuse that Clive and I were known
to be on bad terms with each other. In that case (though I
should probably not desire it) I could understand an old friend's
interference.

But whatever the gossip about us may be, you must know
that we see each other and are to all appearance friendly, so it
should I think be assumed that we are in agreement on those
matters which concern our intimate lives. You say you tell
Will everything, although your married life has been full of
restraints. What reason is there to think that I do not tell
Clive everything? It is perhaps because we neither of us think
much of the world's will or opinion, or that a "conventional
home" is necessarily a happy or good one, that my married

life has not been full of constraints but, on the contrary, full of ease, freedom and complete confidence. Perhaps the peace and strength you talk of can come in other ways than by yielding to the will of the world. It seems to me at any rate rash to assume that it can't, or in fact that there is ever any reason to think that those who force themselves to lead lives according to convention or the will of others are more likely to be "good" (by which I mean to have good or noble feelings) than those who decide to live as seems to them best regardless of other standards.

Vanessa writes wonderfully not only when she is eating someone alive, like Madge Vaughan, but throughout the volume of her letters. "You have a touch in letter-writing that is beyond me. Something unexpected, like coming round a corner in a rose garden and finding it still daylight," Virginia wrote her in August 1908, and the description is right. About her own letters Virginia wrote, "I am either too formal, or too feverish," and she is right there, too. Virginia was the great novelist, but Vanessa was the natural letter writer; she had a gift for letter writing just as she had for making houses beautiful and agreeable. Virginia's letters have passages that surpass anything Vanessa could have written—set pieces that shimmer with her febrile genius—but they lack the ease and unself-consciousness (the qualities on which the epistolary genre draws for its life as a literary genre) by which Vanessa's are consistently marked.

Regina Marler, with her selections, has created a kind of novel-in-letters counterpart of Frances Spalding's sympathetic biography. Each letter illustrates a facet of Vanessa's character and advances the plot of her life. Her relationships with Virginia, Clive, Roger, Duncan, and Julian—the novel-in-letters' other characters—are revealed in moving fullness. The death of Julian, at the age of twenty-nine, in the Spanish Civil War, is the dreadful event toward which the plot inexorably moves. On July 18, 1937, during the Battle of Brunete, he was hit by shrapnel and died of his wounds. Reading Vanessa's letters to him in the two years before his death in the knowledge of what is coming is almost unbearable. In a letter written to him in China, where he was teaching, she writes, "Oh Julian, I can never express what happiness you've given me in my life. I often wonder how such luck has fallen my way. Just having children seemed such incredible delight, but that they should care for me as you make me feel you do, is something beyond all dreaming of—or even wanting. I never expected it or hoped for it, for it seemed enough to care so much oneself." A year later, when he has begun to make plans to go to Spain, she writes, "I woke . . . from an awful nightmare about you, thinking you were dead, and waking saying 'Oh, if only it could all be a dream.'" In July 1937, when, in spite of her anguished arguments, he has gone to Spain, she writes a long, witty letter about gatherings at Charleston and in London attended by, among others, Leonard, Virginia, Quentin, Angelica, T. S. Eliot, and Henri Matisse, and also by James, Dorothy, Pippa, Jane, and Pernel Strachey ("There was slightly overwhelming Strachey atmosphere") and holds up as "extraordinarily sane and unanswerable" an article by Maynard in the *New Statesman* replying to Auden's poem "Spain" and asserting the primacy of "the claims of Peace." Reading the next letter in the book, dated August 11, to Ottoline Morrell, *is* unbearable.

Dearest Ottoline,

I was grateful for your little note. You will forgive me for not writing sooner. I am only beginning to be able to write any letters, but I wanted to thank you.

Do you remember when we first knew each other telling me of your sorrow when your baby son died—I have never forgotten it.

Yours, Vanessa

In another short letter, written five days later, Vanessa acknowledges a condolence from Vita Sackville-West (her sister's former lover) and says, "I cannot ever say how Virginia has helped me. Perhaps some day, not now, you will be able to tell her it's true." After Virginia's suicide, in March 1941, Vanessa wrote to Vita again and came back to her letter of August 1937.

I remember sending that message by you. I think I had a sort of feeling that it would have more effect if you gave it and I expect I was right. How glad I am you gave it. I remember all

> those days after I heard about Julian lying in an unreal state
> and hearing her voice going on and on keeping life going as it
> seemed when otherwise it would have stopped, and late every
> day she came to see me here, the only point in the day one
> could want to come.

Virginia noted in her diary in September 1937, "Nessa's little
message: to me so profoundly touching, thus sent secretly via Vita
that I have 'helped' her more than she can say." The reversal of
roles—Virginia now the strong dispenser of comfort and stability to
the pitifully broken Vanessa—is one of the most beautiful and interesting moments in the Bloomsbury novel. Vanessa's inability to tell
Virginia directly of her love and gratitude is a measure of the depth
of her reserve, the quality that gave her character its immense authority and her household its improbable peacefulness, which strangers
sometimes mistook for hauteur, and her sister—emotional, wildly
imaginative—for indifference.

"I thought when Roger died that I was unhappy," the devastated
Vanessa said to Virginia after Julian's death. Vanessa's affair with
Roger had begun in 1911 and had painfully (for him) ended in
1913, but, like Clive, Roger remained in Vanessa's orbit and continued to function in her life as one of its fundamental structures. As
well as a lover, he had been a mentor and a decisive artistic influence. His postimpressionist show of 1910 had introduced the then
difficult art of Cézanne, Gauguin, van Gogh, Picasso, and Matisse,
among others, to an obligingly derisive English public. ("The exhibition is either an extremely bad joke or a swindle," Wilfred Blunt
wrote in his diary. "The drawing is on the level of that of an un-
taught child of seven or eight years old, the sense of colour that of a
tea-tray painter, the method that of a schoolboy who wipes his fingers on a slate after spitting on them.") Perhaps the most remarkable
of Vanessa's letters to Roger is one she wrote in November 1918
(from Charleston, in the last month of her pregnancy with Angelica), recalling "that first part of our affair," which was

> one of the most exciting times of my life, for apart from the
> new excitement about painting, finding for the first time

someone whose opinion one cared for, who sympathised with and encouraged one, you know I really was in love with you and felt very intimate with you, and it is one of the most exciting things one can do to get to know another person really well. One can only do so, I think, if one's in love with them, even though it may be true that one's also then deluded about them—as I daresay you *were* about me. But I really loved and admired your character and I still do and I expect having been in love with you will always make me have a different feeling about you from what I could have had otherwise, in spite of all the difficulties that have happened since.

Roger's death, in 1934, of a heart attack after a fall, is almost as afflicting as Julian's; Lytton's, in 1932, of stomach cancer, is scarcely less so. Vanessa's letters make us care about these long-dead real people in the way novelists make us care about their newly minted imaginary characters. We weep unashamedly when we read Vanessa's letters reaching out to Dora Carrington, the woman who had been hopelessly in love with Lytton, as Vanessa was in love with Duncan, and to Helen Anrep, who had become Roger's companion after he got over Vanessa. Why do books of letters move us as biographies do not? When we are reading a book of letters, we understand the impulse to write biographies, we feel the intoxication the biographer feels in working with primary sources, the rapture of firsthand encounters with another's lived experience. But this intoxication, this rapture, does not carry over into the text of the biography; it dies on the way. Here, for example, is Virginia writing to Lytton from Cornwall in April 1908:

Then Nessa and Clive and the Baby and the Nurse all came, and we have been so domestic that I have not read, or wrote . . . A child is the very devil—calling out, as I believe, all the worst and least explicable passions of the parents—and the Aunts. When we talk of marriage, friendship or prose, we are suddenly held up by Nessa, who has heard a cry, and then we must all distinguish whether it is Julian's cry, or the cry of the 2 year old, who has an abscess, and uses therefore a different scale.

And here is Frances Spalding:

If Clive was irritated and frustrated, Virginia was experiencing a more agonizing sense of real loss. In Cornwall both
were infuriated by Vanessa's habit of interrupting the conversation in order to discern whether it was Julian or the land-
lady's two-year-old who was crying. The caterwauling increased
their discomfort.

Or Vanessa writing to Clive on October 12, 1921:

Our arrival in Paris was thrilling. You will be sorry you
missed Quentin's first sight of Paris. He and I stood in the
corridor to see it and he told me he was most anxious to see
what it was like as he expected to live there some day. He was
wild with excitement, taking in everything with eyes staring
out of his head, especially as we crossed the Seine, which did
look most lovely. He thought all the colours so different from
England, though it was dark and there was not much to be
seen but coloured lights.

And Spalding:

On the journey out her chief pleasure lay in watching her
son's response to all that they saw. As the train approached
Paris she stood in the corridor with Quentin awaiting the
first sight of the city for, as he told her in his most ceremoni-
ous manner, he was most anxious to see it as he expected to
live there one day.

There is nothing wrong with what Spalding has written in these
extracts. They illustrate normal biographical method. The genre
(like its progenitor, history) functions as a kind of processing plant
where experience is converted into information the way fresh produce is converted into canned vegetables. But, like canned vegetables, biographical narratives are so far removed from their source—so
altered from the plant with soil clinging to its roots that is a letter or

a diary entry—that they carry little conviction. When Virginia complains to Lytton (another high-strung, single, childless intellectual) about what a nuisance the baby is, her voice carries great conviction, and so does Vanessa's when she proudly exclaims over her young son's aestheticism to his aesthete father. When Spalding writes, "In Cornwall both were infuriated," and "On the journey out her chief pleasure lay," we do not quite believe her. Taken from its living context, and with its blood drained out of it, the "information" of biographies is a shriveled, spurious thing. The canniest biographers, aware of the problem, rush massive transfusions of quotation to the scene. The biographies that give the greatest illusion of life, the fullest sense of their subject, are those that quote the most. Spalding's biography is one of these, as is Quentin's—though Quentin, in any case, is exempt from the above criticisms because his nephew's and son's voice carries the authority that no stranger-biographer's voice can. His acute critical intelligence is always being inflected by a fond familial feeling; this does not so much blunt his judgments as give them a kind of benign finality. (When Virginia once characterized an affectionate letter of Quentin's mother as "exquisitely soft and just, like the fall of a cat's paw," she could have been describing her nephew's biography.)

The judgments of Quentin's half sister, Angelica, have a rather different atmosphere. Angelica appears in Vanessa's letters and Virginia's diaries as a radiant, impish child, and then as a beautiful, piquant young woman—a kind of crown of Vanessa's maternal achievement, the lovely flower who provided the "feminine element" (as Vanessa termed it) that the family required to reach its final perfection. But in her book *Deceived with Kindness* (1985), Angelica, now a rather defeated older woman, comes forward to correct our admiring vision of Vanessa and to bring the Bloomsbury legend into line with our blaming and self-pitying times. Angelica is a kind of reincarnation of Madge Vaughan; what Madge adumbrated in her piously accusing letters to Vanessa, Angelica elaborates in her angry and aggrieved book about Vanessa. Madge felt that she could not bring her husband and children to live in a house of such irregularity; Angelica confirms her misgivings. Bloomsbury bohemianism was evidently lost on its youngest heir, who never felt at ease with her family, and would have infinitely preferred to grow up in a household like Madge's, where the children came first and you were unlikely to one day discover that your mother's lover was your real father. The relationship between Duncan and Vanessa—regarded by Spalding and other Bloomsbury aficionados as a testament to Vanessa's magisterial free-spiritedness and as an extraordinarily fruitful artistic union— is regarded by Angelica as simply disreputable and pathological. ("There must have been a strong element of masochism in her love for him, which induced her to accept a situation which did permanent harm to her self-respect . . . She gained companionship with a man she loved on terms unworthy of her whole self.") In 1917 Roger wrote to Vanessa,

> You have done such an extraordinarily difficult thing without any fuss, but thro' all the conventions kept friends with a pernickety creature like Clive, got quit of me and yet kept me your devoted friend, got all the things you need for your own development and yet managed to be a splendid mother . . . You have a genius in your life as well as in your art and both are rare things.

Angelica denies that Vanessa was a splendid mother and believes Vanessa's life was a shambles. Her book introduces into the Bloomsbury legend the most jarring shift in perspective. Until the publication of *Deceived with Kindness* the legend had a smooth, unbroken surface. Efforts from the outside to penetrate it—I think of such books as Louise DeSalvo's *Virginia Woolf: The Impact of Childhood Sexual Abuse on Her Life and Work* (1989) and Roger Poole's less crude but almost as dark and accusing *The Unknown Virginia Woolf* (1978)—succeeded no better than did Madge's and other interfering busybodies' attempt to "help" where no help had been requested.

But Angelica's attack from within is something else. It is a primary document; it cannot be pushed aside, unpleasant and distasteful though it is to see a minor character arise from her corner and proceed to put herself in the center of a rather marvelous story that now threatens to become ugly. An unhappy Quentin attempted to do a little damage control in a review of *Deceived with Kindness* that was first published in *Books and Bookmen* and then in the Charleston *Newsletter.* Treading carefully ("Ought a brother to review his sister's book? Certainly it is an awkward undertaking, made all the more awkward when, as in the present instance, one cannot but express admiration") but firmly ("To say that this is an honest narrative is not to say that it is accurate"), Quentin tries to correct the correction and restore the Bloomsbury story to its old dignity and high style. Occasionally, his irritation with his irritating little sister gets the better of his tact, as when he notes, "My sister was the only young person I then [in the thirties] knew who seemed to take not the slightest interest in politics." He goes on:

> The non-political person must of necessity see the world in terms of personality and individual responsibility, hence of praise or blame. The impersonality of politics which Angelica saw as something inhuman can also lead to milder moral judgments . . . I was sorry for my sister coming as she did to her majority just as the last hopes of peace in Europe vanished, [but] she, as these pages show, had quite other misfortunes to preoccupy her mind.

More than anything else, it is the tone of Angelica's book that sets it apart from other Bloomsbury texts. The note of irony—perhaps because it resounded too insistently in her ears when she was growing up—is entirely absent from her text, an absence that brings into relief Bloomsbury's characteristic obliqueness. Virginia, writing of sorrows at least as afflicting as Angelica's, never allows her stoicism to falter, and rarely fails to hang on to some shred of her natural gaiety. Her niece writes under inspiration of different spirits. When Angelica says that Vanessa

> never realised that, by denying me my real father she was treating me even before my birth as an object, and not as a human being. No wonder she always felt guilt and I resentment, even

though I did not understand the true reason for it; no wonder too that she tried to make it up to me by spoiling me, and
in so doing only inhibited me. As a result I was emotionally
incapacitated.

we withhold our sympathy—as we withheld it from Madge
Vaughan—not because her grievance is without merit, but because
her language is without force. As Madge cloaked and muffled the
complexity and legitimacy of her fears for her children in the ornate
pieties of the Victorian period (which she had brought with her into
the 1920s), so Angelica cloaks and muffles the complexity and legitimacy of her fury at her mother in the streamlined truisms of the
age of mental health.

The man Angelica married (and separated from after many unhappy years) was—the reader who doesn't already know this will fall
out of his chair—Bunny Garnett. On the day Angelica was born,
Bunny, who was then ensconced at Charleston as Duncan's lover,
wrote to Lytton about the new baby: "Its beauty is the remarkable
thing about it. I think of marrying it; when she is twenty I shall be
46—will it be scandalous?" That Bunny's prophecy should have
come true is a twist that seems to belong to another plot, but that
Bunny and Angelica gravitated toward each other is not so remarkable. Like Angelica, Bunny never really belonged among the
Bloomsbury aristocrats. Vanessa put up with him because of Duncan; Lytton and Virginia jeered at his (now hopelessly dated) novels.
(In her diary for 1925, Virginia quotes Lytton on Bunny's latest
work: "Really it's very extraordinary—so arty,—so composed—the
competence terrific, but . . . well, it's like a perfectly restored Inn—Ye
Olde Cocke and Balls, everything tidied up & restored.") Bunny's
three-volume autobiography is permeated with complacency and an
air of bogusness. Every literary society has its Bunny, it seems; so
often the least talented member comes forward as its noisiest, and
most knowing, self-appointed and self-important spokesman.

In what I have written, in separating my Austenian heroines and
heroes from my Gogolian flat characters, I have, like every other

biographer, conveniently forgotten that I am not writing a novel, and that it really isn't for me to say who is good and who is bad, who is noble and who is faintly ridiculous. Life is infinitely less orderly and more bafflingly ambiguous than any novel, and if we pause to remember that Madge and Bunny, and even George and Gerald Duckworth, were actual, multidimensional individuals, whose parents loved them and whose lives were of inestimable preciousness to themselves, we have to face the problem that every biographer faces and none can solve; namely that he is standing in quicksand as he writes. There is no floor under his enterprise, no basis for moral certainty. Every character in a biography contains within himself or herself the potential for a reverse image. The finding of a new cache of letters, the stepping forward of a new witness, the coming into fashion of a new ideology—all these events, and particularly the last one, can destabilize any biographical configuration, overturn any biographical consensus, transform any good character into a bad one, and vice versa. The manuscript of *Deceived with Kindness* was made available to Frances Spalding during the writing of her biography of Vanessa, and though she does not ignore it, she chooses not to allow it to sour her affectionate portrait. Another biographer might have made—a subsequent biographer may well make—a different choice. The distinguished dead are clay in the hands of writers, and chance determines the shapes that their actions and characters assume in the books written about them.

After my inspection of the Charleston house, a walk in the walled garden (which somehow seemed warmer than the icy house), and a visit to the gift shop, I rejoined Christopher Naylor, and, as had been arranged, we drove off for tea with Anne Olivier Bell, Quentin's wife, who is known as Olivier. Quentin would not be at tea, Christopher told me; he was frail and napped in the afternoon. The couple live in a house a mile away, which, like Charleston, is on a huge estate belonging to a Lord Gage, who has managed to hang on to his property (is this why one thinks of *The Cherry Orchard* while at Charleston?) and is one of the supporters of the Charleston Trust. When we arrived at the Bell house, at about four-thirty, it was already dark. Olivier ushered us into a large, warm room with a kitchen at one end and, at the other, a fireplace in which a fire was robustly burning. A long wooden table stood in front of the fire. Olivier is a tall, vigorous woman in her late seventies, with an appealing shy friendliness. One is immediately drawn to her warmth and naturalness, her sensible and matter-of-fact manner, her extreme niceness. She put a kettle on the hob and then showed me (as if this were what her visitors expected) various paintings by Bloomsbury artists. One was a large portrait of Vanessa in a red evening dress with one arm raised voluptuously over her head, painted by Duncan in 1915, and another was Vanessa's portrait of Quentin as a little boy of eight, looking up in the act of writing in a notebook. Neither these paintings nor any of the others was hung to advantage: the portrait of Vanessa was in a hallway at the bottom of a staircase, on a wall too small for it, and the portrait of Quentin, though not quite so badly placed, was not right, either. In *Deceived with Kindness*, Angelica bitterly writes of how "appearances of a purely aesthetic kind were considered of supreme importance" at Charleston ("Hours were spent hanging an old picture in a new place, or in choosing a new colour for the walls"), while she herself was allowed to go out into the world unbrushed and unwashed. Quentin and Olivier's house was entirely without the aestheticism of Charleston. It was comfortable, pleasant, and inviting but aesthetically unremarkable: this was not where their interests lay. Vanessa's dining table at Charleston was round, and she had painted a design on it in yellow, gray, and pink, evocative of the covers she did for Virginia's Hogarth Press books, which for some readers are inextricably bound up with reading Virginia's novels and essays. Quentin and Olivier's table was plain scrubbed wood. Olivier served tea at this table in large earthenware mugs made by Quentin, who, in addition to writing, painting, and teaching, is a potter.

We heard some thumping overhead, and Olivier said, "That's Quentin," and he presently appeared—drawn by curiosity, perhaps. He is a tall man with white hair and a white beard, and he was wearing an artist's smock the color of his blue eyes, which looked at one with a direct, calm gaze. He walked with a cane, with some difficulty. Like Olivier, Quentin immediately pulled one into his orbit of decency, sanity, wholesomeness, fineness. He had a bit of an aura. I asked him what he had thought of Angelica's book. He laughed, and said he had been irritated by Angelica's telling stories he would have wanted to tell himself and getting them wrong, missing the point. He said that the book had been a part of her therapy, and that today she would rewrite it if she could. I asked him a question about Clive. During my tour of Charleston, I had been struck by the amount of space Clive occupied in the house—he had a down-stairs study, an upstairs library, a bedroom, and his own bathroom—and had noted the special character of his rooms. They aren't *out* of character with the rest of the place—they are decorated with Duncan and Vanessa's usual painted panels, windowsills, bed boards, and bookcases—but they are more elegant and more luxurious. The bedroom has an expensive carpet and a pair of ornate Venetian chairs; the study has an elaborate early-nineteenth-century marquetry table. (It had been a wedding present to Clive and Vanessa from his parents.) Clive had evidently wanted his little comforts and conveniences, and had got them. Everybody except poor Angelica seemed to have got what he or she wanted at Charleston. ("The atmosphere is one of liberty and order," Angelica's daughter Henrietta Garnett has written of visits to Charleston during her childhood.) Quentin said of Clive that he was an extremely complex person, and that he had been very fond of him and had taken great pleasure in his company until they fell out over politics.

"Clive was conservative?" I asked. (I had not yet read Quentin's *Bloomsbury*, in which he writes sharply of Clive's book *Civilisation*, published in 1928: "It seemed that Clive Bell felt it more important to order a good meal than to know how to lead a good life," and "Clive Bell sees civilisation as something that exists only in an élite and from which the helots who serve that élite are permanently ex-cluded. The manner in which civilisation is to be preserved is im-material; if it can be maintained by a democracy so much the better, but there is no fundamental objection to a tyranny so long as it maintains a cultured class with unearned incomes.")

"Conservative is putting it very mildly," Quentin said. "You could almost say he was Fascistic."

"Then he and Julian must have fallen out even more," I said.

"Well, no," Quentin said. He explained that he himself was the more left wing of the brothers—in fact, the most left wing of all the Bloomsbury set, though he never joined the Communist Party.

I said that I had assumed Julian's extreme leftness because of his going to Spain in 1937.

"That is a common misconception about Julian," Quentin said, and he went on, "Julian liked wars. He was a very austere person." As Quentin talked about his brother, I felt that he was answering, in part, a question that had "stabbed my heart" when I was reading Vanessa's extraordinarily intimate letters. Some of them, as she herself was aware, were almost love letters, and I had wondered what Quentin's feelings had been as the less obsessively loved son who had survived the favorite's death. But I did not pursue the point. Quentin has negotiated the feat of presiding over the Bloomsbury biographical industry while keeping himself out of the Bloomsbury narrative. He has offered only the barest indication of how he felt when he was growing up in his mother's remarkable household. He is mentioned in the family letters and memoirs and diary entries, of course, but the references are rather sparse and uninformative. (In a few of the Bloomsbury photographs in which he appears we glimpse some of the charm and merriness of the author of *Virginia Woolf.*) He is almost a kind of generic younger son; Julian is always more visible and more fussed over. Julian's large shadow may have given Quentin's character the protection it needed to flourish outside the family orbit. For whatever reason, Quentin has succeeded in living his own life and keeping his own counsel. Now, in his mid-eighties, he evidently feels it safe (as his uncle Leonard felt it safe in *his* eighties) to break his silence and donate his person to the Bloomsbury novel. He has written a memoir, to be published in England in the fall.

Among the books I had bought in the Charleston gift shop (I noticed that neither DeSalvo's nor Poole's book was on sale there) was a thin pamphlet called *Editing Virginia Woolf's Diary* in which Olivier writes of her experiences as the editor of the diaries that Virginia kept between 1915 and 1941. Their publication, in five volumes, has earned her the highest praise for the excellence of their annotations. In the pamphlet, Olivier writes with a voice as distinct as Quentin's, and with a tart note of her own about the invasions of scholars and journalists that followed the publication of *Virginia Woolf*:

> The house became a sort of honey-pot with all these Woolf addicts buzzing around. I had to provide some of the honey in the form of food and drink. Earnest seekers after the truth armed with tape recorders came from Tokyo, Belgrade, or Barcelona; others we came to refer to as "beard-touchers"— those for whom it was obligatory to be able to state "I consulted with Professor Bell" when submitting their doctoral dissertations on *Mythic Patterns in "Flush"* or whatever it might be.

She allows herself a bitter comment: "We have sometimes found it hurtful to read articles or reviews by those we have entertained and informed and given up our time to, to the effect that we operated a sort of Bloomsbury closed shop—a protection racket maintained for the purposes of self-aggrandisement and financial gain." (As Olivier points out in the acknowledgments to volume IV of the diaries, their full publication was possible only because Quentin's share of the royalties issuing from the copyright of Virginia's writings, which he and Angelica inherited from Leonard, were used to pay the costs.) Olivier's tartest comments, however, are reserved for the revisionist works "purporting to demonstrate that both Leonard and Quentin had completely misrepresented [Virginia], and by concealing or cooking the evidence to which only they had access, had been able to present *their* preferred image—and one in which Leonard himself figured as hero." She goes on, "Perhaps the most grotesque manifestations of this line of approach have been those which discern that it was the fundamental antagonism, sometimes fuelled by Virginia's alleged anti-semitism, between her and Leonard which drove her, not only to periods of despair, but to suicide; indeed, it has been suggested that he practically pushed her into the river."

I have to confess that I did not buy *Editing Virginia Woolf's Diary* because I expected it to be interesting. The title is about as enticing as a piece of dry brown bread. What enticed me was the pamphlet's cover, which reproduces one of the minor but, in their way, momentous visual pleasures of the Charleston house. This pleasure—lying on a table beside an armchair in the living room—is a book on whose front cover someone (Duncan, it turns out) has pasted a few geometric shapes of hand-colored paper to form a most handsome and authoritative abstraction of olive green, umber, black, ocher, and blue. The book is a volume of plays of J. M. Synge, inscribed to Duncan from Clive in 1913. Why Duncan decorated it thus, no one knows—perhaps a child had put a glass of milk on it and left a ring, perhaps Duncan just felt like making a collage that day. Whatever its impetus, Duncan's little project comes down to us (Olivier told me she had pulled the book back from the brink of consignment to Sotheby's) as an emblem of the spirit of unceasing, unself-conscious—you could almost say artless—art making by which Charleston was inhabited.

Sitting beside me at the long, scrubbed table, Quentin returned to Angelica's book and to a photograph of Vanessa she included in it, which distressed him perhaps more than anything else in it. "Now, why did she put that picture in?" he said. "It's the only photograph of Vanessa I've ever seen that makes her look ugly. Do you agree?"

I said I did. The picture shows a grim old woman (it is dated 1951, when Vanessa was seventy-two) with thinning gray hair and round black-rimmed glasses; her mouth is turned down at the corners, and she is returning the camera's pitiless gaze with a kind of wounded directness. The photograph bears no resemblance to others of Vanessa that appear in Angelica's book, or to photographs of her that appear in any other Bloomsbury books. Nothing remains in it of the determined schoolgirl of Hyde Park Gate or the beautiful girl in white whom Leonard saw at Cambridge or the serene woman looking up from an easel or presiding over a garden tea table or the Madonna posing with her children. It is a picture out of a different world—a world stripped of beauty and pleasure and culture, the world of Forster's "panic and emptiness," the world after the great cat has pounced. "I really pity people who are not artists most of all, for they have no refuge from the world," Vanessa wrote in 1939 to a friend that Julian had made in China. "I often wonder how life would be tolerable if one could not get detached from it, as even artists without much talent can, as long as they are sincere." In Angelica's ugly picture, Vanessa is caught in a moment of engagement with the intolerable.

In "A Sketch of the Past" Virginia describes "a certain manner" that she and Vanessa were indelibly taught to assume when people came to tea at Hyde Park Gate: "We both learnt the rules of the game of Victorian society so thoroughly that we have never forgotten them," she wrote in 1940.

> We still play the game. It is useful. It has also its beauty, for it is founded upon restraint, sympathy, unselfishness—all civilized qualities. It is helpful in making something seemly out of raw odds and ends . . . But the Victorian manner is perhaps— I'm not sure—a disadvantage in writing. When I read my old *Literary Supplement* articles, I lay the blame for their suavity, their politeness, their sidelong approach, to my tea-table training. I see myself, not reviewing a book, but handing plates of buns to shy young men and asking them: do they take cream and sugar? On the other hand, the surface manner allows one, as I have found, to slip in things that would be inaudible if one marched straight up and spoke out loud.

Angelica has marched straight up and spoken out loud. She has cut her family down to size. She has shown up the civilized, oblique Bloomsbury manner for the hollow thing she believes it to be. She is a kind of counter-Cassandra—she looks back and sees nothing but darkness. Quentin's quarrel with Angelica over her book is more than a sibling's tiff about whose story is right. It is a disagreement about how stories of lives should be told. "To some extent the difference between us is the difference between one who plods and one who flies," Quentin writes with characteristic sidelongness in his review of *Deceived with Kindness*, as he crushingly subjects his sister's flights of accusing generalization to his own tolerant specificity.

The struggle between the obedient, legitimate son of Bloomsbury and its disobliging, illegitimate daughter is an uneven one, and Quentin will prevail. The achievement of his biography, his wise and liberal management of the family papers, and the existence of Charleston (in whose restoration Angelica took an active hand, such is the messiness of life: in a novel, she would never have looked at the place again) ensure the preservation of the Bloomsbury legend in its seductive fauve colors. But Angelica's cry, her hurt child's protest, her disappointed woman's bitterness will leave their trace, like a stain that won't come out of a treasured Persian carpet and eventually becomes part of its beauty.

THE WOMAN WHO HATED WOMEN

1986

The world of Edith Wharton's novels—sometimes erroneously thought to be the actual world of late-nineteenth-century New York—is a dark, nightmarish place peopled by weak, desperate men and destructive, pathetic, narcissistic women. To read the four novels in this volume is to become impressed anew with Wharton's powers as a satirist—you could almost say a black humorist—and to be struck, perhaps for the first time, by the cool modernism of her writing. She is not the wan, old-fashioned realist we have taken her to be; she works not in the delicate traceries of Mrs. Gaskell, but in the black, bold strokes of Evelyn Waugh, Muriel Spark, Don DeLillo. Her books are pervaded by a deep pessimism and an equally profound misogyny.

Wharton's stately autobiography, *A Backward Glance*, written in 1934 when she was seventy-two, is a sort of tour de force of self-control: she tells us exactly what she wants to tell us in a tone that never falters, and she cuts exactly the figure she has chosen to cut. The little betrayals (of complacency, pomposity, self-congratulation) that leak out of so many autobiographies simply do not leak out of Wharton's. It is a remarkable performance, and indeed, the august persona that Wharton created for herself is such a powerful one that her biographer R.W.B. Lewis simply transferred it to the pages of

The Library of America single-volume edition of *The House of Mirth, The Reef, The Custom of the Country*, and *The Age of Innocence* by Edith Wharton

his own stately book; it is to Cynthia Griffin Wolff's restlessly original psychoanalytic literary study, *A Feast of Words*, that we must go
to get beneath the onyx surface formed by *A Backward Glance* and
the Lewis biography, and receive a sense of the troubled human being from whom the literary artist derives.

But if *A Backward Glance* yields no personal secrets, it does not
disappoint the snooper after literary secrets. In at least two places,
Wharton inadvertently lets the figure in the carpet of her fiction come
briefly into view. The first of these rare glimmerings is afforded by a
strange story that Wharton says she heard in her youth in Newport,
Rhode Island, from "a thin young man with intelligent eyes" named
Cecil Spring-Rice, who appeared at a yachting party, told this and
another story, and was never seen by her again. Like an analytic patient prefacing an important self-revelation with the obligatory disclaimer "this isn't very interesting," Wharton writes, "I record our
single encounter only because his delightful talk so illuminated an
otherwise dull afternoon that I have never forgotten the meeting."
She then tells this story:

> A young physician who was also a student of chemistry, and a
> dabbler in strange experiments, employed a little orphan boy
> as assistant. One day he ordered the boy to watch over, and
> stir without stopping, a certain chemical mixture which was
> to serve for a very delicate experiment. At the appointed time
> the chemist came back, and found the mixture successfully
> blent—but beside it lay the little boy, dead of the poisonous
> fumes.
>   The young man, who was very fond of his assistant, was
> horrified at his death, and in despair at having involuntarily
> caused it. He could not understand why the fumes should
> have proved fatal, and wishing to find out, in the interest of
> science, he performed an autopsy, and discovered that the
> boy's heart had been transformed into a mysterious jewel, the
> like of which he had never seen before. The young man had a
> mistress whom he adored, and full of grief, yet excited by this

strange discovery, he brought her the tragic jewel, which was very beautiful, and told her how it had been produced. The lady examined it, and agreed that it was beautiful. "But," she added carelessly, "you must have noticed that I wear no ornaments but earrings. If you want me to wear this jewel, you must get me another one just like it."

With this story we leave the bland everyday world of the autobiography and plunge into the mysterious, symbolic universe of Edith Wharton's fiction, where "strange experiments" (that is, deviations from the social norm) inexorably lead to tragedy, and where the callousness and heartlessness by which this universe is ruled is the callousness and heartlessness of women. There are no bad men in Wharton's fiction. There are weak men and there are foolish men and there are vulgar New Rich men, but no man ever deliberately causes harm to another person; that role is exclusively reserved for women. From the "society of irresponsible pleasure-seekers" that Wharton grimly satirizes in *The House of Mirth* (1905) and holds accountable for the death at twenty-eight of its beautiful, luxury-loving, moneyless heroine, Lily Bart ("A frivolous society can acquire dramatic significance only through what its frivolity destroys," Wharton writes in *A Backward Glance*), she selects a woman, Bertha Dorset, to be the instrument of Lily's ruin.

Bertha is the personification of female treachery and malevolence and, incidentally, sexual voraciousness; she has no private character. When we meet her in the early pages of the novel, making a nuisance of herself on a train, she is rendered with the pouncing strokes of a Pascin drawing: "She was smaller and thinner than Lily Bart, with a restless pliability of pose, as if she could have been crumpled up and run through a ring, like the sinuous draperies she affected. Her small pale face seemed the mere setting of a pair of dark exaggerated eyes, of which the visionary gaze contrasted curiously with her self-assertive tone and gestures; so that, as one of her friends observed, she was like a disembodied spirit who took up a great deal of room."

•

If the spooky Bertha—whose first malign act is to queer Lily's chances for marriage to the boring, priggish but extremely rich Percy Gryce—has the one-dimensionality of evil characters in fairy stories, dreams, and modernist satires, the tragic Lily is similarly "unreal" in her preternatural beauty and passivity. She is the fairy-tale heroine patiently waiting to be rescued, but help never comes. *The House of Mirth* is Wharton's bitterly ironic retelling of the Cinderella story, in which the fairy godmother is a dour and stingy woman named Mrs. Peniston, the aunt who grudgingly doles out Lily's clothes allowance to her and ultimately betrays her; the prince is a plump, "shoppy" Jew named Simon Rosedale, to whom Lily is finally reduced but who will marry her only on the condition that she do something dishonorable; and Lily herself is a sad little party girl whose vanity, craving for luxury, and pathological fear of what she calls "dinginess" make her vulnerable to the machinations of Bertha.

Cynthia Wolff, in her extraordinary analysis of *Ethan Frome*, sees Ethan as an embodiment of the death instinct, and this reading is germane to Lily Bart as well. Lily's death by an overdose of sleeping potion is a logical extension of her life, of the Sleeping Beauty existence from which she is never roused. Throughout the book, Wharton has planted—like small hidden road signs to the nirvana that is Lily's destination—descriptions of the luxurious, soft, dimly lit guest bedrooms through which Lily passes on her journey. The first of this series of wombs is contrasted to the harsh, rough world outside:

> As she entered her bedroom, with its softly-shaded lights, her lace dressing-gown lying across the silken bedspread, her little embroidered slippers before the fire, a vase of carnations filling the air with perfume, and the last novels and magazines lying uncut on a table beside the reading-lamp, she had a vision of Miss Farish's cramped flat, with its cheap conveniences and hideous wall-papers. No; she was not made for mean and shabby surroundings.

Gerty Farish represents the alternative to Lily's futile, parasitic existence in fashionable society—she is a plain young woman who lives in a small flat on very little money and works with the poor—

but she actually is no alternative at all, for according to the novel's strict archetypal code, the plain and the beautiful simply belong to different universes. When Gerty is held up to Lily as an exemplar of the independence that Lily has claimed to be impossible for moneyless young women like herself, Lily cruelly points out, "But I said marriageable."

"Being a very normal person, she preferred men to women, and often terrified the latter with a cold stare," Mrs. Gordon Bell, a friend of Wharton's, recalls in Percy Lubbock's waspish memoir, *Portrait of Edith Wharton*, adding, "Many women who only knew her slightly have said to me, 'She looks at me as if I were a worm.'" With Undine Spragg, the antiheroine of *The Custom of the Country* (1913), Wharton takes her cold dislike of women to a height of venomousness previously unknown in American letters, and probably never surpassed. Undine's face is lovely, but her soul is as dingy as Gerty Farish's flat. Ralph Marvell, one of her unfortunate husbands, reflects on "the bareness of the small half-lit place in which his wife's spirit fluttered."

Undine is one of the Invaders, as Wharton calls the people with new money who are taking over New York from the gentle, enervated old aristocracy. Her simple, indulgent father, Abner Spragg, comes to New York from a town called Apex with Mrs. Spragg and Undine and sets up residence at the Stentorian Hotel, on the West Side, to launch Undine in society. Underneath Undine's small-town naïveté and her vulgarisms and gaucheness lies a vast destructive energy that propels her toward her improbable social goals. In turn, she marries Marvell, a member of the Old New York aristocracy; Raymond de Chelles, a French aristocrat; and, finally, Elmer Moffat, a raucous fellow-Invader from Undine's hometown who has become so rich and powerful that he has taken to collecting art.

As the nepenthean guest bedrooms of *The House of Mirth* set that novel's tone of deadly languor, so does a series of airless, hideously ugly, and decreasingly luxurious American hotels to which the elder Spraggs are reduced by Undine's voracious demands for money provide *The Custom of the Country* with its most mordant trope of alienation. We meet the family in the "sodden splendour" of the Stentorian breakfast room, a

> sumptuous stuffy room, where coffee-fumes hung perpetually under the emblazoned ceiling and the spongy carpet might have absorbed a year's crumbs without a sweeping. About them sat other pallid families, richly dressed, and silently eating their way through a bill-of-fare which seemed to have ransacked the globe for gastronomic incompatibilities; and in the middle of the room a knot of equally pallid waiters, engaged in languid conversation, turned their backs by common consent on the persons they were supposed to serve.

At the end, the Spraggs are in the Malibran, "a tall narrow structure resembling a grain-elevator divided into cells, where linoleum and lincrusta simulated the stucco and marble of the Stentorian, and fagged business men and their families consumed the watery stews dispensed by 'coloured help' in the grey twilight of a basement dining-room."

Undine is Becky Sharp stripped of all charm, spirit, and warmth, the adventuress pared down to her pathology, but a pathology that is invested with a kind of magical malignancy. Undine's name, as Mrs. Spragg earnestly informs Ralph during his courtship of her daughter, comes from "a hair-waver father put on the market the week she was born . . . It's from undoolay, you know, the French for crimping." But Undine is also the name of a legendary water sprite, and by presenting her tacky protagonist as a creature of the deeps— a cold, bloodless being, a Lorelei luring men to their deaths— Wharton seeks to make it credible that any man of substance would look at her twice. The attempt is not wholly successful.

Like George Eliot's Rosamund Vincy, Undine inspires in her creator a kind of loathing that makes the reader nervous even as it powerfully works on him; like Eliot's account of Lydgate's sufferings at the hands of Rosamund in *Middlemarch*, Wharton's account of Marvell's sufferings at the hands of Undine has less the even-handedness of omniscient authorship than it has the partisanship of love—love for the castrated male. Unlike Eliot, however, Wharton offers no alternative; no wonderful woman—no Dorothea Brooke—appears in *The Custom of the Country* or in any other Wharton work. Ellen Olenska, the heroine of *The Age of Innocence* (1920), is supposed to be a wonderful woman, but in fact she is a fantasy figure—an idea, a spirit as disembodied as Bertha Dorset. She seems to be drawn from Anna Karenina, but she has none of Anna's elating and heartrending actuality. Throughout the novel Ellen remains frozen into a kind of simulacrum of the vision of the charming and radiant Anna that Vronsky first fell in love with; the character never develops beyond that vision. Ellen's fan of eagle feathers, her monkey-fur muff, the artistic atmosphere of her house, her exotic flowers and unconventional clothes are the stuff of which she is made; she is almost pure sign.

The true "heroine" of the book is Newland Archer (several critics have pointed out the name's connection to James's Isabel Archer), who, like Ralph Marvell in *The Custom of the Country* and Lawrence Selden in *The House of Mirth*, lives a dilettantish half-life of longing ("Something he knew he had missed: the flower of life," Archer reflects at the novel's powerful end) and is the culminating figure in Wharton's pantheon of unmanned men. (In Newland's case, the castrating female comes in the guise of the conventional "nice" young woman of good society who traps him into loveless marriage.)

George Darrow, the suave hero of *The Reef* (1912), deviates from the formula in being a seducer and manipulator of women, rather than their victim; but Wharton—as if herself under his spell—extends to him the same sympathy she extends to Marvell, Selden, and Newland. *The Reef* has been called Wharton's most Jamesian novel, but it is merely her least cleverly plotted one. James would never have committed the solecism of narration that Wharton commits in *The Reef*—telling the story of a secret relationship forward instead of backward in time, thus bringing into glaring relief the incredible coincidence by which the characters of her eccentric fable of sexual guilt are brought under one roof. James would have begun the novel with the characters securely in position.

•

The second place in *A Backward Glance* where Wharton reveals more about her art than she appears to realize is a passage criticizing the late novels of Henry James, whose close friend she became in middle age. ("His friendship has been the pride and honour of my life," she wrote with moving truth to a friend during James's last illness, in 1915.)

She says:

His latest novels, for all their profound moral beauty, seemed to me more and more lacking in atmosphere, more and more severed from that thick nourishing human air in which we all live and move. The characters in "The Wings of the Dove" and "The Golden Bowl" seem isolated in a Crookes tube for our inspection: his stage was cleared like that of the Théâtre Français in the good old days when no chair or table was introduced that was not relevant to the action (a good rule for the stage, but an unnecessary embarrassment to fiction). Preoccupied by this, I one day said to him: "What was your idea in suspending the four principal characters in 'The Golden Bowl' in the void? What sort of life did they lead when they were not watching each other, and fencing with each other? Why have you stripped them of all the human fringes we necessarily trail after us through life?"

With uncharacteristic obtuseness, Wharton goes on to describe James's profound puzzlement at her words—for the void that Wharton describes is, of course, not James's, but her own, and it is precisely where she has pruned the fringes of naturalism most ruthlessly that she achieves her most powerful and individual effects. Her strongest work (*Ethan Frome, The House of Mirth, The Custom of the Country*) has a stylization and abstraction, a quality of "madeness" that propels it out of the sphere of nineteenth-century realism and nudges it toward the self-reflexive literary experimentation of the twentieth century. In the primal horror of *Ethan Frome*, in the brittle pathos of *The House of Mirth*, and in the satiric surrealism of *The Custom of the Country*, Wharton most commandingly comes into her own as a literary artist. If she is an artist from whom we shrink a little and to whom we finally deny the highest rank, she remains—as Q. D. Leavis very fairly put it in her 1938 essay on Wharton in *Scrutiny*—"a remarkable novelist if not a large-sized one, and while there are few great novelists there are not even so many remarkable ones that we can afford to let her be overlooked."

SALINGER'S CIGARETTES

2001

When J. D. Salinger's "Hapworth 16, 1924"—a very long and very strange story in the form of a letter from camp written by Seymour Glass when he was seven—appeared in *The New Yorker* in June 1965, it was greeted with unhappy, even embarrassed silence. It seemed to confirm the growing critical consensus that Salinger was going to hell in a handbasket. By the late fifties, when the stories "Franny" and "Zooey" and "Raise High the Roof Beam, Carpenters" were coming out in the magazine, Salinger was no longer the universally beloved author of *The Catcher in the Rye*; he was now the seriously annoying creator of the Glass family.

When "Franny" and "Zooey" appeared in book form in 1961, a flood of pent-up resentment was released. The critical reception—by, among others, Alfred Kazin, Mary McCarthy, Joan Didion, and John Updike—was more like a public birching than an ordinary occasion of failure to please. "Zooey" had already been pronounced "an interminable, an appallingly bad story," by Maxwell Geismar* and "a piece of shapeless self-indulgence" by George Steiner.† Now Alfred Kazin, in an essay sardonically entitled "J. D. Salinger: 'Everybody's Favorite,'" set forth the terms on which Salinger would be relegated to the margins of literature for doting on the "horribly

---

* "The Wise Child and the New Yorker School of Fiction," in *American Moderns: From Rebellion to Conformity* (Hill and Wang, 1958).
† "The Salinger Industry," *The Nation*, November 14, 1959.

precocious" Glasses. "I am sorry to have to use the word 'cute' in respect to Salinger," Kazin wrote, "but there is absolutely no other word that for me so accurately typifies the self-conscious charm and prankishness of his own writing and his extraordinary cherishing of his favorite Glass characters."* McCarthy peevishly wrote: "Again the theme is the good people against the stupid phonies, and the good is still all in the family, like a family-owned 'closed' corporation . . . Outside are the phonies, vainly signaling to be let in." And: "Why did [Seymour] kill himself? Because he had married a phony, whom he worshiped for her 'simplicity, her terrible honesty'? . . . Or because he had been lying, his author had been lying, and it was all terrible, and he was a fake?"†

Didion dismissed *Franny and Zooey* as "finally spurious, and what makes it spurious is Salinger's tendency to flatter the essential triviality within each of his readers, his predilection for giving instructions for living. What gives the book its extremely potent appeal is precisely that it is self-help copy: it emerges finally as *Positive Thinking* for the upper middle classes, as *Double Your Energy and Live Without Fatigue* for Sarah Lawrence girls."‡ Even kindly John Updike's sadism was aroused. He mocked Salinger for his rendering of a character who is "just one of the remote millions coarse and foolish enough to be born outside the Glass family," and charged Salinger with portraying the Glasses "not to particularize imaginary people but to instill in the reader a mood of blind worship, tinged with envy." "Salinger loves the Glasses more than God loves them. He loves them too exclusively. Their invention has become a hermitage for him. He loves them to the detriment of artistic moderation. 'Zooey' is just too long."§

Today "Zooey" does not seem too long, and is arguably Salinger's masterpiece. Rereading it and its companion piece, "Franny," is no less rewarding than rereading *The Great Gatsby*. It remains brilliant and is in no essential sense dated. It is the contemporary criticism that has dated. Like the contemporary criticism of *Olympia*, for example, which jeered at Manet for his crude indecency, or

---

* *Atlantic Monthly*, August 1961.
† "J. D. Salinger's Closed Circuit," *Harper's Magazine*, October 1962.
‡ "Finally (Fashionably) Spurious," *National Review*, November 18, 1961.
§ "Anxious Days for the Glass Family," *The New York Times Book Review*, September 17, 1961.

that of *War and Peace*, which condescended to Tolstoy for the inept
"shapelessness" of the novel, it now seems magnificently misguided.
However—as T. J. Clark and Gary Saul Morson have shown in their
respective exemplary studies of Manet and Tolstoy*—negative contemporary criticism of a masterpiece can be helpful to later critics,
acting as a kind of radar that picks up the ping of the work's originality. The "mistakes" and "excesses" that early critics complain of are
often precisely the innovations that have given the work its power.†

In the case of Salinger's critics, it is their extraordinary rage
against the Glasses that points us toward Salinger's innovations. I
don't know of any other case where literary characters have aroused
such animosity, and where a writer of fiction has been so severely
censured for failing to understand the offensiveness of his creations.
In fact, Salinger understood the offensiveness of his creations perfectly well. "Zooey"'s narrator, Buddy Glass, wryly cites the view of
some of the listeners to the quiz show *It's a Wise Child*, on which all
the Glass children had appeared in turn, "that the Glasses were a
bunch of insufferably 'superior' little bastards that should have been
drowned or gassed at birth." The seven-year-old letter writer in
"Hapworth" reports that "I have been trying like hell since our arrival to leave a wide margin for human ill-will, fear, jealousy, and
gnawing dislike of the uncommonplace." Throughout the Glass
stories—as well as in *Catcher*—Salinger presents his abnormal heroes in the context of the normal world's dislike and fear of them.
These works are fables of otherness—versions of Kafka's *Metamorphosis*. However, Salinger's design is not as easy to make out as
Kafka's. His Gregor Samsas are not overtly disgusting and threatening; they have retained their human shape and speech and are
even, in the case of Franny and Zooey, spectacularly good-looking.

---

* T. J. Clark, *The Painting of Modern Life: Paris in the Art of Manet and His Followers*
(Princeton University Press, 1984); Gary Saul Morson, *Hidden in Plain View: Narrative
and Creative Potentials in 'War and Peace'* (Stanford University Press, 1987).

† Evidently understanding this, Updike ended his review with a handsome concession:
"When all reservations have been entered, in the correctly unctuous and apprehensive tone,
about the direction [Salinger] has taken, it remains to acknowledge that it is a direction,
and that the refusal to rest content, the willingness to risk excess on behalf of one's obsessions, is what distinguishes artists from entertainers, and what makes some artists adventur-
ers on behalf of us all."

Nor is his vision unrelentingly tragic; it characteristically oscillates between the tragic and the comic. But with the possible exception of the older daughter, Boo Boo, who grew up to become a suburban wife and mother, none of the Glass children is able to live comfortably in the world. They are out of place. They might as well be large insects. The critics' aversion points us toward their underlying freakishness, and toward Salinger's own literary deviance and irony.

Ten years before the "interminable" and "shapeless" "Zooey" appeared in *The New Yorker*, a very short and well-made story called "A Perfect Day for Bananafish" appeared there, and traced the last few hours in the life of a young man who kills himself in the story's last sentence by putting a revolver to his temple. At the time, readers had no inkling that Seymour Glass—as the young man was called— would become a famous literary character, and that this was anything but a self-contained story about a suicidal depressive and his staggeringly shallow and unhelpful wife, Muriel. It is only in retrospect that we can see that the story is a kind of miniature and somewhat oversharp version of the allegory that the Glass family stories would enact.

The story, which takes place at a Florida resort where the husband and wife are vacationing, is divided into two sections. In the first we overhear a telephone conversation between the wife and her mother in New York, which mordantly renders the bourgeois world of received ideas and relentless department-store shopping in which the women are comfortably and obliviously ensconced. The second section takes place on the beach, where the despairing Seymour is conversing with a little girl named Sybil Carpenter, whose mother has told her to "run and play" while she goes to the hotel to have a martini with a friend. Seymour is revealed as a man who is wonderful with children, not talking down to them, but rather, past them, as thus:

> "My daddy's coming tomorrow on a nairiplane," Sybil said, kicking sand.
> "Not in my face, baby," the young man said, putting his

hand on Sybil's ankle. "Well, it's about time he got here, your daddy. I've been expecting him hourly. Hourly."

"Where's the lady?" Sybil said.

"The lady?" The young man brushed some sand out of his thin hair. "That's hard to say, Sybil. She may be in any one of a thousand places. At the hairdresser's. Having her hair dyed mink. Or making dolls for poor children, in her room."

Seymour is the Myshkin-like figure whose death inhabits the Glass family stories. But as he appears in "Bananafish," he isn't quite right for the role. He is too witty and too crazy. (When he leaves the beach and goes back to the hotel to kill himself, his behavior in the elevator is that of a bellicose maniac.) Salinger takes care of the problem by disclaiming authorship of "Bananafish." In "Seymour: An Introduction," he allows Buddy Glass, the second-oldest brother and the story's narrator, to claim authorship of "Bananafish" (as well as of *Catcher* and the story "Teddy") and then to admit that his portrait of Seymour is wrong—is really a self-portrait. This is the sort of "prankishness" one imagines Kazin to have been complaining about and that no longer—after fifty years of postmodern experimentation (and five Zuckerman books by Philip Roth)—sticks in our craw. If our authors want to confess to the precariousness and handmade-ness of their enterprise, who are we to protest? Salinger would also considerably amplify and complicate the simple, harsh sketch of the regular world that "Bananafish" renders. But he would permanently retain the dualism of "Bananafish," the view of the world as a battleground between the normal and the abnormal, the ordinary and the extraordinary, the talentless and the gifted, the well and the sick.

In "Zooey" we find the two youngest Glass children, Franny and Zooey, in their parents' large apartment on the Upper East Side of Manhattan. Salinger's use of recognizable places in New York and his ear for colloquial speech give the work a deceptive surface realism that obscures its fundamental fantastic character. The Glass family apartment is at once a faithfully, almost tenderly, rendered, cluttered, shabby middle-class New York apartment and a kind of lair, a mountain fastness to which Salinger's strange creations retreat to be with their own kind. Twenty-year-old Franny, who is brilliant and kind as well as exceptionally pretty, has come home from college after suffering a nervous collapse during a football weekend. In the shorter story "Franny," which serves as a kind of prologue to "Zooey," we have already seen her in the alien outer world, vainly struggling against her antipathy to her boyfriend, Lane Coutell. If the mother and daughter in "Bananafish" represented the least admirable features of mid-century female bourgeois culture, so Lane is an almost equally unprepossessing manifestation of 1950s male culture. He is a smug and pretentious and condescending young man. Over lunch in a fancy restaurant, the conversation between Franny and Lane grows ever more unpleasant as he obliviously boasts about his paper on Flaubert's mot juste, for which he received an A, and she tries less and less hard to hide her impatient disdain.

Lane is not alone as an object of Franny's jaundiced scrutiny. "Everything everybody does is so—I don't know—not wrong, or even mean, or even stupid necessarily. But just so tiny and meaningless and—sad making," she tells him. The one thing she finds meaningful is a little book she carries around with her called *The Way of a Pilgrim*, which proposes that the incessant repetition of the prayer "Lord Jesus Christ, have mercy on me" will bring about mystical experience. Lane is as unimpressed with the "Jesus Prayer" as Franny is with his Flaubert paper. As the breach between the pair widens, another agon is played out, that of food. Lane orders a large meal of snails, frogs' legs, and salad, which he eats with gusto, and Franny (to his irritation) orders a glass of milk, from which she takes a few tiny sips, and a chicken sandwich, which she leaves untouched.

As we follow Lane's consumption of his lunch (Salinger shows him chewing, cutting, buttering, even exhorting his frogs' legs to "sit still"), we also watch—with the bated breath of parents of anorexics—Franny's nonconsumption of hers. At the end of the story she falls into a faint. In "Zooey," at the Glass apartment, the drama of food continues as the daughter continues to refuse to eat. As in *Metamorphosis* (and in its pendant "The Hunger Artist"), the person who is other, the misfit, is unable to eat the food normal people eat. He finds it repellent. Kafka's heroes die of their revulsion, as does Salinger's hero Seymour. (Though Seymour shoots himself, there is a suggestion that he, too, must be some sort of hunger artist. When he is on the beach with the little girl he tells her a cautionary tale about underwater creatures called bananafish, who crawl into holes where they gorge themselves on bananas and get so enlarged that they cannot get out again, and die.) In "Zooey," Franny is pulled back from the brink by her brother. The story has some of the atmosphere of the Greek myths about return from the underworld and the Bible stories in which dead children are resurrected.

"Neither you nor Buddy knows how to talk to people you don't like. Don't love, really," Bessie Glass tells Zooey. She adds, "You can't live in the world with such strong likes and dislikes." But Buddy and Zooey do, in fact, live in the world, if uncomfortably. Buddy is a college teacher, Zooey a television actor. They have passed through crises like Franny's. They are misfits—Mary McCarthy will always be cross with them—but they are not Seymours. They will live. Now the job at hand is to bring Franny out of her dangerous state of disgust. As she lies fitfully sleeping in the Glass living room on a Monday morning, the mother urges the son to get going with the rescue mission.

The conversation takes place in a bathroom. Zooey is in the bathtub with a shower curtain drawn decorously around him—a red nylon shower curtain with canary-yellow sharps, flats, and clefs printed on it—and the mother is sitting on the toilet seat. (The influence of the story's genteel first publisher, William Shawn, may be adduced from the fact that Salinger never comes right out and says where the mother is sitting.) Both are smoking. In his essay on Salinger, Kazin writes with heavy irony, "Someday there will be learned theses on *The Use of the Ash Tray in J.D. Salinger's Stories*; no other writer has made so much of Americans lighting up, reaching for the ash tray, setting up the ash tray with one hand while with the other they reach for a ringing telephone." Kazin's observation is true, but his irony is misplaced. The smoking in Salinger is well worth tracking. There is nothing idle or random about the cigarettes and cigars that appear in his stories, or with the characters' dealings with them. In "Raise High the Roof Beam, Carpenters," Salinger achieves a brilliant effect with the lighting of a cigar that has been held unlit by a small old deaf-mute man during the first ninety pages of the story; and in "Zooey" another cigar is instrumental in the dawning of a recognition. The cigarettes that the mother and son smoke in the bathroom play less noticeable but no less noteworthy roles in the progress of the story.

Like the food in "Franny," the cigarettes in "Zooey" enact a kind of parallel plot. Cigarettes offer (or used to offer) the writer a great range of metaphoric possibilities. They have lives and deaths. They glow and they turn to ashes. They need attention. They create smoke. They make a mess. As we listen to Bessie Glass and Zooey talk, we follow the fortunes of their cigarettes. Some of them go out for lack of attention. Others threaten to burn the smoker's fingers. Our sense of the mother and son's aliveness, and of the life-and-death character of their discussion, is heightened by the perpetual presence of these inanimate yet animatable objects.

Bessie and her husband, Les, respectively Irish-Catholic and Jewish, are a pair of retired vaudeville dancers; they closed down their act when the fourth of their seven children was born, and Les took some sort of vague job "in radio." He is himself a vague, recessive figure, an absence. (Note the name.) He is never physically described, nor does his Jewishness play a part in the narrative. One of the things that really got up Maxwell Geismar's nose was what he saw as Salinger's craven refusal to admit that all his characters were Jewish. Of *Catcher*, Geismar wrote, "The locale of the New York sections is obviously that of a comfortable middle-class urban Jewish society where, however, all the leading figures have become beautifully Anglicized. Holden and Phoebe Caulfield: what perfect American social register names which are presented to us in both a social and a psychological void!" (In his discussion of "Zooey," Geismar drily noted that the family cat, Bloomberg, "is apparently the only honest Jewish character in the tale.") As it happens, Salinger is himself honestly half Jewish: his mother, née Marie Jillich, was an Irish-Catholic who, however, changed her name to Miriam and passed herself off as a Jew after she married Salinger's father, Sol, with the result that Salinger and his older sister, Doris, grew up believing they were wholly Jewish; only when Doris was nineteen, and after Salinger had been bar mitzvahed, were they told the surprising truth.

The connection between this piece of biography and Salinger's refusal to be an American Jewish writer writing about Jews in America is impossible to fully sort out, of course, given Salinger's reticence; we can only assume that it exists. But the refusal itself is what is significant. Geismar is acute to note it—but obtuse, I think, to condemn it. The "void" of which he speaks is a defining condition of Salinger's art. The preternatural vividness of Salinger's characters, our feeling that we have already met them, that they are portraits directly drawn from New York life, is an illusion. Salinger's references to Central Park and Madison Avenue and Bonwit Teller, and the Manhattanish cadences of his characters' speech, are like the false leads that give a detective story its suspense. In Salinger's fiction we never really quite know where we are, even as we constantly bump up against familiar landmarks. *The Catcher in the Rye*, though putatively set in an alien nighttime New York, evokes the familiar terrifying dark forest of fairy tales, through which the hero blunders until dawn. Near the end of "Zooey," its hero picks up a glass paperweight from his mother's desk and shakes it to create a snowstorm around the snowman with a stovepipe hat within. So, we might say, Salinger creates the storms that whirl around his characters' heads in the close, hermetically sealed world in which they live.

Salinger will often literally set his scenes in small, sealed-off spaces—such as, for example, the limousine in which the central scene of "Raise High the Roof Beam, Carpenters" is set. In "Franny" there is a startling moment when Lane, waiting for Franny to come back from the ladies' room, looks across the restaurant and sees someone he knows. It is startling because until this moment we had no awareness of there being anyone else in the restaurant. Salinger had typically isolated Franny and Lane at their table, so that we saw nothing and heard nothing but their conversation and the remarks of the waiter who attended to them.

The bathroom scene in "Zooey" is perhaps the consummate example of this hermeticity. As if the space of the bathroom were still not small enough, there is a space-within-a-space formed by the shower curtain drawn around the tub in which Zooey sits with a lit cigarette parked on the soap dish. The scene is one of the most remarkable mother-and-son scenes in literature. Before the drawing of the curtain occasioned by the mother's entrance, the immersed Zooey, drawing on his "dampish" cigarette, reads a four-year-old letter from Buddy, in which, among other things (such as encouraging Zooey in his decision to become an actor rather than going for a Ph.D.), Buddy tells Zooey to "be kinder to Bessie . . . when you can. I don't think I mean because she's our mother, but because she's weary. You will after you're thirty or so, when everybody slows down a little (even you, maybe), but try harder now. It isn't enough to treat her with the doting brutality of an apache dancer toward his partner."

The apache dance begins with Bessie's entrance:

"Do you know how long you've been in that tub? Exactly forty-five—"

"Don't tell me! Just don't tell me, Bessie."

"What do you mean, don't tell you?"

"Just what I said. Leave me the goddam illusion you haven't been out there counting the minutes I've—"

"Nobody's been counting any minutes, young man," Mrs. Glass said.

Bessie is a stout middle-aged woman dressed in a garment Buddy calls her "pre-notification of death uniform"—a midnight-blue Japanese kimono, whose pockets are stuffed with things like screws, nails, hinges, faucet handles, and ball-bearing casters, along with several packs of king-size cigarettes and matches, and who is as unlike the other women in her "not unfashionable" apartment building as her children are unlike the other people in the world at large. The other women in the building own fur coats and, like Muriel and her mother, spend their days shopping at Bonwit Teller and Saks Fifth Avenue. Bessie "looked, first, as if she never, never left the building at all, but that if she did she would be wearing a dark shawl and she would be going in the direction of O'Connell Street, there to claim the body of one of her half-Irish, half-Jewish sons, who, through some clerical error, had just been shot dead by the Black and Tans." At the same time, her way of holding a cigarette between the ends of two fingers

> tended to blow to some literary hell one's first, strong (and still perfectly tenable) impression that an invisible Dubliner's shawl covered her shoulders. Not only were her fingers of an extraordinary length and shapeliness—such as, very generally speaking, one wouldn't have expected of a medium stout woman's fingers—but they featured, as it were, a somewhat imperial-looking tremor; a deposed Balkan queen or a retired favorite courtesan might have had such an elegant tremor.

Bessie also has great legs. But her most significant attribute—the one that gives "Zooey"'s comedy its tragic underside (and raises the stakes of its outcome)—is her grief:

> It was a very touch and go business, in 1955, to get a wholly plausible reading from Mrs. Glass's face, and especially from her enormous blue eyes. Where once, a few years earlier, her eyes alone could break the news (either to people or to bathmats) that two of her sons were dead, one by suicide (her favorite, her most intricately calibrated, her kindest son), and one killed in World War II (her only truly lighthearted son)—where once Bessie Glass's eyes alone could report these facts, with an eloquence and a seeming passion for detail that neither her husband nor any of her adult surviving children could bear to look at, let alone take in, now in 1955, she was apt to use this same terrible Celtic equipment to break the news, usually at the front door, that the new delivery boy hadn't brought the leg of lamb in time for dinner or that some remote Hollywood starlet's marriage was on the rocks.

All families of suicides are alike. They wear a kind of permanent letter *S* on their chests. Their guilt is never assuaged. Their anxiety never lifts. They are freaks among families in the way prodigies are freaks among individuals. Walter died tragically but "normally." Seymour haunts the family like a member of the Undead. At the beginning of "Zooey," Buddy (who again brashly claims authorship of Salinger's work) describes it as a love story, and it is true that the affection the family members feel for one another is an almost palpable presence. But it is also (what family story isn't?) a hate story. Ambivalence fills the air of the bathroom in which mother and son sit. The son behind the curtain repeatedly protests the mother's invasion of his privacy—even as he ensures that she remain rooted to the spot, transfixed by his relentless wit. She dutifully plays her straight-man role. When she grumbles about Franny's unhealthy diet, for example ("I don't think it's at all impossible that the kind of food that child takes into her system hasn't a lot to do with this whole entire funny business . . . You can't go on abusing the body indefinitely, year in, year out—regardless of what you think"), she only opens the way for a new flight of aggressive fancy:

> "You're absolutely right. You're absolutely right. It's staggering how you jump straight the hell into the heart of a matter. I'm goosebumps all over . . . By God, you inspire me. You inflame me, Bessie. You know what you've done? Do you realize what you've done? You've given this whole goddam issue a fresh, new, Biblical slant. I wrote four papers in college on the Crucifixion—five, really—and every one of them worried me half crazy because I thought something was missing. Now I know what it was. Now it's clear to me. I see Christ in an entirely different light. His unhealthy fanaticism. His rudeness to those nice, sane, conservative, tax-paying Pharisees. Oh, this is exciting! In your simple, straightforward bigoted way, Bessie, you've sounded the missing keynote of the whole New Testament. Improper diet. Christ lived on cheeseburgers and Cokes. For all we know he probably fed the mult—"
>
> "Just stop that, now," Mrs. Glass broke in, her voice quiet but dangerous. "Oh I'd like to put a diaper on that mouth of yours."

When Zooey gets out of the tub, the mother leaves the bathroom, only to return when he is half dressed and shaving. During this second visit ("Ah! What a pleasant and gracious surprise!" the fresh son says when she enters. "Don't sit down! Let me drink you in first") she touches his bare back and remarks on its beauty. ("You're getting so broad and lovely," she says.) His response is to sharply recoil in a way we recall two other Salinger characters to have recoiled. One is the little girl in "Bananafish," who says "Hey!" when Seymour impulsively kisses the arch of her foot after she says that she saw a bananafish. The other is Holden Caulfield, who jumps up and says "What the hellya doing?" when he wakes up in the apartment of the one good teacher he ever had, Mr. Antolini, to find him sitting beside the bed patting his head. "Don't, willya?" Zooey says to his mother; and when she says, "Don't what?" he replies, "Just don't, that's all. Don't admire my goddam back."

The rescue fantasy from which *Catcher* takes its title—Holden imagines himself standing at the edge of a cliff at the end of a rye field where thousands of children are playing, catching any child who starts going over the cliff—bears on the whole of Salinger's enterprise. Salinger is himself a kind of catcher of the children and young adults who appear in his stories and are in danger of falling—threatened by the adults who are supposed to be protecting them but cannot keep their hands off them. The frank pleasure Bessie Glass takes in the sight of her son's body is represented as the breaching of a boundary, as "something perverty" (in Holden's term). Even a good teacher like Mr. Antolini or a good parent like Bessie (or a good psychotic like Seymour) cannot be counted on, will ultimately fail the child in the test of disinterest. The young must stick together; only they can save each other. Thus, in *Catcher*, Phoebe saves Holden, and, in "Zooey," Zooey saves Franny. But where Phoebe, in *Catcher*, was "normal," in opposition to the off-center Holden, Franny and Zooey are peas in a pod. They have the Glass disease; they suffer from a kind of allergy to human frailty. The pettiness, vulgarity, banality, and vanity that few of us are free of, and thus can tolerate in others, are like ragweed for Salinger's helplessly uncontaminated heroes and heroines.

•

The second half of "Zooey" is occupied with Zooey's blind-leading-
the-blind attempt to propel Franny back into the world he himself
stumbles about in. Interestingly, he does not consider his sister's
(and his own) condition of hypercriticality congenital, but believes it
to have been caused by the older brothers, who at an early age in-
doctrinated them in Eastern religion (as well as a kind of East-
inflected Christianity). ("We wanted you both to know who and
what Jesus and Gautama and Lao-tse and Shankaracharya and
Huineng and Sri Ramakrishna, etc., were before you knew too
much or anything about Homer or Shakespeare or even Blake or
Whitman, let alone George Washington and his cherry tree or the
definition of a peninsula or how to parse a sentence," Buddy writes
in his letter to Zooey.) "We're freaks, the two of us, Franny and I,"
Zooey says to Bessie:

> "I'm a twenty-five-year-old freak, and she's a twenty-year-old
> freak, and both those bastards are responsible . . . I could
> murder them both without batting an eyelash. The great
> teachers. The great emancipators. My God. I can't even sit
> down to lunch with a man any more and hold up my end of
> a decent conversation. I either get so bored or so goddam
> preachy that if the son of a bitch had any sense, he'd break his
> chair over my head."

As Franny wanly lies on the living-room sofa under an afghan,
with the Jewish cat snuggled up against her, Zooey makes his
pitch—and gets nowhere for an excruciatingly long time. The
charge that the story was "interminable" doubtless derived from
Salinger's unwillingness—at whatever cost to the speed of his narrative—to scant the magnitude of Franny's retreat from life.

Finally, Zooey resorts to an interesting stratagem—he leaves the
living room and calls Franny on a telephone extension in the apartment, first pretending he is Buddy and then admitting he is himself.
Salinger permits us to overhear both sides of the conversation, but
to see only Franny, who has taken the telephone in her parents' bedroom and is sitting tensely upright on one of the twin beds, smoking a cigarette, putting it out, and attempting to light another with

her free hand. As Zooey talks—"If it's the religious life you want, you ought to know right now that you're missing out on every single goddam religious action that's going on around this house. You don't even have sense enough to drink when somebody brings you a cup of consecrated chicken soup—which is the only kind of chicken soup Bessie ever brings to anybody around this madhouse"— Franny's body language tells us that his message is coming through. The cure that could not be effected in the large, light-filled living room is achieved in the dark closet of the telephone conversation. Franny will eat from now on. Also, she will not carry out her threat of giving up acting because of "the stupidity of audiences," of "the goddam 'unskilled laughter' coming from the fifth row." "That's none of your business, Franny," Zooey says. "An artist's only concern is to shoot for some kind of perfection, and on his own terms, not anyone else's." Zooey's final offering, which causes Franny to hold the phone with both hands "for joy, apparently," is the now famous concept of the Fat Lady in the audience, who is Everyman, and who is Christ. I would have preferred that Salinger had stopped at the chicken soup and the artist's minding of his own business. Salinger rarely puts a foot wrong; but with the Fat Lady, I'm afraid he takes a tumble into condescension.

Although Salinger stopped publishing after the appearance of "Hapworth," he evidently has never stopped writing, and someday there may be dozens, maybe hundreds, more Glass stories to read and re-read. On the dust jacket of the 1961 Little, Brown edition of *Franny and Zooey*, Salinger wrote an author's note about his enterprise:

> Both stories are early, critical entries in a narrative series I'm doing about a family of settlers in twentieth-century New York, the Glasses. It is a long-term project, patently an ambitious one, and there is a real-enough danger, I suppose, that sooner or later I'll bog down, perhaps disappear entirely, in my own methods, locutions, and mannerisms. On the whole, though, I'm very hopeful. I love working on these Glass stories, I've been waiting for them most of my life, and I think I

have fairly decent, monomaniacal plans to finish them with due care and all-available skill.

The image of the patiently and confidently "waiting" writer is arresting, as is the term "settlers," with its connotations of uncharted territory and danger and hardship.

Salinger's own perilous journey away from the world has brought many misfortunes down on his head. His modest wish for privacy was perceived as a provocation and met with hostility, much like the hostility toward the Glasses. Eventually it offered an irresistible opportunity for commercial exploitation. The pain caused Salinger by the crass, vengeful memoirs of, respectively, his former girlfriend, Joyce Maynard,* and his daughter, Margaret,† may be imagined. A redeeming moment occurred a few weeks after the publication of the latter book, when a letter by, of all people, Margaret's younger brother, Matt, an actor who lives in New York, appeared in *The New York Observer.* He was writing to object to his sister's book. "I would hate to think I were responsible for her book selling one single extra copy, but I am also unable not to plant a small flag of protest over what she has done, and much of what she has to say." Matt went on to write of his sister's "troubled mind" and of the "gothic tales of our supposed childhood" she had liked to tell and that he had not challenged because he thought they had therapeutic value for her. He continued:

> Of course, I can't say with any authority that she is consciously making anything up. I just know that I grew up in a very different house, with two very different parents from those my sister describes. I do not remember even one instance of my mother hitting either my sister or me. Not one. Nor do I remember any instance of my father "abusing" my mother in any way whatsoever. The only sometimes frightening presence I remember in the house, in fact, was my sister (the same person who in her book self-servingly casts herself as my benign

* *At Home in the World* (Picador, 1998).
† *Dream Catcher* (Washington Square Press, 2000).

protector)! She remembers a father who couldn't "tie his own shoe-laces" and I remember a man who helped me learn how to tie mine, and even—specifically—how to close off the end of a lace again once the plastic had worn away.

What is astonishing, almost eerie, about the letter is the sound that comes out of it—the singular and instantly recognizable sound of Salinger, which we haven't heard for nearly forty years (and to which the daughter's heavy drone could not be more unrelated). Whether Salinger is the rat his girlfriend and daughter say he is will endlessly occupy his biographers and cannot change anything in his art. The breaking of ranks in Salinger's actual family only under- scores the unbreakable solidarity of his imaginary one. "At least you know there won't be any goddam ulterior motives in this mad- house," Zooey tells Franny. "Whatever we are, we're not fishy, buddy." "Close on the heels of kindness, originality is one of the most thrilling things in the world, also the most rare!" Seymour writes in "Hapworth." What is thrilling about that sentence is, of course, the order in which kindness and originality are put. And what makes reading Salinger such a consistently bracing experience is our sense of always being in the presence of something that— whatever it is—isn't fishy.

CAPITALIST PASTORALE

2009

When I was ten, I read a novel called *A Girl of the Limberlost* that made a deep impression on me. I assumed that its author, Gene Stratton-Porter, was a man, and gave the matter no further thought. I read the book, written in 1909, at a small New Hampshire girls' camp—run by an elderly Congregationalist minister and his wife and itself past its prime—curled up on a worn velvet sofa in an outbuilding called the Lodge, whose walls were hung with Indian blankets and sepia photographs of girls in togas doing eurythmic dances in a forest clearing. It was 1944, and civilian America was undergoing a regimen of wartime austerity by which it was never more than mildly discommoded, but that imparted a sort of scratchy gray wool feel to the atmosphere. The lack of gas and the rationing of meat touched us campers—we had to walk the three and a half miles to the lake where we swam, and we ate a lot of creamed codfish—but did not register on us as deprivations.

For a child living in a culture of limited and somewhat monotonous resources, *A Girl of the Limberlost*—the story of an Indiana girl who starts out in severe material distress and ends up with everything a girl could possibly want—had special resonance. When

---

A Girl of the Limberlost, Freckles, The Harvester, Her Father's Daughter, and *The Keeper of the Bees* by Gene Stratton-Porter; *Gene Stratton-Porter: Novelist and Naturalist* by Judith Reick Long; and *The Lady of the Limberlost: The Life and Letters of Gene Stratton-Porter* by Jeannette Porter Meehan

I reread the book in the 1980s (I found it at a library sale), I felt that I was reentering an imaginative world whose grip on my own imagination had never loosened. The opening scene—Elnora Comstock's arrival at a small-town high school dressed in rough farm clothes, in mortifying contrast to the "bevy of daintily clad, sweet-smelling things that might have been birds, or flowers, or possibly gaily dressed, happy young girls"—came back to me with the force of a seminal memory.

As the plot unfolded, almost every turn had a familiar ring. When a kindly neighbor named Wesley Stinton and his wife, Margaret, take pity on Elnora and go shopping at the local dry goods store for the clothes that will propel her into the ranks of the daintily clad, I could all but recite their purchases of fabric for "bright and pretty, but simple and plain" school dresses ("four pieces of crisp gingham, a pale blue, a pink, a gray with green stripes and a rich brown and blue plaid"), along with ribbons, belts, a hat, umbrella, shoes, boots, and toiletries. But my greatest shock of recognition was reserved for the final "neat and genteel" purchase of a brown leather lunch box:

> inside was a space for sandwiches, a little porcelain box for cold meat or fried chicken, another for salad, a glass with a lid which screwed on, held by a ring in a corner, for custard or jelly, a flask for tea or milk, a beautiful little knife, fork, and spoon fastened in holders, and a place for a napkin.
>
> Margaret was almost crying over it.

So was I. As the novel progresses, the box appears and reappears, almost like a character, its ingenious compartments filled with delicious homemade food. But it is as an empty vessel that it makes its deepest impression. What better emblem of childhood than an object designed around a state of expectation? The good things not yet in the lunch box connect with deep feelings of childhood optimism. The high promise of the lunch box heralds the novel's own happy denouement and, perhaps, even its long life as a classic text of girlhood fulfillment.

•

Gene Stratton-Porter (originally Geneva) was a plump, bossy woman of enormous energy and enterprise who is vaguely remembered today as a sentimental novelist and (incorrectly) as a sort of proto-environmentalist. She was born in 1863 on a farm in Wabash, Indiana, the unplanned last of twelve children, and began to write after her marriage to a druggist and banker named Charles Dorwin Porter, thirteen years her senior. Her early writings were studies of bird life, illustrated with black-and-white photographs that she took herself with great effort. When the nature writing did not bring in money, Stratton-Porter turned to fiction and promptly became a bestselling author. By the time of her death in an automobile accident in 1924, her novels had sold more than seven million copies and she herself was a millionaire.

Money wasn't enough, however; Stratton-Porter wanted recognition as a literary artist. "I am desperately tired, as I have often told you," she wrote to a friend, "of having the high-grade literary critics of the country give a second- and at times a third-class rating to my literary work because I would not write of complexes and rank materialism."

In fact, materialism (or consumerism, as we now call it) is at the heart of Stratton-Porter's literary enterprise. Her heroes and heroines burn with desire for money and goods, though their naked acquisitiveness is clothed in the homespun mantle of the Protestant work ethic: unless you work for it, you can't have it. Accordingly, Elnora will accept the Stintons' wonderful purchases only if she can repay them for each item with money she has earned. In her darkest hour (her awful clothes aren't her only problem—she also needs money for tuition and books) she sees a sign in the window of a bank that leads her to the Bird Woman (a character based on the author), who is offering high cash prices for specimens of moths and butterflies. Elnora, as it happens, has hundreds of moths and butterflies stashed away in a wooden case in a swampy wilderness called the Limberlost (based on an actual area of that name). As Dreiser's Caroline Meeber sells her body to men to escape poverty and acquire the pretty things she craves, so Elnora sells moths to the Bird Woman (who in turn sells them to foreign collectors). Elnora's continuing quest for marketable lepidoptera permits her to become a popular, nicely dressed high school girl.

A Girl of the Limberlost is a Cinderella story whose wicked stepmother, in an interesting twist, is the heroine's real mother. She is a crazy person, deranged by grief for a husband who was sucked into a quagmire before her eyes when she was pregnant with Elnora. Elnora grows up actively disliked by her mother—blamed for the death of the husband—and treated with harsh unkindness. The mother's derangement extends to her finances—she believes herself poor, though her land is full of valuable trees and has oil beneath its surface. Cutting down timber and drilling for oil would permit her to provide comfortably for Elnora. But she refuses to allow it. "Cut down Robert's trees! Tear up his land! Cover everything with horrid, greasy oil! I'll die first!" she says.

Far from commending her for her environmental correctness, Stratton-Porter treats the mother's refusal to lumber and drill as a symptom of her madness. In 1909, commercial exploitation of the wilderness was as unexceptionable as pig farming and beekeeping. When the ecosystem of the actual Limberlost, where Stratton-Porter did her work on birds, was destroyed by lumbering and oil drilling, she simply moved her nature operations elsewhere; there was still plenty of elsewhere. And when the mother in the novel learns that the husband for whom she has been grieving for eighteen years was a philanderer who drowned while sneaking home from an assignation, she demonstrates her return to sanity by expressing her willingness to "sell some timber and put a few oil wells where they don't show much."

The unobjected-to destruction of the Limberlost also figured in Stratton-Porter's previous novel, *Freckles* (1904), whose impoverished boy hero struggles as Elnora does for a place in the world of buying and selling and ends up a rich man with an Irish title. He was found on the streets of Chicago as an infant, with his right hand horrifyingly cut off, and after a bleak childhood in an orphanage, he arrives at the Limberlost, where a fatherly lumberman named McLean, a partner in a Grand Rapids lumber company, hires him to patrol the trail and guard the valuable trees that are soon to become Grand Rapids furniture:

Of the thousands who saw their faces reflected on the polished surfaces of that furniture and found comfort in its use,
few there were to whom it suggested mighty forests and
trackless swamps, and the man, big of soul and body, who cut
his way through them, and with the eye of experience doomed
the proud trees that were now entering the homes of civiliza-
tion for service.

Freckles was the first of the consumerist fairy tales packaged as
nature novels that brought Stratton-Porter to the forefront of early-
twentieth-century American popular fiction. In it she performs the
brilliant feat of fudging that permits the reader to feel ennobled
by the natural world while rooting for its extirpation. It isn't that
Stratton-Porter's feeling for nature wasn't genuine. She once wrote
to a reader who asked what church she belonged to that she didn't
go to church because "I prefer to continue in the relationship I feel
is established between me and my Creator through a lifetime of nature study." She went on:

> I would advocate holding services out-of-doors in summer,
> giving as my reason that God so manifests Himself in the
> trees, flowers, and grass that to be among His creations puts
> one in a devotional frame of mind, gives better air to breathe,
> and puts worship on a natural basis, as it was in the begin-
> ning, when Christ taught the people beside the sea and in
> the open.

And yet when Freckles exclaims, "Do you suppose Heaven is any
finer than that?" he is not talking about a forest glade in spring
carpeted with violets and hepatica, but about the "polished floors,
sparkling glass, and fine furnishings" of the Bird Woman's house
during a party, when it is "all ablaze with lights, perfumed with
flowers, and filled with elegantly dressed people."

After *Freckles*, Stratton-Porter never again so baldly celebrated the
destruction of the natural environment in the name of "service."

Henceforth her entrepreneurial heroes and heroines confine their commodifications of nature to moths, medicinal herbs, and bees. But their attachment to the world of commerce grows ever stronger. In *The Harvester* (1911), Stratton-Porter's greatest bestseller and arguably her worst book, she achieves a kind of apotheosis of shopping. Her hero, David Langston, lives alone in the woods, like Thoreau, but unlike Thoreau he doesn't criticize the townspeople for their hapless acquisitiveness. He himself is constantly rushing into town to buy things. He has a good income from the medicinal herbs he gathers and sells to drug companies, and is fixing up a house he has built for the woman he plans to marry—a woman who appeared to him in a vision, and who presently appears in real life in the form of another hard-up girl.

Like Elnora Comstock, Ruth Jameson—known as the Girl throughout the novel, as David Langdon is called the Harvester—won't take money she hasn't earned, or things she can't pay for, but weirdly agrees to enter into a not-for-real marriage (like a marriage for a green card) so that she may live in the Harvester's house. The Harvester hopes that in time the marriage will become a marriage more than in name. In a kind of reverse *Taming of the Shrew* scenario, he woos the Girl with nourishing meals and tasteful decor. "This adjoining is your bathroom," he tells her, and goes on:

> "I put in towels, soaps, brushes, and everything I could think of, and there is hot water ready for you—rain water, too."
>
> The Girl followed and looked into a shining little bathroom, with its white porcelain tub and wash bowl, enamelled wood-work, dainty green walls, and white curtains and towels. She could see no accessory she knew of that was missing, and there were many things to which she never had been accustomed.

Actually, the Girl is no slouch at label recognition. "Just as I thought!" she exclaims after inspecting the corner of a coverlet. "It's a genuine Peter Hartman!" (It is painful to think that the name Ralph Lauren may one day mean as little as that of Peter Hartman.) In the pages that follow, the Harvester shops for beds and sofas and curtains for the not yet furnished parts of the house, and puts special effort into the room to be occupied by the housekeeper. "Rogers," he tells the man who comes with the van bringing the furniture,

> "hang those ruffled embroidered curtains. Observe that whereas mere guest beds are plain white, this has a touch of brass. Where guest rugs are floor coverings, this is a work of art. Where guest brushes are celluloid, these are enamelled, and the dresser cover is hand embroidered . . . Watch the bounce of these springs and the thickness of this mattress and pad."

When the Girl expresses disbelief at the idea of treating a housekeeper better than a guest, the Harvester reasonably explains:

> "Friends come and go, but a good housekeeper remains and is a business proposition—one that if conducted rightly for both parties and on a strictly common-sense basis, gives you living comfort."

But the housekeeper never comes. No servant (or wife) could live up to the Harvester's standards. He may be the most maniacally neat hero in literature. On taking his beloved to sit under an oak on a hilltop, he fussily "spread the rug and held one end of it against the tree trunk to protect the Girl's dress." When the sound of an arriving car roused him in the middle of the night, he "swung his feet to the floor, setting each in a slipper beside the bed." His house is like a five-star hotel: "rooms shining, beds fresh, fireplaces filled and waiting a match, ice chest cool." His personal hygiene is no less outstanding. He is always jumping into the lake and changing into fresh white clothes.

The Harvester is clean in another sense of the word. In *A Girl of the Limberlost*, Elnora's upper-class suitor, Philip Ammon, makes a point of telling her, "I've kept myself clean," meaning—what else?—that he has refrained from sex. The house-proud Harvester is similarly sex deprived, but he goes beyond private self-denial to public crusading. In a speech delivered before a medical society in New

York (to which he is peddling his herbal remedies), he rants about
the evil social consequences of uncleanness:

> "The next time any of you are called upon to address a body
> of men, tell them to learn for themselves and to teach their
> sons, and to hold them at the critical hour, even by sweat and
> blood, to a clean life; for in this way only can feeble-minded
> homes, alms-houses, and the scarlet woman be abolished. In
> this way only can men arise to full physical and mental force,
> and become the fathers of a race to whom the struggle for
> clean manhood will not be the battle it is with us.
>
> "By the distorted faces, by the misshapen bodies, by marks
> of degeneracy, recognizable to your practised eyes, everywhere
> on the streets . . . I conjure you men to live up to your high
> and holy privilege, and tell all men that they can be clean, if
> they will."

The Harvester is such a nutty book that by the time you come to
this passage it seems like just another of its forays into the crackpot-
tery of its period. According to her biographer, Judith Reick Long,
Gene Stratton-Porter never revised or cut; her novels—like the Harvester's hysterical sermon—just came pouring out of her. But racial
theories were no passing fancy with her. They became the central
theme of a noxious novel called *Her Father's Daughter*, written in
1921, after she had moved to Los Angeles and enthusiastically em-
braced the hatred for Chinese and Japanese immigrants by which
early-twentieth-century California was seized. Its seventeen-year-
old heroine, Linda Strong, talks like this:

> "The white man has dominated by his colour so far in the
> history of the world, but it is written in the Books that when
> the men of colour acquire our culture and combine it with
> their own methods of living and rate of production, they are
> going to bring forth greater numbers, better equipped for the
> battle of life, than we are. When they have got our last secret,
> constructive or scientific, they will take it, and living in a way
> that we would not, reproducing in numbers we don't, they

will beat us at any game we start, if we don't take warning while we are in the ascendancy, and keep there."

And this:

"There's an undercurrent of something deep and subtle going on in this country right now . . . If California does not wake up very shortly and very thoroughly she is going to pay an awful price for the luxury she is experiencing while she pampers herself with the service of the Japanese, just as the South has pampered herself for generations with the service of the negroes. When the negroes learn what there is to know, then the day of retribution will be at hand."

The plot of *Her Father's Daughter* revolves around a Japanese A student in a Los Angeles high school, named Oka Sayye, who is actually a thirty-year-old man planted there by the Japanese government for God knows what reason, but who is clearly such a threat to the white world that in the end he has to be remorselessly pushed off a cliff by the heroine's Irish housekeeper. I'm not kidding.

Suspecting that Oka Sayye is not what he pretends to be, and in any case incensed by the very thought of a nonwhite leading the class, Linda reproaches another A student named (yes) Donald Whiting for his supine acceptance of second place. She taunts him with the idea

"that a boy as big as you and as strong as you and with as good brain and your opportunities has allowed a little brown Jap to cross the Pacific Ocean and in a totally strange country to learn a language foreign to him, and, with the same books and the same chances, to beat you at your own game."

Donald meekly asks, "Linda, tell me how I can beat that little cocoanut-headed Jap."

In this atrocious book (I said that *The Harvester* was Stratton-Porter's worst book, because this one is really in a different league), Stratton-Porter puts her talent for describing desirable consumer objects to the task of describing undesirable racial traits: "I have never seen anything so mask-like as the stolid little square head on that Jap," Linda says to Donald. "I have never seen anything I dislike more than the oily, stiff, black hair standing up on it like menacing bristles." Consumerism is not absent from the book—parallel to the yellow-peril plot is another Cinderella story, this one featuring a wicked stepsister, Eileen, who deprives Linda of the pretty clothes and dainty furnishings that are her due.

Like Elnora, Linda finds a way of extracting money from nature: she collects desert plants and writes a lucrative magazine column about the delectable dishes she makes from them. But here even the Cinderella plot has a racist twist. Stratton-Porter improves on the original Cinderella story by severing the blood connection between the heroine and her nasty sibling: Linda finds a document in a secret compartment in her late father's study, from which she learns that Eileen was not his biological daughter. Blood tells all.

Judith Reick Long notes in her biography that *Her Father's Daughter* "caused no ripples in Gene Stratton-Porter's readership" and in general "met with few complaints." (*The Literary Review* went so far as to praise its "wholesome charm," she writes.) In *The Great Gatsby*, F. Scott Fitzgerald gives us a nice sense of where white supremacy was situated in the thinking of 1920s America. In drawing the portrait of his deeply unpleasant character Tom Buchanan, he has him extravagantly praise a book called *The Rise of the Colored Empires* by a writer named Goddard: " 'The idea is if we don't look out the white race will be—will be utterly submerged. It's all scientific stuff; it's been proved . . . This fellow has worked out the whole thing. It's up to us, who are the dominant race, to watch out or these other races will have control of things.' "

Fitzgerald used Goddard's book as a novelist writing today might use a New Age book to establish a character's intellectual nullity. He based Goddard on a real writer named Lothrop Stoddard, whose book *The Rising Tide of Color Against White World-Supremacy* (1920) sometimes reads as if Stratton-Porter had written it—"clean, virile, genius-bearing blood, streaming down the ages through the unerring action of heredity"—and surely had been read by her. She had probably also read *The Passing of the Great Race* (1916) by the equally fervent racist Madison Grant—a book Adolf Hitler is said to have called "my bible."*

When, during the 1980s and 1990s, Indiana University Press re-issued eight of Stratton-Porter's novels (as literature for "young adults"), it wisely didn't go near *Her Father's Daughter*, though it did include *The Keeper of the Bees* (1925), a work about a World War I veteran with an incurable shrapnel wound, whose weirdness almost surpasses that of *The Harvester*. But while other nineteenth- and early-twentieth-century sentimental novels have fallen by the wayside, as dull as they are ridiculous, even the most risible of Stratton-Porter's works remain oddly readable. One mocks them but goes on turning their pages. Stratton-Porter had the crucial ability of the popular novelist to make the reader want to know what happens next to people in whose existence he does not for one minute believe. But she had something else as well.

In a perceptive study called "Class, Gender, and Sexuality in Gene Stratton-Porter's *Freckles*," Lawrence Jay Dessner, dwelling on some of the book's more conspicuous excesses, notes:

> This relentless insistence, this lack of moderation, this sensa-tionalism in [*Freckles*'s] language is so customary, so seem-ingly habitual, that one feels the presence of presumably unconscious expressive needs. It is as if the novel's intellectual and ideological muddle is merely a superficial layer of flotsam bobbing on a boiling sea of emotion.

Dessner adds, with nice dryness, "*Freckles* is not a work to sup-port a faith in the political progressiveness of popular fiction." But Dessner's image of a boiling sea of emotion as the element in which Stratton-Porter's fiction is suspended offers a clue to its power. She often uses the phrase "she panted" instead of "she said," and the novels themselves have the atmosphere of someone breathlessly run-ning around inside them, ordering their cuckoo plots and scattering

---

* See Trevor Butterworth's review of Timothy Ryback's *Hitler's Private Library: The Books That Shaped His Life* (Knopf, 2008), *Bookforum*, December/January 2009.

their pernicious notions in a kind of passion of uncontrolled and uncontrollable feeling. Her peaceable kingdom—where birds and moths and small mammals lie down with oil tycoons and lumber barons, and elegant bathroom fixtures and lovely things to eat and lawn dresses and eugenics and God and fringed gentians are all mixed up together—is the product of an imagination of almost life-threatening febrility.

If a sense of "unconscious expressive needs" wafts out of all imaginative literature, it is rare to find it so floridly present in bestselling sentimental fiction. In an article called "The Why of the Best Seller," published in 1921 in *The Bookman*, the critic William Lyon Phelps valiantly struggled to define the character of Gene Stratton-Porter's achievement. He was reduced to saying, "She is a public institution, like Yellowstone Park," and "If she is not a literary artist, she is anyhow a wonderful woman." (This after deploring *Her Father's Daughter*.)

In a memoir called *The Lady of the Limberlost* (1928), Stratton-Porter's daughter, Jeannette Porter Meehan, defended her mother's apparent mawkishness:

> Mother *knew* both sides of life, but she chose to write only about one side. She knew the stern realities, the immorality, and the seamy, disgusting sidelights of life. But why write about them? Every one has his own trouble and heartache, so why not give the world something happy to read, and make them see visions of idealised life? Surely this does more good than sordid tales of sex filth that only lead to morbid and diseased thinking.

But in fact, read a certain way, the novels have much to offer dirty minds. For example, the way Dessner, under the sway of Eve Kosofsky Sedgwick's *Between Men: English Literature and Male Homosocial Desire*, reads the queer stuff going on between Freckles and McLean ("the perfervid, the ecstatic—may one say the erotic?—relationship between Freckles and McLean") and sees the stump of Freckles's missing hand as a "shame-provoking, phallic-shaped member." Stratton-Porter generally kept her interest in sex filth below the level of consciousness, but in *The Harvester* she allowed it to surface with almost embarrassing explicitness. The Girl predictably succumbs to the charms of her benefactor-decorator (Stratton-Porter liked to portray him asleep, looking like a Rockwell Kent Aryan hero, "his lithe figure stretched the length of the bed," "the strong, manly features, the fine brow and chin" etched by the light of the moon)—but she is sexless. After one of her sad attempts at a kiss, he witheringly tells her, "That was the loving caress of a ten-year-old girl to a big brother she admired. That's all!" and stalks off to talk to his dog Belshazzar about his sex starvation. Presently, he decides on a bold step: "Excuse me if I give you a demonstration of the real thing, just to furnish you an idea of how it should be." After the demonstration,

> she lifted her handkerchief and pressed it against her lips, as she whispered in an awed voice, "My gracious Heaven, is *that* the kind of a kiss he is expecting me to give *him*? Why, I couldn't—not to save my life."

In the end, the Harvester accepts the counsel of a lewd old lady named Granny Moreland:

> "If you're going to bar a woman from being a wife 'til she knows what you mean by love, you'll stop about nine tenths of the weddings in the world, and t'other tenth will be women that no decent-minded man would jine with."

Granny checks her facts with a doctor:

> "I told him you'd tell him that no clean, sweet-minded girl ever had known nor ever would know what love means to a man 'til he marries her and teaches her. Ain't it so, Doc?"
> "It certainly is."

(Ian McEwan's *On Chesil Beach* takes a mordant look at the conduct of this pedagogy in mid-twentieth-century England.)

•

In *A Girl of the Limberlost*, there is a scene of voyeurism so vividly rendered that I have retained a picture of it in my mind over the years, assuming that I was recalling one of the book's art nouveau illustrations by Wladyslaw T. Benda. In fact, no such illustration exists—the image derives from my mind's eye. What I see is a man in a tree on a dark night, looking through a window into a lighted room where a girl in a nightgown is reading at a table. In Stratton-Porter's description:

> He could see the throb of her breast under its thin covering and smell the fragrance of the tossing hair. He could see the narrow bed with its pieced calico cover, the whitewashed walls with gay lithographs, and every crevice stuck full of twigs with dangling cocoons . . . But nothing was worth a glance save the perfect face and form within reach by one spring through the rotten mosquito bar. He gripped the limb above that on which he stood, licked his lips, and breathed through his throat to be sure he was making no sound.

It is a measure of what children pick up without knowing exactly what they are taking in that my uninformed ten-year-old self grasped and was excited by the scene's obvious sense of sexual threat. Though not spelled out, the implications of "throb of her breast," "within reach by one spring," "licked his lips" were not lost on me. Of course, the rape is averted: Elnora starts talking to herself, as Stratton-Porter's characters are given to doing when she needs them to, and her innocent babble converts the would-be predator into a blubbering, sentimental fool who restores the money he has stolen from Elnora's hiding place in the Limberlost and leaves her a note of warning against his fellow lowlifes.

A Girl of the Limberlost is Stratton-Porter's best book. Alone among the novels, it escapes the wild veerings of her mind into strange, crankish byways. Its single touch of racism—and it is recognizable as racism only in the light of *Her Father's Daughter* and *The Harvester*—is the drastic skin peel the reformed mother gives herself to remove the brown complexion she acquired while working outdoors without a sunbonnet; a white skin is part of her program of looking nice in front of Elnora's classmates. And Elnora is Stratton-Porter's best heroine. Her strict morality and goodness are accompanied by a straightforwardness, almost a brusqueness of manner that sets her off from the saccharine heroines of conventional sentimental fiction. She has a lot to put up with, and she puts up with it with endearing good-enough grace.

Edith Carr, *A Girl of the Limberlost*'s bad girl, is another unusual creation. She is beautiful, rich, and spoiled, but has a dimension of neuroticism that sets her off from her conventional counterparts. There is an atmosphere around her—and her peculiar faithful follower Hart Henderson—that evokes the beautiful damned characters Fitzgerald created twenty years later. Philip Ammon (né Mammon?) is about as wooden as a character can get—but then Prince Charming is no Pierre Bezukhov, either. *A Girl of the Limberlost*'s strong mythic understructure, the Aladdin's cave glitter it imparts to the modest material rewards of Elnora's enterprise and hard work secures it a special place in Stratton-Porter's oeuvre—and in American popular art.

In 1922 Stratton-Porter wrote a long poem called *The Fire Bird*, about an Indian maiden who brings divine retribution on herself, in which she believed she had achieved the high art that eluded her in her novels. Her one fear, as she wrote to a friend, was that "it is one of those things so very high class, so for the few understanding ones, that I have the very gravest doubts as to whether I could market it if I wanted to." The poem did get published, but has long been out of print. It isn't as bad as you might think; it's merely boring.

Stratton-Porter gave a party for herself in Los Angeles to celebrate *The Fire Bird*'s publication. She invited 115 people and wore "a new evening dress of orchid chiffon velvet, looking, my friends were kind enough to say, the best they ever had seen me." (This is from a letter that Jeannette Porter Meehan quotes in *The Lady of the Limberlost*.) The house was decorated with red and white flowers and large branches on which stuffed cardinals, "insured at one hundred dollars each and loaned me from one of the museums of the city," were perched. There was music (" 'The Pastoral Symphony' with the bird notes done on a flute"), an hour-long reading from *The Fire Bird*, and a buffet supper of roasted turkey and spiced ham and salad and cake and ice cream. "A number of people who were present told me that it was the most unique and the most beautiful party ever given in Los Angeles." (Freckles had clearly seen nothing when he rhapsodized about the Bird Woman's party in Indiana.)

Two years later, Stratton-Porter was dead, at sixty-one; she was killed when a Los Angeles streetcar rammed into her chauffeur-driven limousine, one of two she owned. She had just finished *The Keeper of the Bees* at her new fourteen-room redwood vacation house on Catalina Island, to which she had retreated with a cook, a driver, two secretaries, and "a little Yaqui Indian" while awaiting the completion of an eleven-thousand-square-foot, twenty-two-room Tudor-style mansion in Bel Air.

The book was dictated from a hammock slung between two oaks on a hillside and sometimes reads as if the author's attention were elsewhere. At the start of the novel, its hero, Jamie Mac-Farlane, flees a veterans' hospital at a California hot spring, where he has been unsuccessfully treated for his shrapnel wound (and from which he is about to be transferred to the dread Camp Kearney, where everyone is or will become tubercular), and makes his way to the seaside house and garden of a moribund beekeeper, who asks him to look after the bees when he collapses and is hospitalized. MacFarlane learns beekeeping from an annoying child called the Little Scout and gets mixed up with a woman called the Storm Girl, whom he meets on a rock jutting out of the Pacific Ocean during a storm and obligingly weds the next day to give her unborn child (the Shame Baby) a name.

None of this is believable, and much of it is tedious. Only when she is dealing with the minute and sometimes disgusting particulars of MacFarlane's medical condition does Stratton-Porter fully draw us (and perhaps herself) into her story. As she scrutinizes her hero's bloody bandages and traces his chronic infection to the germs bred by the "hot, chemically saturated boiling spring water" piped through the veterans' hospital, she returns to the boiling sea of emotion that is the breeding ground for her inspiration. She invests the story of MacFarlane's cure by bathing in cold Pacific water and never eating starches and meats in the same meal with a thrilling significance. Putting her characteristic feverish intensity in the service of the medical fads of her day, she once again strikes the note to which her contemporaries vibrated, and to which we ourselves may helplessly, if somewhat more mutedly, respond. Imagine a Jane Brody column written by Charlotte Brontë and you will have a sense of Stratton-Porter's singular feat.

THE GENIUS OF THE GLASS HOUSE

1999

In a short essay in the voluminous catalog that accompanies the exhibition *Julia Margaret Cameron's Women*, Phyllis Rose notes that "Cameron's women do not smile. Their poses embody sorrow, resignation, composure, solemnity, and love, determined love, love which will have a hard time of it." Rose goes on to write of the illness, disaster, and defeat that perpetually hovered over the lives of Victorian women. But there were causes closer to hand for the tragic address of Cameron's women. Cameron used a photographic apparatus—fifteen- by twelve-inch glass plates and a lens of thirty-inch focal length—that required exposures of between *three and ten minutes*. Here is an account of a sitting by one of the unsmiling women, quoted by Helmut Gernsheim in his book *Julia Margaret Cameron: Her Life and Photographic Work* (1948 and 1974):

> Mrs. Cameron put a crown on my head and posed me as the heroic queen. This was somewhat tedious, but not half so bad as the exposure . . . The exposure began. A minute went over and I felt as if I must scream; another minute, and the sensation was as if my eyes were coming out of my head; a third, and the back of my neck appeared to be afflicted with palsy; a fourth, and the crown, which was too large, began to slip down my forehead . . .

As it proved, the sitter's excruciations were for naught. The photograph was ruined during the fifth minute by Cameron's husband, Charles, a distinguished retired colonial official with a magnificent white beard, who would affably lend himself to his wife's enterprise to play a Merlin or Lear as the occasion required, but who was unfortunately given to "unconquerable fits of hilarity which always came in the wrong places." When Charles "began to laugh audibly . . . this was too much for my self-possession, and I was obliged to join the dear old gentleman."

We have been affectionately laughing at Julia Cameron for more than half a century; her reputation as a major photographer is inextricably entangled with the legend of her endearing ridiculousness. Virginia Woolf, who was Cameron's great-niece, set the legend in motion in 1926 in a biographical essay she wrote for the Hogarth Press monograph *Victorian Photographs of Famous Men and Fair Women* by Julia Margaret Cameron. Three years earlier, Woolf had written a farce called *Freshwater* (a sort of *Patience* manqué, named for Freshwater Bay on the Isle of Wight, where Charles and Julia lived) in which she poked fun at the Victorian cult of beauty and rendered her great-aunt as one of its more exalted high priestesses. She described Cameron as "a brown-faced gypsylike-looking old woman, wearing a green shawl, fastened by an enormous cameo," and gave her this speech:

> All my sisters were beautiful, but I had genius. They were the brides of men, but I am the bride of Art. I have sought the beautiful in the most unlikely places. I have searched the police force at Freshwater, and not a man have I found with calves worthy of Sir Galahad. But, as I said to the Chief Constable, "Without beauty, constable, what is order? Without life, what is law?" Why should I continue to have my silver protected by a race of men whose legs are aesthetically abhorrent to me? If a burglar came and he were beautiful, I should say to him: Take my fish knives! Take my cruets, my bread baskets and my soup tureens. What you take is nothing to what you give, your calves, your beautiful calves.

Woolf's essay on her great-aunt, though less broadly Gilbertian than her farce, sustains the comic note. It begins with a wild story about Cameron's reprobate father, James Pattle, a colonial official stationed in Calcutta who died of drink in 1845 and whose corpse, according to the story, was sent back to England in a cask of rum that exploded on the sea journey and caused the death by horror of his widow—as well as the destruction of the ship, which itself exploded when the rum, running out of the cask, ignited. The tall tale of the father who couldn't be contained in his sepulchre of spirits is told to illustrate the "indomitable vitality" of the stock from which Cameron sprang. She was one of seven sisters celebrated for their energy, strong-mindedness, and, in all but one case, spectacular beauty. Julia Margaret was the exception. She "was without her sisters' beauty," Woolf writes, and goes on to substantiate the charge with the testimony of another great-niece, who had known Cameron as a child and recalled her as "short and squat, with none of the Pattle grace and beauty about her . . . Dressed in dark clothes, stained with chemicals from her photography (and smelling of them too), with a plump eager face and a voice husky, and a little harsh, yet in some way compelling and even charming."

Cameron's unattractiveness—her role as the woman who loved beauty but didn't herself possess it—is a pivot of the legend. When we look at Cameron's pictures of fair women (almost without exception her female sitters were young and pretty), we see, as a kind of afterimage, the gypsylike crone in the stained black dress who was their creator. Cameron's pictures also inescapably evoke the Victorian household over which she presided, with its fish knives and cruets and soup tureens, its maids and cooks and gardeners, its children and grandchildren and streams of visitors, among them the famous men (Tennyson, Carlyle, Browning, Darwin, Longfellow, among others) whom Cameron lured into the chicken house she had converted into a studio, and upon whose likenesses her artistic reputation for a long time largely rested.

We recall, further, that Cameron started photographing only at the age of forty-eight, with a camera her daughter and son-in-law supplied to divert her while the jocund Mr. Cameron was away looking after a failing coffee plantation and she was alone in the house at Freshwater Bay suffering from depression and anxiety. "It may amuse you, mother, to try to photograph during your solitude at Freshwater," were the words that accompanied the fateful gift. Hitherto, Cameron had lived the life of a well-to-do Victorian married woman who dabbled in poetry and fiction while raising her six children, and made a reputation for herself as a person of irrepressible, almost pathological generosity. Helmut Gernsheim, who elaborated what Woolf had adumbrated, tells wonderful anecdotes about the presents Cameron would force on the people she fell in love with, most notably the poet Henry Taylor (who had been a runner-up to Tennyson for poet laureate and now is only known to Victorian specialists) and his wife, Alice. Cameron's largesse took the form of rare rugs, shawls, jewelry, and decorative objects she and Charles brought from Calcutta when they returned to England in 1848, which Cameron proceeded to dispense as if they were throat lozenges. Gernsheim cites a man who "was sitting in a train with Henry Taylor at Waterloo Station when a disheveled lady rushed up at the last moment and flung a Persian rug in through the window as a present for Henry Taylor, who immediately—the train had started to move—heaved it out of the window onto the platform."

Another story Gernsheim tells about Cameron's relentless benevolence toward the Taylors concerns a "particularly valuable shawl" that Alice Taylor had accepted

> only under the threat that otherwise it would be thrown into the fire. After an interval to allow Mrs. Cameron's feelings to calm down, it was returned, and nothing more was said. But it was impossible to defeat Mrs. Cameron. She sold the shawl, and with the proceeds bought an expensive invalid sofa which she presented in Mrs. Taylor's name to the hospital for incurables at Putney. The matter came to light many months later when Alice Taylor had occasion to visit the hospital and, to her astonishment, saw her name inscribed as donor.

The resourcefulness Cameron developed in the course of her subjugation of the Taylors (according to Gernsheim, Cameron "told

Mrs. Taylor that before the year was over she would love her like a sister," and Mrs. Taylor evidently did) stood her in good stead when she began to "try to photograph." Photography in the 1860s was not for sissies. You did not snap the shutter and someone else did the rest. What you had to do was akin to Marie Curie's extraction of radium from pitchblende. The wet collodion process (then the state-of-the-art method) required a combination of dexterity and stamina that only the most fanatically motivated of amateurs could command. "I worked fruitlessly, but not hopelessly," Cameron wrote in an unfinished autobiographical account called *Annals of My Glass House.* "I began with no knowledge of the art. I did not know where to place my dark box, how to focus my sitter, and my first picture I effaced to my consternation by rubbing my hand over the filmy side of the glass . . . when holding it triumphantly to dry."

Cameron's defeat was characteristically short-lived; she rapidly mastered the collodion process and went on to produce photographs by which not only her immediate family was charmed ("My husband from first to last has watched every picture with delight, and it is my daily habit to run to him with every glass upon which a fresh glory is newly stamped, and to listen to his enthusiastic applause," she wrote in *Annals*, and went on in her breathless, unstinting way to report that "this habit of running into the dining room with my wet pictures has stained such an immense quantity of table linen with nitrite of silver, indelible stains, that I should have been banished from any less indulgent household"), but which won the praise of a larger world and presently came to number among the monuments of photography. However, not all of Cameron's photographs became monuments.

Early on, a distinction was drawn between the photographs of single individuals and the group pictures (Cameron called them "fancy-subject" pictures), in which two or more costumed (or, in the case of children, nude or seminude) sitters enacted, under Cameron's direction, scenes from the Bible, mythology, Shakespeare, or Tennyson. In the critical essay that followed Woolf's biographical one in *Famous Men and Fair Women*, Roger Fry set the terms of the yes-and-no discourse on Cameron's photography that was to remain in place for more than half a century. He heaped praise on the individual portraits, placing them in "the universal and dateless world" of Rembrandt, and dismissed the group pictures as so much Victorian ephemera. "These must all be judged as failures from an aesthetic standpoint," he wrote of the fancy-subject pictures, mystifyingly excepting a photograph called *The Rosebud Garden of Girls*. Gernsheim, who had escalated Woolf's remarks about Cameron's looks to "Julia was charmingly, hopelessly, pathetically plain," similarly heightened the harshness of Fry's estimate of the fancy-subject pictures: "If the majority of Mrs. Cameron's subject pictures seem to us affected, ludicrous and amateurish, and appear in our opinion to be failures, how masterly, on the other hand, are her straightforward, truthful portraits, which are entirely free from false sentiment, and which compensate for the errors of taste in her studies." Subsequent writers on Cameron, among them Cecil Beaton, Edward Lucie-Smith, Quentin Bell, Brian Hill, and Ben Maddow, unquestioningly perpetuated the idea that only some of her work was worth looking at, and that a lot of it was an embarrassment.

In 1984 a book with the quiet title *Julia Margaret Cameron, 1815–1879* was published in England, and it almost crackled with the indignation of its author, an Oxford professor named Mike Weaver, who couldn't bear the way Cameron and her work had been, as he saw it, condescended to and misjudged by Woolf, Fry, et al. Here is Weaver's testy commentary on the legend of the wacky great-aunt:

> The story that her children gave her a camera to pacify her while [Charles Cameron] was away . . . is another of those many anecdotes which aim to rob her of her dignity as woman and artist, and have taken the place of criticism of her work . . . The anecdotes attempt to turn her into a blue-stocking. She is depicted as obsessed with old-fashioned shawls, with fingers stained with chemicals (what do women know about science?) . . . Some have suggested it was all too much for poor Charles and other alleged "victims," but there is no sign of conflict between them, rather a sense of deep and lasting

relationship based on mutual admiration. She was the Mrs. Gaskell of photography. She seems to have accepted maternity and marriage as high and holy offices, and lived an active life in which art relieved her from daily household cares. She was not an invalid, not repressed, and not inadequate. She was a nice-looking woman, who was a fine person. Her sisters, all younger than her, for all their famed beauty, could not hold a candle to her. A Christian artist, she submitted her passions and her pride to the will of others, and, above all, to God. If it were not so unfashionable, I would have called her a genius . . .

Far from dismissing the fancy-subject pictures as kitsch, Weaver holds them up as the essential core of Cameron's oeuvre, the culminating expression of the Christian piety by which, in his view, all her photography is animated—the "straightforward," secular-seeming portraits no less than the explicitly religious compositions—and to which her aesthetic ambition was always subservient. What Gernsheim saw as "false sentiment" and "errors of taste," Weaver sees as an enterprise of confident seriousness and sincerity. Weaver proposes the typological tradition of Bible reading—whereby characters and themes in the Hebrew scriptures are identified as prefigurations of characters and themes in the New Testament (Rachel at the well anticipating the angel at the tomb, for example, or the infant Samuel anticipating the infant Jesus)—as a model for the decoding of the problematic group pictures. Through his study of Anna Jameson's *Sacred and Legendary Art*, among other nineteenth-century texts, Weaver imagines himself into the imagination of Cameron, where, he believes, the Bible, classical mythology, Shakespeare's plays, and Tennyson's poems were fused into a single vision of ideal beauty. The vision's matrix was the Renaissance, medieval, and Pre-Raphaelite art with which Cameron, as a woman of culture, was intimately familiar.

In a second book, *Whisper of the Muse*, Weaver expands and deepens his account of Cameron as a major religious artist, further naturalizing her "magnificent contribution" in the now very far country of Victorian Christian aesthetic theory (John Henry Newman, John

Keble, and Charles Cameron, who had written an essay on the sublime, are among his sources). He continues to spring at the throats of "those who charge her with eccentricity." "They deserve our indignation. It is a cheap calumny against a completely *centered* woman," he writes.

Weaver's fierce reappraisal has been very influential. The fancy-subject pictures have become the object of appreciative study, and the funny stories about the woman "of ardent speech and picturesque behavior" are no longer routinely retailed. Sylvia Wolf, the curator of the *Cameron's Women* show, almost entirely excludes them from her sober-sided feminist catalog essay, from which Cameron emerges as a woman of no particular oddness. Weaver's empathic understanding of Cameron—his insistence that we approach her as an advanced Christian thinker rather than as the heroine of a screwball comedy—has obviously had weight with Wolf. The trouble is that Cameron *was* the heroine of a screwball comedy. There is too much evidence of the picturesque behavior for it to be summarily dismissed as a calumny. Virginia Woolf and Gernsheim did not invent the anecdotes: they gratefully took them from Cameron's contemporaries (notably her best friend, the painter G. F. Watts, and her good friend Annie Thackeray) and, most tellingly, from Cameron herself. It is, after all, from Cameron's own *Annals* that the story of the camera given "to amuse you, mother" derives, as does the image of Cameron rushing into the dining room and dripping silver nitrite all over the linen of the table at which poor Charles is trying to eat.

But above all, it is the photographs themselves that confirm the *You Can't Take It with You* character of life at Freshwater and that oblige us to demur from Weaver's presentation of Cameron as a Raphael or Giotto of the camera. If Cameron's Madonna and Child pictures and her illustrations of scenes from Tennyson seem less silly to us than they did to the puritanical modernists, even the most catholic of postmodernists will have to acknowledge that these photographs bear unmistakable traces of the conditions under which they were taken, and that these conditions were often comical. In a group picture in the *Cameron's Women* show called *May Day*, for example, the five flower-bedecked figures look as if they had been brought together not to celebrate the annual renewal of life, but to illustrate the memoir of the lady who said she felt as if her eyes were coming out of her head. A little girl in the foreground (who, in actuality, was a little boy named Freddy Gould, the son of a local fisherman) stares into the middle distance with an unforgettably glazed expression of resigned misery. Another subject picture—a Madonna and Child composition called *Goodness*—would be more aptly named *Sulkiness*, after the expression of the child who is representing the infant Jesus, and who obviously hates every minute of her modeling assignment.

These traces, of course, are what give the photographs their life and charm. If Cameron had succeeded in her project of making seamless works of illustrative art, her work would be among the curiosities of Victorian photography—such as Henry Peach Robinson's waxen *Fading Away* and Oscar Gustave Rejlander's extravagantly awful *The Two Ways of Life*—rather than among its most vital images. Cameron liked to make albums of her photographs and to thrust them upon friends and influential people in rather the way she thrust shawls on the Taylors. (Lord Overstone, Victor Hugo, and George Eliot were among the sometimes puzzled objects of her largesse. It is also said that she tipped porters with photographs.) These collections were not family albums. They were intended not to fix the fleeting moments of family life, but to record Cameron's triumphant progress through the precincts of High Art. And yet, in many respects, Cameron's compositions have more connection to the family album pictures of recalcitrant relatives who have been herded together for the obligatory group picture than they do to the masterpieces of Western painting. In Raphael and Giotto there are no infant Christs whose faces are blurred because they moved, or who are looking at the viewer with frank hatred. Gernsheim wrote of Cameron's illustrations of Tennyson as attempts to do "something photography cannot and should not be made to do . . . When she tried to illustrate an action, the results are reminiscent of poor amateur theatricals, and are unintentionally comic. In these she has certainly overshot the mark of what is acceptable—to our generation—in artificiality." Gernsheim added that "most attempts to illustrate the unreal by a medium whose main contribution to art lies in its realism are doomed to failure."

But it is precisely the camera's realism—its stubborn obsession with the surface of things—that has given Cameron's theatricality and artificiality its atmosphere of truth. It is the truth of the sitting, rather than the fiction that all the dressing up was in aid of, that wafts out of these wonderful and strange, not-quite-in-focus photographs. They are what they are: pictures of housemaids and nieces and husbands and village children who are dressed up as Madonnas and infant Jesuses and John the Baptists and Lancelots and Guineveres and trying desperately hard to sit still. The way each sitter endures his or her ordeal is the collective action of the photograph, its "plot," so to speak. When we look at a narrative painting, we can suspend our disbelief; when we look at a narrative photograph, we cannot. We are always aware of the photograph's doubleness—of each figure's imaginary *and* real persona. Theater can transcend its doubleness, can make us believe (for at least some of the time) that we are seeing only Lear or Medea. Still photographs of theatrical scenes can never escape being pictures of actors. What gives Cameron's pictures of actors their special quality—their status as treasures of photography of an unfathomably peculiar sort—is their singular combination of amateurism and artistry.

Weaver's characterization of Cameron as a genius does not seem to me exaggerated in regard to her grasp of the possibilities offered by photography for transcendent formal achievement. "I longed to arrest all beauty that came before me," Cameron wrote in her *Annals.* Every amateur photographer knows this feeling. But only a few amateurs (Lartigue is another) have understood what is involved in this arrest. For a beautiful child's beauty to survive the camera's withering gaze, much propitiatory activity by the photographer is required. Cameron knew, for example, that the clothes children normally wear (in Victorian times no less than in ours) are among the camera's most potent weapons against the pedophilia of the photographing aunt or grandmother. Instead of a beautiful child, the camera will deliver a competition between a face and a dress or snowsuit, a clash between the delicacy and translucency of young skin and the coarse materiality of fashionable dress. A great-niece of Cameron's named Laura Gurney recalled the day when she and her sister Rachel were "pressed into the service of the camera [as] . . . two Angels of the Nativity, and to sustain them we were scantily clad and each had a heavy pair of swan wings fastened to her narrow shoulders, while Aunt Julia, with ungentle hand, tousled our hair to get rid of its prim nursery look." But clearly Aunt Julia knew what she was doing to give her vision of childhood beauty its best possible shot at being transmitted onto the wet glass plate. If it would be too much to say that Cameron chose religious and literary themes simply as an escape from Victorian costume, there is no question that her draperies and veils and turbans and crowns and coats of mail gave her a considerable aesthetic advantage over the studio photographers and fellow amateurs who took their sitters as they came.

Cameron had other strategies for throwing a veil of romance over the zany goings-on in the chicken house. In her essay "Cupid's Pencil of Light: Julia Margaret Cameron and the Maternalization of Photography,"* Carol Armstrong wonderfully reads a photograph of old Mr. Cameron, dressed as Merlin, posed with an unknown sitter dressed as the sorceress Vivien (who is pointing a finger at Charles's head as if it were a lady's small revolver), as "an allegorical figuration of Cameron herself as photographic sorceress, quite a bit younger than her husband, directing the bemused patriarch to hold his pose, commanding him to be still (and stop his giggling), and magically, indexically, enchanting him, transforming him into Merlin, all through the bewitching witchcraft of photography."

One of Cameron's most potent spells was the soft focus into which—at first unwittingly (she evidently initially had the wrong lens for her camera) and then by design—she consistently cast her images. One has only to imagine her fancy-subject pictures as taken by Richard Avedon's or Annie Leibovitz's pitilessly sharp lenses to

* *October*, vol. 76 (Spring 1996).

understand the role soft focus plays in the sense these pictures give of being traces of impossible dreams rather than mere laughable attempts to fool the eye. Cameron's lighting further heightens the oneiric character of her work. She kept her glass house fairly dark, which prolonged the torture of the sittings but permitted her to put into play what Quentin Bell called her "Venetian understanding of chiaroscuro." A photograph called *The Passing of Arthur*, which has often been jeered at for its artificiality and theatricality, and which Gernsheim holds up as one of the very worst of the fancy-subject pictures, has always given me a secret thrill, to which I now feel free to confess. The picture shows, in Gernsheim's derisively vivid description,

> the mortally wounded king [lying] in the stately barge (a simple makeshift boat with broomsticks for mast and oar jutting out into the white muslin curtains representing water), resting his head in the lap of one of the Queens, and looking rather suspicious of his strange surroundings. Unfortunately the boat is too small to contain the three mourning Queens, so the other two have to stand behind it. Half a dozen villagers muffled in monks' cowls made by Mrs. Cameron's maids lurk in the background . . .

But the accompanying illustration does not support Gernsheim's mockery. Far from looking ridiculous, *The Passing of Arthur* is a kind of crowning image of Cameron's imaginative enterprise. Yes, the broomsticks and the muslin curtains are there, but they are insignificant. For once, the homely truth of the sitting gives right of place to the romantic fantasy of its director. The picture, a night scene, is magical and mysterious. Gernsheim compared Cameron's fancy-subject pictures to poor amateur theatricals. *The Passing of Arthur* puts me in mind of good amateur theatricals I have seen, and recall with shameless delight.

Cameron is reported to have said—on the occasion of declining to photograph Mrs. Charles Darwin—that "no woman must be photographed between the ages of eighteen and seventy." How firmly Cameron adhered to her program of ruthless ageism is evident from the *Cameron's Women* show, in which one dewily fresh young woman after another is on view. These are the "fair women" of the Hogarth Press monograph, who now reappear unescorted. Sylvia Wolf, accounting for her decision to banish the "famous men," writes that she finds Cameron's portraits of women "different from her portraits of men—more complex and enigmatic somehow."

However, in one respect at least, the portraits of the famous men (who are middle-aged or elderly) and those of the fair women are not dissimilar: both reflect Cameron's love of hair. Her close-ups of Tennyson, Carlyle, Darwin, Longfellow, Taylor, Watts, and Charles Cameron are as much celebrations of beards as of Victorian eminence. (In the case of her remarkable portrait of Sir John Herschel, who was clean-shaven, Cameron made the seventy-five-year-old astronomer wash his white hair before the sitting so that it would fly out to form a kind of mad scientist's shock around his head.) Hair is similarly prominent in the portraits of Mary Ann Hillier (who was Cameron's parlor maid and posed for her as the Mother of God so frequently that she was called Madonna around the house), Cyllena Wilson (an adopted daughter), Alice Liddell (Lewis Carroll's Alice, now grown), Annie Chinery (Cameron's daughter-in-law), Mary Ryan (another maid), May Prinsep (a niece), and Julia Jackson (another niece and future mother of Virginia Woolf), who, among others, form the cast of the *Cameron's Women* show. Like the little girls whose hair was mussed to rid it of its prim nursery look, the bigger girls were made to undo their buns and chignons so that their hair would poetically stream or flow or twist around their faces.

A profile portrait of Hillier, entitled *The Angel at the Tomb*, in which a massive tangle of freshly washed hair occupies half the frame, could serve as a companion piece for the Herschel portrait. In two portraits of Alice Liddell, entitled, respectively, *Pomona* and *Alethea*, the boundary between a dense profusion of leaves and flowers and the sitter's long, loose hair is breached—as if to express Cameron's Morris-like delight in all things that grow and twine.

Her practice of portraying the famous men in their own illustrious person while (with some exceptions) rendering the fair women as biblical or literary characters might suggest a certain sexism.* But the photographs themselves tell a more egalitarian story. They show no evidence that Cameron's heart beat any less rapidly and jumpily when she photographed her maid than when she photographed the poet laureate. Perhaps she dared less with men in the hair-mussing and clothes-changing department (though she did manage to throw a gray blanket across Tennyson's shoulders and possibly even to tousle his hair when she took the photograph that came to be known as the *Dirty Monk* portrait). But the intensity of the photographer-subject relationship was no less in the case of the servant than in that of the great man.

In 1864, her fellow amateur photographer Lewis Carroll visited the Isle of Wight and wrote to his sister about a "mutual exhibition of photographs" he had had with Cameron. "Hers are all taken purposely out of focus—some are very picturesque—some merely hideous—however, she talks of them as if they were triumphs of art." Certainly Cameron never doubted herself. In her *Annals* she found it "too comical" that Tennyson should have preferred a portrait of himself by a studio photographer named Mayall to her *Dirty Monk* portrait. She dismissed a devastating review of her work in *The Journal of the Photographic Society of London*, writing: "[It] would have dispirited me very much had I not valued that criticism at its worth. It was unsparing and too manifestly unjust for me to attend to it."

Sylvia Wolf has put many remarkable photographs on view in her show, but I'm not sure she has done Cameron the feminist justice

---

* One of the exceptions was Julia Jackson, who had inherited the Pattle beauty and whom Cameron obsessively photographed—always as herself—in the years before and after her first marriage to Herbert Duckworth. Another was Cameron's only daughter, Julia Norman—the daughter who gave her the camera—whom Cameron scarcely ever photographed. A rare portrait of Julia Norman at the age of twenty-eight, which appeared in *Famous Men and Fair Women* and appears in the *Cameron's Women* show, renders her as a woman of a rather startlingly different type of beauty from that to which Cameron was habitually drawn. It shows a dark, strong-featured woman dressed in black, her sad, almost grim face framed by a dark veil; she is looking down, and she could be one of the nameless widows who appear in news photographs from war-torn Near Eastern or Mediterranean places. However, it was her husband who was to become a widower: she died in childbirth in 1873, at the age of thirty-four, leaving six children. None of Cameron's biographers have enlarged on the relationship between mother and daughter, around which there hovers a certain atmosphere of unease.

she believes she has. As in any all-woman or all-man gathering, a certain artificiality and self-consciousness adheres to the occasion. (A couple of costumed men appear—Henry Taylor as King Aha-suerus in one group picture and as Friar Laurence in another, and an anonymous sitter as Lancelot—but they are recessive, like the male escorts in women's fashion pictures.) The famous-men portraits may have once been overvalued, but without them the world of Camer-on's photography is diminished. The beauty that Cameron found, and in a surprising number of cases was able to arrest, among the aging and aged men of the Victorian literary and art establishment is a cornerstone of her achievement. (Her refusal to photograph ag-ing and aged women is an obvious measure of her understanding of biology's misogyny.) According to Gernsheim, Cameron once took a visitor to a bedroom in her house where Charles had retreated and lay fast asleep. "Pointing to him, she said, 'Behold the most beauti-ful old man on earth!' When out of the room the stranger inquired, 'Who is he, is he a model?' to which Mrs. Cameron proudly replied: 'He is my husband.'" The banishment of the beautiful old men—like the ban on the funny stories—is surely only a temporary ob-struction standing in the way of the enlivening force of the Cameron revival.

GOOD PICTURES

2004

1

On January 7, 1971, Diane Arbus conducted interviews with prospective students of a photography master class she would teach that winter—the last winter of her life—and wrote about the interviewees thus:

> . . . one after another would parade into this empty room like as if I was a burlesque producer or a pimp . . . their pictures mostly bored me and I had a slight feeling like I didn't know what was wrong with 'em, they werent after all so wildly different from Good pictures, except there was that mysterious thing . . . I didn't want to look at them, as if it might be catching and I would end up learning from the students how to take just such boring pix as those.*

If the threat of taking boring pix hangs over every photographer of ambition, Diane Arbus was perhaps more conscious of it than any other photographer. Her photographs relentlessly tell us how interesting they are; they dare us to look away from them. If our favorite thing in the world is not to look at pictures of freaks and transvestites and nudists and mentally retarded people, this cuts no ice with Arbus. She forces us to acknowledge that these are no ordinary unpleasant pictures of society's discards. They are photographs only

---

* Letter to Allan Arbus and Mariclare Costello, January 11, 1971.

Diane Arbus could have taken. The question of whether they are also great works of photography remains undetermined thirty years after her death. Arbus is not universally beloved the way, say, Walker Evans is. Interestingly (and fittingly), she herself did not love Evans. Of the 1971 Evans retrospective at MoMA she wrote, "First I was totally whammied by it. Like THERE is a photographer, it was so endless and pristine. Then by the third time I saw it I realized how it really bores me. Can't bear most of what he photographs."*

There are those who can't bear most of what Arbus photographs. Writing in *The New York Review of Books* in 1984, the late Jonathan Lieberson complained that "her photographs call too much attention to her, one is too much reminded that her success as a photographer consists in her 'figuring' herself into a strange situation and too much invited to ask how she did it." Comparing Arbus's "cold, dead elegance" to the messy naturalism of Weegee, Lieberson concluded that "there is something life-denying, at any rate not quite human, about it that prevents it from being altogether first-rate." More recently, Jed Perl wrote in *The New Republic*: "if directness is photography's glory, it is also liable to be manipulated, used as a sort of all-purpose rhetorical device, until frankness itself becomes a form of obfuscation or artiness—which is a fair description, I think, of the work of Diane Arbus." Perl went on to describe Arbus as "one of those devious bohemians who celebrate other people's eccentricities and are all the while aggrandizing their own narcissistically pessimistic view of the world," and to bitterly note that "the woman and her work are exerting as strong an attraction today as they did at the time of the posthumous retrospective at the Museum of Modern Art in 1972."

The occasion for Lieberson's calm disdain was the publication of Patricia Bosworth's unauthorized biography of Arbus. Perl's excited harshness was set off by the publication of a huge new book of Arbus's photographs entitled *Revelations* that accompanies a retrospective at the San Francisco Museum of Modern Art and is gener-

* Letter to Allan Arbus and Mariclare Costello, January 31, 1971.

ating a galling aura of success. Two excellent sympathetic essays on
Arbus—one by Judith Thurman in *The New Yorker* and the other
by Arthur Lubow in *The New York Times Magazine*—have but-
tressed the sense of a notable cultural event, as have ubiquitous
shorter positive notices. The new book adds many new photographs
to the Arbus oeuvre and offers an authorized version of Arbus's life.
It adds, as such publications are designed to do, great luster to the
figure of Arbus; it makes a kind of institution of her. But it also, unwittingly and perhaps inevitably, blurs the radicalism of the achievement that has made her life an object of avid interest.

The Bosworth biography, which was largely based on Bosworth's
interviews with self-promoting contemporaries—ungentlemanly men
who couldn't resist boasting of sleeping with Arbus and faithless
women who couldn't wait to betray Arbus's confidences—was almost
universally disliked. "A pall of smut hangs over the book," Lieberson icily wrote, deploring the portrait of Arbus that emerges as
"brooding and morbid and sexually perverse, slightly absurd as she
runs about asking her friends if they know any 'battered people' or
'freaks' she can photograph."

Although *Revelations* never mentions Bosworth's book, it
contains an obvious corrective to it in the form of a biographical
account, entitled "A Chronology," written by Doon Arbus, Diane's older daughter, and Elisabeth Sussman, one of the curators of
the San Francisco show. Here, in the place of the base metal of unreliable, self-serving hearsay, we have the solid gold of letters and
diary entries and compositions written by Arbus herself. These are
quoted at length and accompanied by great numbers of photographs of family members and friends and Arbus herself. And guess
what? Arbus comes out looking just as brooding and morbid and
sexually perverse and absurd. Where Bosworth, for example, offered
secondhand and sometimes thirdhand accounts of the sex orgies
Arbus participated in and photographed, the "Chronology" actually shows a photograph of a naked Arbus lying across the lap of a
half-dressed black man. Quotations from the letters to which Bosworth was denied access similarly corroborate the impression of
waifish unwholesomeness that Bosworth's book gives. "I need to be
forlorn and anonymous in order to be truly happy," Arbus writes to

a friend in 1967; and, writing from London in 1970, "Nobody seems miserable, drunk, crippled, mad, or desperate. I finally found a few vulgar things in the suburbs, but nothing sordid yet." In her afterword, Doon Arbus writes that the "Chronology" "amounts to a kind of autobiography." But it amounts to no such thing. Autobiography is the art of choosing what you want the world to know about you. Arbus had no more say in what would be quoted from her letters and journals than she had in what her contemporaries would blab into a tape recorder.

In a memoir of Arbus published in *Ms.* magazine in 1972, Doon recalls the wrestling matches in bed she had with her mother:

> She always beat me. Every time. And when I think of it now, I have the feeling she tricked me into losing. I was always worried about being too rough with her . . . and always, I think, a little embarrassed by her enthusiasm for the contest, so that I would start to laugh, laugh too hard to concentrate, and it would end with me pinned on my back and her smiling placidly down at me.

The positions are now reversed. Doon is smiling down on Arbus. Doon has achieved a fame of her own for the draconian control she has exercised as executor of the Arbus estate. She has withheld permission to reproduce Arbus's photographs from writers who either refused to submit texts for her approval or balked at making the changes she proposed. In October 1993 the journal *October* printed a box explaining why there were no illustrations accompanying an essay on Arbus by Carol Armstrong. *October* had submitted the text to Doon and received a five-page single-spaced letter proposing changes that meddled with content and were, of course, unacceptable. Thirteen years earlier, Ingrid Sischy, editor of *Artforum*, also had chosen to forgo illustrations for an article on Arbus by Shelley Rice. "Permission would be granted only on the condition that the article be read before a permission decision could be reached. *Artforum* is not willing to accommodate compromising stipulations," Sischy wrote in her editor's note. Doon defends her obstructionism in an afterword in *Revelations*:

[Diane Arbus] was turning into a phenomenon and that phenomenon, while posing no threat to her, began endangering
the pictures. She had achieved a form of immunity but the
photographs had not. The photographs needed me. Well, they
needed someone. Someone to keep track of them, to safe-
guard them—however unsuccessfully—from an onslaught of
theory and interpretation, as if translating images into words
were the only way to make them visible.

It is a measure of the power Doon wields in the Arbus world that
no one dared to protect her against saying something so breathtak-
ingly silly in print. Theory and interpretation, far from threatening
works of art, keep them alive. Even negative interpretations like
Lieberson's and Perl's are tributes to Arbus's vitality. Doon sees danger where none exists, and misses seeing it where it does. Photographers need to be protected not against critics' words, but against
photography's plenitude. If a photographer's achievement is not to
be buried under an avalanche of images, his offerings to the world
must be drastically pruned. As candidates for Good pictures are
extracted from contact sheets, so a photographer's extraordinary
work needs to be culled from his merely good work.

Revelations is hardly the first collection to illustrate the truism that
in photography, more is less. The bulky books of Cartier-Bresson's
photographs that followed the small, perfect book of his photographs of the thirties and forties put out by the Museum of Modern
Art in 1947 are among the more egregious examples of this kind of
editorial misguidedness. But that the keeper of the Rhine gold of
Arbus's photography should have so miscalculated is surprising. Doon
had it right thirty years ago when she edited and designed, in collaboration with Arbus's friend Marvin Israel, the book called *Diane
Arbus: An Aperture Monograph*. The eighty images in this incomparable collection constitute the body of work by which Arbus
has been known and judged. Almost every image is an example of
Arbus's style at its most essential and inimitable, and the book as a
whole represents photographic publishing at its most distinguished.

The order in which the eighty images appear is neither chrono-
logical nor determined by subject, but has a mysterious, brilliant
logic. As one leafs through the book, one is drawn into Arbus's
world in the way one is drawn into the world of a novel. That all the
photographs appear on right-hand pages facing left-hand pages
blank except for a title and date gives them a weight and force they
would surely not have in a more economic arrangement. We read
the photographs more slowly and, by so doing, more firmly grasp
their artfulness. The content of Arbus's photographs is more talked
about than their form, but the content would not be what it is
without the form. She did not just go out and take quik pix of her
freaks and transvestites and nudists. As the *Aperture* book underscores with its repetitive series of frontal portraits, she got them to
pose for her, and whenever possible, she placed them against a
plain background. Arbus is hardly the first photographer to have
understood the aesthetic value of the plain background, but her
superimposition of this formalist device on the subject matter that
was the traditional domain of informal, documentary photography
is her own distinctive gesture. In the view of Arbus's admirers, the
"cold, dead elegance" of her pictures, far from being something
to complain about, is precisely what gives them their transfixing
power.

The most novel feature of the *Aperture Monograph*, and perhaps the editors' canniest move, is the absence of any prefatory
critical text. Instead, there are fifteen pages of short fragments of
Arbus's speech and writing—derived largely from a tape recording
made by one of the students in the 1971 class, as well as from interviews and letters—from which Arbus emerges with the vividness
(and some of the speech mannerisms) of a Salinger character. As
rendered by the fragments, Arbus is as brilliant and likable and
amusing and off-kilter as a Glass. Here she is on the people she
photographs:

> Actually, they tend to like me. I'm extremely likable with
> them. I think I'm kind of two-faced. I'm very ingratiating. It
> really kind of annoys me. I'm just sort of a little too nice.
> Everything is Ooooo. I hear myself saying, "How terrific,"

and there's this woman making a face. I really mean it's terrific. I don't mean I wish I looked like that. I don't mean I
wish my children looked like that. I don't mean in my private
life I want to kiss you. But I mean that's amazingly, undeniably something.

And on freaks:

Freaks was a thing I photographed a lot . . . There's a quality
of legend about freaks. Like a person in a fairy tale who stops
you and demands that you answer a riddle. Most people go
through life dreading they'll have a traumatic experience.
Freaks were born with their trauma. They've already passed
their test in life. They're aristocrats.

And on her own achievement:

I do feel I have some slight corner on something about the
quality of things. I mean it's very subtle and a little embarrassing to me, but I really believe there are things which nobody would see unless I photographed them.

This is all very disarming (what a clever rhetorical stroke that
"a little embarrassing to me" is) and it hovers over the pictures. A
photograph may be worth a thousand words, but a photograph and
words—the right words—are an unbeatable combination. Looking
at Arbus's pictures of freaks in the light of her remark about the test
they've passed in life is to look at them with new eyes.

Revelations, in contrast, causes us to look at Arbus's work with tired
eyes. The book reminds me of a porch I know with a lovely view of
a valley, but where no one ever sits, because it is crammed from floor
to ceiling with mattresses, broken chairs, TV sets, piles of dishes,
cat carriers, baby strollers, farm implements, unfinished woodwork-
ing projects, cartons of back issues of *Popular Mechanics,* black plastic bags filled with who knows what. *Revelations,* following a recent

trend of gigantism among the publications that accompany museum photography shows,* is similarly encumbered. In addition to the 104-page "Chronology" (itself crammed with illustrations) and Doon's afterword, there is a long essay by the other curator of the San Francisco exhibition, Sandra S. Phillips, also heavily illustrated; a short essay on Arbus's darkroom technique by Neil Selkirk, who had worked with Arbus and printed her photographs after her death; eleven pages of biographical notes by Jeff L. Rosenheim, associate curator of photography at the Metropolitan Museum, on people who appear in the "Chronology"; fourteen pages of footnotes; the obligatory director's letter by Neal Benezra of the San Francisco Museum; and a sponsor's statement by Charles Schwab.

But what distinguishes the book from other recent SUVs of photography publishing, and makes them inoffensive in comparison, is the way Arbus's photographs are presented. There is no one place in the book devoted to the work. Instead, someone had the horrible idea of mingling Arbus's photographs with the various texts. You look at a few pages of Arbus photographs and then bump into one of the texts. Then there are more Arbus photographs, and then another bump. This is no way to look at photographs. Nor should photographs be bled over to the opposite page, so that two inches are in effect chopped off. Some of Arbus's best-known images—the Russian dwarfs at home, the Christmas tree in a living room in Levittown, the couple in the woods at the nudist colony—are manhandled in this way. The new photographs, with a few exceptions, only subtract from our sense of Arbus's achievement. The collection feels padded. Its cluttered cover, showing a double exposure of Arbus's face superimposed on a night view of Times Square, presages the clutter within. The *Aperture Monograph*, with its serene and uncanny cover image of twins in dark corduroy dresses posed against a white background, is secure in its canonical status.

---

* For example, the modest book of photographs accompanying the 1971 Walker Evans show at MoMA (the one Arbus found so boring) contained a single essay by John Szarkowski; the grand book accompanying the 2000 Walker Evans show at the Metropolitan Museum contained six essays.

2

Arbus came from a wealthy family—her father, David Nemerov, was the owner of the Russeks department store on Fifth Avenue—but it was evidently not the kind of wealthy family that shares its wealth with the children after they grow up. Diane married Allan Arbus at the age of eighteen, and until they amicably separated and then divorced in the late sixties, the couple supported themselves and their two children by working as advertising and fashion photographers. They worked as a team—Allan did the actual photographing, and Diane fussed with the models' clothes and thought up the ideas (rather conventional ones, not at all Arbus-like) for the photographs. Arbus started taking her own photographs on the side and gradually began to get assignments from such magazines as *Esquire* and *Harper's Bazaar.*

In 1963, seeking a recommendation for a Guggenheim grant, she brought some of her photographs to John Szarkowski, head of the Museum of Modern Art's photography department, who was unimpressed. As Szarkowski told Doon Arbus in 1972, "I didn't really like them. I didn't think they were quite pictures somehow. But they were very forceful. You really felt somebody who was just enormously ambitious, really ambitious. Not in any cheap way. In the most serious way. Someone who was going to stand for no minor successes." Szarkowski soon came to think better of Arbus's work, and in 1967 he included thirty of her photographs in a show at the museum called *New Documents*, featuring two other innovative photographers, Lee Friedlander and Gary Winogrand.

But in spite of her major success as a Szarkowski annointee, and as the recipient of two Guggenheims (one in 1964 and the other in 1966), Arbus had to struggle to support herself after she and Allan closed down the commercial photography business and went their separate ways. To augment her income, she was sometimes obliged to put her artistic ambition aside and do work that simply brought in money. One such project of necessity was a private commission in December 1969 to photograph a rich and successful New York actor and theatrical producer named Konrad Matthaei and his wife, Gay, and three children, Marcella, Leslie, and Konrad, Jr., at their East Side town house during a Christmas family gathering. Arbus exposed twenty-eight rolls of film on the two-day project and received a flat fee as well as fees for the prints the family ordered from contact sheets and work prints she submitted. Nothing was known of the Matthaei shoot until the fall of 1999, when Gay and the older daughter, Marcella, came forward with dozens of prints and twenty-eight contact sheets and offered them on loan to the Mount Holyoke College Art Museum for public viewing. (Gay Matthaei was a Holyoke alumna.) From this offering comes the exhibition, and an accompanying book, called *Diane Arbus: Family Albums*, originally at Mount Holyoke and now at the Grey Art Gallery at NYU.

The title derives from a marginal scribble in a letter Arbus wrote in 1968 to Peter Crookston, an editor at the London *Sunday Times*, about a book of photographs she wanted to produce but "which I keep postponing." "The working title . . . is *Family Album*," she told Crookston, and went on, "I mean I am not working on it except to photograph like I would anyway, so all I have is a title and a publisher and sort of sweet lust for things I want in it." In the same letter, Arbus delivered herself of her famous line: "I think all families are creepy in a way."

In the perceptive essays they have written for the accompanying book, John Pultz, associate professor of art history at the University of Kansas, and Anthony W. Lee, associate professor of art history at Mount Holyoke, both begin by quoting Arbus's marginal scribble—and then go on to write the way they probably would anyway, taking up such subjects as (Pultz) the magazine culture of the fifties and sixties and (Lee, in a longer essay) postwar Jewish-American identity, cold war culture, the influence on Arbus of Walker Evans and August Sander, and John Szarkowski's promotion of photography as a modernist art form. Their efforts to connect everything they say to the family-album theme—to the idea that Arbus's mature work reflects a special obsession with the family—are ingenious but not always persuasive. Don't we all have families, and aren't we all obsessed with them on some level?

There are two parts to the *Family Albums* exhibition and book. The original idea had been to show only the Matthaei pictures. But this was thought "too narrow" (as the director of the Mount Holy-oke museum, Marianne Doezema, put it to me) by the university presses approached to do the book, so a mollifying extra group of pictures was tacked on—photographs of Mae West, Bennett Cerf, Marguerite Oswald, Ozzie and Harriet Nelson, Tokyo Rose, and Blaze Starr, among others, that Arbus took for *Esquire* in the six-ties. Unlike the Matthaei pictures, the *Esquire* pictures are not un-known. They appeared in a book called *Diane Arbus: Magazine Work* (1984), edited and designed by Doon Arbus and Marvin Is-rael, though this time without art. What has never been seen before are the contact sheets from which the published *Esquire* photo-graphs derive.

It is fascinating to peer at the many pictures Arbus took of each celebrity and to ponder and even sometimes question the choices she (or the editors) made. Unfortunately, however, one can do so only if one attends the exhibition, for as the book was going to press, the Arbus Estate made one of its characteristic moves of re-pression. Lee and Pultz were obliged to pull the contact sheets of the *Esquire* pictures from their book. (The show, evidently, is out of the reach of the estate and the *Esquire* contact sheets remain in it.)

As if this prepublication tsuris weren't enough, the younger Matthaei daughter, Leslie, suddenly decided she didn't want any pictures of herself published. This forced Lee and Pultz to remove from the book every print and contact image in which Leslie ap-pears, alone or in a group. Here, perhaps even more urgently than with the *Esquire* contacts, it is advisable to see the show for what it reveals about Arbus's photographic practice.

In the section of his essay devoted to the Matthaei commission, Anthony Lee, a little cruelly perhaps, elaborates on the celebrity Konrad Matthaei enjoyed when Arbus came to photograph him and his kin in December 1969. Matthaei, Lee writes, "was becoming an enormous mover and shaker on the New York theater scene, was intimate with the city's, indeed the country's, most famous stage actors and actresses, and was held as a fast-rising star whose good fortune was only beginning." His town house, Lee notes, was filled with eighteenth-century French furniture and paintings by Monet and Renoir; he and Gay regularly appeared in newspaper and magazine society columns. Lee cannot resist quoting from a clipping that the guileless Konrad had produced from his files: "Mr. Matthaei wears a fitted double-breasted suit by Pierre Cardin, brown with a purple over-check, and a lavender shirt and tie. 'I was heavily Paul Stuart oriented,' he wryly remarks, 'before I discovered Cardin.'"

The uncut Matthaei contact sheets straightforwardly tell the story of Arbus's two-day-long struggle with her commission. Family gatherings are no place for photographers of even minor ambition. The photographs they yield are necessarily messy, shapeless, unbeautiful. The photographs Arbus took of the Matthaeis and their relatives at the dinner table and in decorous horseplay in the living room are no different from the photographs today's Instamatic cameras have made it unnecessary to hire professional photographers to take. Arbus tried to put a little order into her pictures by posing family members in a row on a sofa over which the Monet hung or in groups in one of the ornately draped windows. But these images, too, are indistinguishable from the worthless snapshots some annoying relative can always be counted on to take at Christmas and Thanksgiving. Finally, Arbus began taking people off in pairs or alone to other parts of the house to photograph against plain backgrounds. She took some pictures of a girlishly dressed older woman, Konrad's mother, who in other circumstances might have given Arbus good value for her ongoing project of documenting, as she put it, "the point between what you want people to know about you and what you can't help people knowing about you." But the older Mrs. Matthaei was clearly not the person with whom to pursue this dangerous inquiry. When she posed alone for Arbus, Arbus simply accepted Mrs. Matthaei's idea of herself as a woman with a nice smile and good legs. This left the children. With them Arbus was finally able to solve the koan of how to please the family and not disgrace herself as an artist. Her quarry was the two daughters. She had already used up a roll of film on little velvet-suited Konrad, Jr., posing for her on his free-form rocking horse and never ceasing to look banally cute. Marcella and Leslie, ages eleven and nine, in their white party dresses, held out the greatest promise of pictures that would not give offense but might be Good.

When I went to see the Mount Holyoke show, I naturally sought out the missing pictures of Leslie and immediately understood why she had not wanted them preserved in a book. Leslie, an attractive girl, is the disobliging daughter, the Cordelia of the shoot. In almost every photograph, she sulks, glares, frowns, looks tense and grim and sometimes even outright malevolent. In his discussion of the Matthaei commission, Lee quotes an account Germaine Greer gave Patricia Bosworth of a photographic session with Arbus that

> developed into sort of a duel between us, because I resisted being photographed like that—close-up with all my pores and lines showing! She kept asking me all sorts of personal questions, and I became aware that she would only shoot when my face was showing tension or concern or boredom or annoyance (and there was plenty of that, let me tell you), but because she was a woman I didn't tell her to fuck off. If she'd been a man, I'd have kicked her in the balls.

Lee goes on to write that "unlike Greer, neither Gay nor Marcella Matthaei recalls wanting to kick Arbus in her balls," but Leslie might recall otherwise: her resistance to Arbus's project is almost palpably evident. Arbus's too-niceness didn't do its usual work on this thorny girl. Leslie hated every moment of being photographed. In one exceptional moment, Arbus extracted a reluctant smile from the girl. She stands next to her sister—who also looks amused—in an uncharacteristically relaxed pose, with her hands thrust deep into the pockets of her short white satin sheath dress. Something pleasant has passed between the girls and Arbus.

But pictures of pretty, smiling girls were not what Arbus was after. Marcella gave Arbus what Leslie refused her. The two portraits of Marcella that Lee and Pultz reproduce in the book are true Arbus photographs. They have the strangeness and uncanniness with which Arbus's best work is tinged. They belong among the pictures of the man wearing a bra and stockings and the twins in corduroy dresses and the albino sword swallower and the nudist couple. Like these subjects, Marcella unwittingly collaborated with Arbus on her project of defamiliarization. The portraits of Marcella—one full-figure to the knees, and the other of head and torso—show a girl with long hair and bangs that come down over her eyes who is standing so erect and looking so straight ahead of her that she might be a caryatid. The fierce gravity of her strong features further enhances the sense of stone. Her short, sleeveless white dress of a crocheted material, which might look tacky on another girl, looks like a costume from myth on this girl. To contrast the pictures of balky little Leslie with those of monumental Marcella is to understand something about the fictive nature of Arbus's work. The pictures of Leslie are pictures that illustrate photography's ready realism, its appetite for fact. They record the literal truth of Leslie's fury and misery. The pictures of Marcella show the defeat of photography's literalism. They take us far from the family gathering—indeed from any occasion but that of the encounter between Arbus and Marcella in which the fiction of the photograph was forged.

How Arbus got Marcella to look the way she did (a way no real-life eleven-year-old girl looks), how she elicited from her the magnificent grotesquerie by which the portrait is marked, remains her artist's secret. From Lee's interviews and correspondence with Gay, Konrad, and Marcella Matthaei, he gathered that Arbus's manner with the family was "pleasant but reticent" and that "she did not interrogate or interact with her subjects—in fact, barely spoke to them." The close-up portrait of Marcella is reproduced on the cover of *Family Albums* and on the various announcements relating to the book and the exhibition. Walter Benjamin's famous notion in his essay "The Work of Art in the Age of Mechanical Reproduction" that works of art lose their aura once it becomes possible to reproduce them does not apply to photography itself. On the contrary, each time a photograph is reproduced it acquires aura. Even a photograph of no special distinction will take on aura if it is reproduced over and over again. The distinguished portrait of Marcella—hidden from the world's view for thirty years—gleams out of Arbus's photographic universe like a new star.

EDWARD WESTON'S WOMEN

2002

In 1975 I wrote a review of a retrospective of Edward Weston's photographs at the Museum of Modern Art for *The New York Times.* I
was allowed an illustration, but the one I chose—the well-known
pear-shaped nude, a starkly abstract study of a woman's bottom—
was considered too racy by the *Times* of that time, and I was obliged
to accept a staid substitute: a seated female nude in which the model
had so arranged her body that nothing of it showed but bent legs
and thighs and arms and the top of an inclined head. A few years
later, I had occasion to look at that staid picture again and to see
with amusement something I and obviously the *Times* had not noticed in 1975: if you look very closely at the intersection of the
woman's thighs, a few wisps of pubic hair are visible. I had been
led to this discovery by the photograph's model, Charis Wilson,
Weston's second wife, who wrote a remembrance of Weston in a
book of his nudes published in 1977, and recalled of the picture that
"he was never happy with the shadow on the right arm, and I was
never happy with the crooked hair part and the bobby pins. But
when I see the picture unexpectedly, I remember most vividly Edward examining the print with a magnifying glass to decide if the
few visible pubic hairs would prevent him from shipping it through
the mails."

Margrethe Mather and Edward Weston: A Passionate Collaboration by Beth Gates Warren;
and *Through Another Lens: My Years with Edward Weston* by Charis Wilson and Wendy
Madar

The photograph was taken in 1936. In 1946, when the Modern gave Weston his first retrospective, it was still against the law to send nudes showing pubic hair through the mail, and the museum seriously debated whether to show any of Weston's nudes at all. (It finally took its life in its hands and showed them. Nothing happened.) Weston's biographer, Ben Maddow, quotes Weston's satiric letter to Nancy and Beaumont Newhall of the Modern's photography department, "re 'public hair'" (as he liked to call it): "By all means tell your Board that P.H. has been definitely a part of my development as an artist, tell them it has been the most important part, that I like it brown, black, red or golden, curly or straight, all sizes and shapes. If that does not move them let me know."

Weston's bitter jest contains a truth evident to anyone familiar with his history. Weston's erotic and artistic activities are so tightly interwoven that it is impossible to write of one without the other. It is known (from Weston's journals) that most of the women who posed for his nudes and portraits—arguably his best work—slept with him (usually after the sitting) and were sources for him of enormous creative energy.

Margrethe Mather, the first of these all-important models, was, as Maddow writes of her, "a small, very pretty, and exceptionally intelligent woman . . . mostly, though not wholly, a lesbian," and a mysterious, elusive object of desire: "Edward Weston fell desperately in love with her. The sons [by his then wife, Flora] remember barging noisily into the studio darkroom in search of dad, to find him locked in embrace with Margrethe; but she would let things go no further, and this semi-platonic relationship tormented him for nearly ten years."

At the time, Weston was living in the Los Angeles suburb of Tropico, earning his living as a studio portrait photographer and striving, with his after-hours work, to make a name for himself in the world of art photography. Mather's delicate Garboesque beauty and ineradicably sad expression made her an ideal subject for the soft-focus, painterly style in which Weston then worked. His longing for Mather—which was finally and rather mystifyingly fulfilled on the eve of his two-year-long trip to Mexico with another love—has been a fixture of writing about Weston, as has the question of her influence on his work. ("It is . . . difficult to ascertain the undoubtedly strong influence on Edward Weston's photographic ideas of a very bright and neurotic woman, whom he not only photographed, but eventually made his partner at the studio," Maddow writes of Mather.) Unfortunately, the document that might have cleared these matters up—a journal kept by Weston during the years of his association with Mather—was destroyed by him in 1923 in a moment of self-disgust. A few months later, Weston repented of his act, writing in a new journal:

> I . . . regret destroying my day book prior to Mexico: if badly written, it recorded a vital period, all my life with M.M., the first important person in my life, and perhaps even now, though personal contact has gone, the most important. Can I ever write in retrospect? Or will there be someday a renewed contact? It was a mad but beautiful life and love!*

When Mather met Weston, she was a pictorialist photographer herself, at least on the same level of achievement as he was. But whereas Weston went on taking pictures—and experimenting with new forms and styles—to become one of the great figures of photography, Mather stopped photographing in the thirties and thus became a mere character in the story of Weston's artistic innovations and heroic encounters with P.H. *Margrethe Mather and Edward Weston: A Passionate Collaboration* by Beth Gates Warren is a mournful reminder of the short attention span of the gods of reputation. If an artist doesn't keep producing, if he remains out of sight too long, he falls by the wayside. The book's illustrations demonstrate the excellence of Mather's work—twenty-two plates by Weston are interspersed with sixty-six plates by Mather, and the work of the obscure photographer by no means suffers from the comparison. As a pictorialist, Mather serenely holds her own. Leafing through the

---

* *The Daybooks of Edward Weston*, vol. 1, *Mexico*, edited by Nancy Newhall (Aperture, 1973), p. 145.

book without looking at the captions, one can confidently identify the Westons only when Mather appears in them. Each photographer masterfully executes the program of early-twentieth-century art photography, with its love of mist and murk and shadow and all things Japanese. But after 1930 (there was a single brief flurry of renewed activity in 1931), Mather allowed the flame of her talent to subside and then to go out.

Mather's early history, a tale out of Dreiser, as Beth Gates Warren tells it in her book's short text, causes one to wonder how the flame ever got lit. She was born Emma Caroline Youngren in Salt Lake City and at the age of three—following the death of her mother—was sent to live with an aunt who was a housekeeper for a man named Joseph Cole Mather. When Emma came of age, she adopted the name Margrethe Mather, moved to California, and became a prostitute. Even after becoming a photographer and bohemian and political activist (she moved in a circle of Emma Goldman disciples), she continued turning tricks to supplement her income. The source of this arresting information is an extremely rum memoir by a man named William Justema, a pattern designer, whose unreliability Warren acknowledges ("recent research has now qualified a good deal of the information in Justema's casually recorded, undocumented, and highly readable telling of her story"), but whose narrative she cannot resist. Under Gresham's law of biography, good stories drive out true ones. The true story here is that we don't know whether Mather was actually a prostitute or whether Justema (or Mather herself) mischievously invented the story.*

Mather and Justema met around 1921, when he was sixteen and she was thirty-five, and soon thereafter began what he calls "a joint existence of quite exceptional austerity and decadence." (He moved into a room across the street from her studio, where he slept, but spent days and evenings with her.) She was "our breadwinner and my surrogate mother," and he was who knows what. At this time

---

* Justema's memoir appears in a catalog of 123 photographs by Mather published in 1979 by the Center for Creative Photography at the University of Arizona.

Mather was working as Weston's partner in his Tropico studio, but from Justema's (and Warren's) account her movements between Weston and Justema are hard to figure out, no less to imagine. She and Justema went on strange, drastic diets, frequented the Chinese theater, sold pornographic drawings made by Justema, and in 1931 collaborated on a remarkable exhibit of pictures of objects arranged in patterns by Justema and photographed by Mather. What Mather did as Weston's partner and collaborator remains tantalizingly unclear. Mather spent the last twenty years of her life with, in Warren's characterization, "a garrulous, hard-drinking man named George Lipton," helping him run his struggling antiques business. She died of multiple sclerosis in 1952 at the age of sixty-six.

Warren's research led her to the many awards Mather received between 1915 and 1925 in the pictorialist salons, and to the camera clubs with which she was associated (she founded one called the Camera Pictorialists of Los Angeles), but not to the beginnings of her engagement with photography—to the moment when the girl who picked up businessmen in hotel lobbies picked up a camera. This remains part of the mist in which Mather remains obscured. Warren is preparing a full-scale biography of Mather and Weston, and perhaps she will eventually penetrate the mist. From her interim report—as from Justema's crazy memoir—we receive a clear impression of the disorder of Mather's life but only a hazy and confusing idea of Mather herself. A rare and most appealing glimpse of her—and of poor Flora Weston—emerges from a letter she wrote in 1922 (quoted by Maddow):

> She [Flora] wept around here one a.m . . . blaming herself for holding Edward back—I told her . . . that she was responsible for Edward's success—without the balance of her and the children—the forced responsibility—Edward would have been like the rest of us—dreaming—living in attics—living a free life (Oh God!) etc. etc. not growing and producing as he had . . . Flora seemed grateful for my words but soon forgot them.

Charis Wilson, in *Through Another Lens: My Years with Edward Weston*, writes of a chance encounter with Mather in 1937, when she and Weston were walking down the street in Glendale, California. Wilson, who was twenty-eight years younger than Weston and the subject of some of his most brilliant nudes, was curious about the first of her predecessors:

> We approached a middle-aged woman who had stopped in front of a secondhand furniture store . . . While she and Edward talked, I looked for some trace of the young woman Edward had known since 1912 and made portraits and nudes of in the early 1920s—that woman of mystery and romance who had cast such a spell over young Edward Henry Weston.

But, she concludes, "I could not detect evidence of that past." What Wilson delicately refrains from saying, a crueler person—the photographer Willard Van Dyke—(quoted by Maddow) has no compunction about waspishly reporting: "I met Margrethe Mather just once. At that time she was fat and not very attractive, and was living with a homosexual . . . She had none of that beauty left, and her mind was not at all attractive."

But even the kindlier writer, then a beautiful young woman in her twenties, cannot break free (and who of us can?) of the idea that exceptional beauty in youth is a defining characteristic, whose loss is a diminishment of the inner as well as the outer person. And thus, for all of Warren's efforts to secure Mather's reputation as a photographer and to invest her vague, sad life story with meaning, Mather's exceptional beauty—immortalized by Weston's photographs (as well as by Imogen Cunningham's)—will probably continue to be what she is known for. What Helen of Troy did in her spare time and what she was "really like" are not questions that torture us. I said earlier that Mather's pictorialist photographs do not suffer in comparison with Weston's; but in one respect they do: none of her photographs portray a person as beautiful as herself.

Edward Weston's grandly eclectic taste in P.H. did not extend to other parts of the anatomy; he was as picky about the faces and forms of his female models as he was about the skins and shapes of his peppers and cabbages. (In his commercial work he could not, of course, be picky, and his daybooks are full of remarks about the "obese and wrinkled hags" who came to his studio and whose portraits he contemptuously retouched.) Weston's daybooks are also stuffed with references to his conquests. "Why this tide of women? Why do they all come at once? Here I am, isolated, hardly leaving my work rooms, but they come, they seek me out,—and yield (or do *I* yield?)," he writes in an entry of February 10, 1927, and, again, on April 24, "What have I, that brings these many women to offer themselves to me? I do not go out of my way seeking them,—I am not a stalwart virile male, exuding sex, nor am I the romantic, mooning poet type some love, nor the dashing Don Juan bent on conquest. Now it is B."*

But though he evidently serviced all the women who came to him, he by no means photographed them all. The nudes for which Weston is known portray a small and select company, from which most of his lovers are excluded. His nudes can indeed be characterized as "passionate collaborations," in which Weston's passion for a certain kind of beauty and a woman embodying that beauty come together with an almost audible bang.

Charis Wilson is the foremost of these collaborators, and unlike Mather, she comes to us very well described, making a dashing first appearance in Maddow's biography. "Charis was a new sort of a person," Maddow writes, "common in Europe at the time, but just beginning to flourish in America: well-to-do, well-educated, quick, frank, aristocratic, but coarse and open about sex and the less interesting functions." Wilson and Weston met at a concert in Carmel, California, in 1934, when she was twenty and he was forty-eight. In his journal of December 9, 1934, Weston writes of the encounter, "I saw this tall, beautiful girl, with finely proportioned body, intelligent face well-freckled, blue eyes, golden brown hair to shoulders,— and had to meet." Wilson was soon posing for him and sleeping with him. Weston writes thus of the transition from one activity to the other:

* *The Daybooks of Edward Weston*, vol. 2, *California*, edited by Nancy Newhall (Aperture, 1973), pp. 4 and 18.

The first nudes of C. were easily amongst the finest I had done, perhaps the finest. I was definitely interested now, and knew that she knew I was. I felt a response. But I am slow, even when I feel sure, especially if I am deeply moved. I did not wait long before making the second series which was made on April 22, a day to always remember. I knew now what was coming; eyes don't lie and she wore no mask. Even so I opened a bottle of wine to help build up my ego. You see I really wanted C. hence my hesitation.

And I worked with hesitation; photography had a bad second place. I made some eighteen negatives, delaying always delaying, until at last she lay there below me waiting, holding my eyes with hers. And I was lost and have been ever since. A new and important chapter in my life opened on Sunday afternoon, April 22, 1934.

After eight months we are closer together than ever. Perhaps C. will be remembered as the great love of my life. Already I have achieved certain heights reached with no other love.

In her memoir, Wilson reverently reprints (as Maddow before her had done) this farrago of male conceit and girls-book bathos. She is content to be remembered as Weston's great love. She was passionately in love with him herself. The impulse to write a memoir came from the "painful jolt" she received on reading Maddow's biography, which, she felt, "makes Edward out to be something of a fanatic—humorless and egotistic." Whereas "the truth is that Edward loved jokes, spoofs, and general rigmarole, and cared nothing for conventional notions of dignity." (Maddow had by no means made Weston as unsympathetic as Wilson believed he had; his portrait is complex—and thus unacceptable to an intimate.) Wilson began making notes for a corrective memoir of her fun-loving ex (she and Weston were divorced in 1945), but it wasn't until the 1990s, when she was in her eighties, and a younger friend offered her assistance, that the memoir finally got written. It therefore isn't what it would have been if written by Wilson in her prime and unaided, though the voice that emerges from it is by no means feeble or unappealing.

•

Wilson believes that much of the trouble with Maddow's portrait of Weston is that he relied too heavily on Weston's surviving journal, which Weston himself felt to be unreliable. "I find far too many belly-aches; it is too personal, and a record of a not so nice person," he wrote to Nancy Newhall in 1948. "I usually wrote to let off steam so the diary gives a one-sided picture which I do not like." But Wilson's own journal—the log she kept during her travels with Weston on two successive Guggenheim grants—puts another obstacle in the way of our understanding of Weston. Wilson is not a boring writer, but her dogged dependence on the log makes her one. For a good half of the book she relentlessly reports the day-by-day progress of the trips—every wilderness area reached, every person stayed with, every tree or mountain photographed, every inconvenience suffered. Weston recedes from view as the mass of floridly uninteresting information grows.

For all that, Wilson achieves at least some of her aim of portraying Weston as lovable and of conveying the pleasure and excitement of her life with him. It was a life of both deliberate and (because of the Depression) imposed simplicity. Weston made a fetish of living in opposition to bourgeois custom, and Wilson, who had had an unhappy childhood in a mansion, was glad to join him in his California dreaming life of meals of raw vegetables and fruits and nuts and living quarters furnished only with a bed covered with a red serape. She was as solemn about sex as he was. People were in those days.

Her belief in Weston's greatness was absolute, and the selflessness of her dedication to his career is moving. It is also surprising—it contradicts Maddow's description of her as "a new sort of a person" and doesn't accord with the impression of her we receive from Weston's photographs. In them she has a bodily ease, almost a languor, and a drop-dead expression on her face that are hardly the characteristics of a put-upon artist's wife. Like his photographs of Mather, Weston's photographs of Wilson take much of their special sparkle from the subject's stunning beauty and presence. The 1977 book of Weston's nudes, many of them of Wilson, brought, she writes, "a rush of attention in my direction."

Suddenly I was a prime source—and a prime subject. It seemed that everywhere I turned I would see another image of myself, sitting in the doorway or stretched on the sand or perched on a model stand. I once emerged from a New York subway to face a soiled city wall plastered with posters of myself as I had looked fifty years earlier, sitting against a boulder in the High Sierra, my head swathed against mosquito attack, with a look of exhaustion on my face—since identified regularly by critics as "sensuality."

This photograph, however Wilson remembers the circumstances of its making, is indeed sensual, probably the sexiest of all of Weston's pictures of her. She sits with her legs spread and her hands crossed over the inner thighs. That she is wearing trousers and high lace-up boots only adds to the sexiness, you could even say dirtiness, of the picture. The face, wrapped in a scarf as a Bedouin might wrap it, stares at the viewer and beyond him. It is a very young face, perhaps a little sullen, certainly not unaware of the provocativeness of the pose, but refusing to register it. One's eye goes back and forth between the hands and the face, alternating between the hands' downward direction and the face's straight-ahead one. I don't know of another photograph that puts the eye through such paces.

It was taken in 1937 at Lake Ediza in the Yosemite wilderness, during the first Guggenheim trip. In *Through Another Lens*, Wilson writes of how Weston almost didn't get the Guggenheim. After working for days on his grant proposal, he threw out everything he had written and confined himself to this terse statement: "I wish to continue an epic series of photographs of the West, begun about 1929; this will include a range from satires on advertising to ranch life, from beach kelp to the mountains. The publication of the above seems assured."

Weston was given to know by a person at the Guggenheim Foundation who wished him well that the committee of judges would be put off, possibly even insulted, by his Cordelia-esque terseness, and told to mend his speech. He did so. Like other desperately needy Depression artists, he could not afford to be willful. With Wilson's help he wrote the five-page essay, full of hot air, that these occasions require. But before applying himself to the task, by way of explaining his original reticence, he wonderfully justifies it: "I felt the need for brevity and simplicity because I realized that any analysis I could give in words, of my viewpoint, aims, way of work,—must of necessity be incomplete—because it is these very things that I can only express fully through my work,—in other words that is why I am a photographer."

The Lake Ediza picture turns out to be one of the few memorable images to come out of the Guggenheim trip. As one regrets Wilson's Guggenheim journal, so one wonders whether the Guggenheim trip itself wasn't a mistake—whether Weston wouldn't have been better off staying home and taking modest but entrancing pictures of Wilson instead of grandiloquent but often uninteresting ones of nature. But then again, if he had stayed home, we wouldn't have the Lake Ediza photograph, and surely one extraordinary photograph is worth a thousand negligible ones.

NUDES WITHOUT DESIRE

2002

In the mid-1960s, a most entertaining solution to a biographical mystery was offered by Mary Lutyens. The mystery concerned the six-year-long unconsummated marriage of John Ruskin and Effie Gray, which was annulled in 1854 after Effie revealed to her father that Ruskin had still not "[made] me his Wife." "He alleged various reasons," Effie wrote: "Hatred to children, religious motives, a desire to preserve my beauty, and finally this last year he told me his true reason . . . that he had imagined women were quite different to what he saw I was, and that the reason he did not make me his Wife was because he was disgusted with my person the first evening 10th April." In a statement Ruskin wrote for his lawyer during the annulment proceedings, he corroborated Effie's account: "It may be thought strange that I could abstain from a woman who to most people was so attractive. But though her face was beautiful, her person was not formed to excite passion. On the contrary, there were certain circumstances in her person which completely checked it."

What did Ruskin see on his wedding night that repelled him so? What were the "circumstances" of Effie's unclothed body that caused him to shrink from her for six years? Mary Lutyens ingeniously proposed that "Ruskin suffered a traumatic shock on his wedding night when he discovered that Effie had pubic hair. Nothing had prepared him for this. He had never been to an art school and none of the pictures and statues on public exhibition at that

time depicted female nudes with hair anywhere on their bodies."*
"In his ignorance he believed her to be uniquely disfigured,"
Lutyens wrote in another discussion of the subject.†

Lutyens's imaginative reconstruction of the awful wedding
night—the author of *The Seven Lamps of Architecture* gazing with
petrified horror at his bride's pubic bush—takes its tragicomic force
from our shared memories of all the marmoreal vulvas we have seen
in museums and in books like Kenneth Clark's *The Nude*. Ruskin's
belief that his wife was abnormal came not so much from his ignorance of female anatomy as from his knowledge of Western art. *He
had imagined women were quite different.* If he had never seen a
painting or a sculpture of a nude woman, the "circumstances" of
Effie's body might not have seemed so strange, so like a betrayal.
They might even have been arousing. Of course, Ruskin was not the
only arty young man whose sex life was derailed by early museum
visits. Clark himself displays an aversion to the human body in *The
Nude*—he writes of "shapeless, pitiful" art school models, of "the
pitiful inadequacy of the flesh," of the "inherent pitifulness of the
body"—that could have come only of formative art experience. "In
almost every detail the body is not the shape that art had led us to
believe it should be," Clark rather artlessly remarks, as if a boy's or a
girl's first sight of his mother's or father's or nurse's naked body is
naturally preceded by the sight of Titian's *Venus of Urbino* or Prax-
iteles' *Hermes*.

Photography, which might have been expected to arrive on the scene
as a kind of rescue mission of the body, bent on restoring it to its
native naked state, in fact only perpetuated and elaborated the styl-
izations and bowdlerizations of art. Leafing through books of early
nude photography, such as Graham Ovenden and Peter Mendes's
Victorian Erotic Photography and Serge Nazarieff's *Early Erotic Photography*, one is only secondarily struck by the photographs' eroti-
cism; the first, overwhelming impression is of their debt to painting.

---

* Mary Lutyens, *Millais and the Ruskins* (Vanguard, 1967), p. 156.
† *Young Mrs. Ruskin in Venice*, edited by Mary Lutyens (Vanguard, 1965), p. 21.

That many of these daguerreotypes and calotypes were made as figure studies for painters—and in several cases can be linked to actual paintings they covertly assisted—only complicates the plot of the art/photography relationship. It does not change the fact that the early photographers of nudes posed their models, arranged their backgrounds, and took their pictures with salon painting dictating their every move.

One of the best known of the photographs linked to a painting is Julien Vallou de Villeneuve's camera study, taken around 1850, of a nude woman holding a drapery to herself, standing beside a chair with her head averted; it is believed to be the source of the nude woman holding a drapery to herself who stands in the center of Gustave Courbet's masterpiece *The Painter's Studio*, looking over the seated painter's shoulder as he works. In comparing the two nudes—especially when seeing them both in black and white, as Aaron Sharf reproduces them on page 131 of his book *Art and Photography* (1968)—one is impressed with how much more real, even more photographic, the painting is. Villeneuve was a painter and a lithographer before he became a photographer, with a taste for "anaemic, erotic scenes of feminine intrigue and despair, of would-be lovers hidden in boudoirs," as Sharf characterizes his lithographs of the 1820s and 1830s. When he took up photography, he simply continued his sentimental program. In the photograph associated with *The Painter's Studio*, Villeneuve works within well-trodden conventions of narrative painting—his nude could be a Susanna hiding her nakedness from the elders or a nymph surprised by a god or a satyr. In another respect—in the rather desperate way she is clutching the drapery and trying to hide her body with it—she could be an allegorical figure representing photography's fear of unmediated actuality. The realist Courbet, in contrast, regards it with poignant fearlessness. His nude, in the intensity of her absorption in the painter's activity, has allowed her drapery to fall away from her body, which is posed in profile and shows a protuberant belly and outthrust buttock and full, round breast. This is a most vital and real and sexy woman. Her body, though not idealized, is hardly "shapeless" and "pitiful." She holds the drapery more out of habit than prudery; she is an artist's model, a working woman (the drapery is one of her working tools) thoroughly accustomed to nakedness. The contribution of the Villeneuve photograph to the Courbet masterpiece was surely a minor one; it gave Courbet a hint, perhaps, about the rendering of the angle of the model's shoulders and head. Whatever nineteenth-century photographers of the nude gave to contemporary art, they took back a thousandfold in their own abject dependency on it.

In the twentieth century, photographers of the nude continued to borrow from art—largely from symbolist, postimpressionist, and modernist painting and sculpture—but less abjectly. These borrowers believed they were making art themselves, and some actually succeeded in doing so. Edward Weston pursued the nude genre more assiduously—and, I think, more brilliantly—than any other practitioner. His earliest nudes, made in the teens and early twenties of the century, look as if he had been studying paintings by Whistler and Munch as well as photographs by the Photo-Secessionists. In the mid-twenties his gaze shifted to the European abstract art that the Armory Show of 1913 had introduced to provincial America and that the cranky but prescient Stieglitz kept on view in his 291 Gallery. In 1927 Weston wrote in his journal of his search "for simplified forms . . . in the nude body." A year earlier—in an act that his biographer Ben Maddow sees as seminal for the abstract work to come—Weston photographed the toilet in his flat in Mexico City. " 'Form follows function'—who said this I don't know—but the writer spoke well," Weston wrote, and continued,

> I have been photographing our toilet—that glossy enameled receptacle of extraordinary beauty . . . Never did the Greeks reach a more significant consummation to their culture—and it somehow reminded me, in the glory of its chaste convolutions and in its swelling, sweeping, forward movement of finely progressing contours—of the "Victory of Samothrace."

Maddow tactfully notes that "in this new venture, [Weston] was following a precedent which was perhaps stored below the surface of his memory: the famous urinal that Marcel Duchamp sent to the historic Armory Show . . . which had been photographed by Stieglitz at the time." Whatever its etiology, *Excusado* (as Weston named the photograph) is a work of remarkable presence and force. In its beauty of form and complexity of texture it might even be thought to surpass the abstract nudes—the famous pear-shaped nude, for example—that followed. Be that as it may, Weston's nudes of the late twenties and thirties—his studies of limbs and breasts and buttocks that resemble the pared-down forms of modernist sculpture and functionalist design—belong among the works of photography that most convincingly support its artistic claims. They not only imitate but are works of modernist art.

"His nudes are indeed examples of strict, yet marvelous form," Maddow writes—and adds, "But the function—and there is no need to specify which function—refuses to vanish, remains inextricable in the photographs, and can never be wholly theorized away, even by the photographer who made them." In the opening chapter of *The Nude*, Clark extends the "function" to every artistic representation of the unclothed body, writing that "no nude, however abstract, should fail to arouse in the spectator some vestige of erotic feeling, even though it be only the faintest shadow." But by the end of the book, Clark is obliged to create a category called "the alternative convention" to accommodate the fat, flabby, or aging bodies (rendered by Dürer, Rembrandt, Rouault, Cézanne, Rodin, among others) that do not turn him on and thus make a mockery of the early dictum. That Clark allowed this contradiction (and several others) to remain in his text may not be mere inattentiveness. It may be a signaling of his recognition that the subject is more unruly and complex than he anticipated and than his sleek treatise can handle.

Two exhibitions of photographic nudes by Irving Penn—one at the Metropolitan Museum and the other at the Whitney—give further evidence of the nude genre's resistance to easy generalization. Indeed, both exhibitions have an atmosphere of difficulty and unease that is at odds with the crisp confidence of their respective catalog essays. The fifty nudes in the Met show are selected from photographs

made in 1949–50, but not shown until 1980, when the Marlborough Gallery exhibited seventy-six of them under the rubric *Earthly
Bodies*. (The Met has retained the rubric.) The Marlborough show
was an event in photography—nudes like these had never before
been seen. Rosalind Krauss, who wrote the Marlborough catalog
essay, gamely struggled with the photographs' strange originality
and offered an original and strange argument that related the work
(and all of photography) to collage. Little else was written about the
nudes. A kind of awed hush settled around them. In her catalog essay Maria Morris Hambourg is content to assume the greatness of
the work and to tell us how adorable the eighty-two-year-old photographer is. "A gentle man who scarcely speaks above a whisper,
Penn is unfailingly polite," she writes, and continues,

> Attired like any American in blue jeans and sneakers, he has
> the unassuming modesty of a simple man, which he likes to
> think he is, or a monk. Although he avoids unnecessary chat-
> ter, he is a preternaturally good listener . . . He is completely
> present and seems to have all the time in the world for you.
> This exquisite sensitivity is wedded to a highly analytical and
> decisive mind and a meticulous and unsparing professional
> demeanor . . . Beneath this public face is a supremely tender
> soul protected, like a younger brother, by an absolutist's will.

Even as I pick on Hambourg, I sympathize with her plight. Penn's
nudes are slippery. They almost force one to talk about anything
and everything but themselves. And this may be where their singu-
larity lies. The photographs immediately raise questions about their
making. One doesn't take them in and only later wonder how they
came to look the way they do. These photographs (in most cases)
have been meddled with—and meddled with in such striking ways
that the image takes second place to the technique by which it was
produced. Like the nudes of Weston's classic period, the Penn nudes
are faceless fragments of the body that evoke the forms of modernist
art. But where Weston delivered his modernism through ordinary
photographic means, Penn released his images only after putting
them through an extraordinary darkroom ordeal. Step one was to
obliterate the image by overexposing the printing paper to such a

degree that it turned completely black in the developer. Step two was to put the black paper into a bleach solution that turned it white. Step Three was to put the white paper into a solution that coaxed back the image, but only up to a point—the point where the earthly bodies exhibit an unearthly pallor and, in certain cases (such as the catalog cover picture), a flat abstractness that human bodies assume only in primitive and modernist art.

Another difference between Penn's nudes and Weston's lies in the type of body they depict and in the photographer's relationship with his models. Weston photographed lissome young women with whom he only rarely didn't sleep. Penn photographed heavy women (in the majority of cases) whom (in all cases, including a few slender women who posed for him in the early days of his project) he kept at a monkish distance. The women were strangers, hired artists' models. "The relationship between us was professional, without a hint of sexual response. Anything else would have made pictures like these impossible," Penn reported in his book *Passage: A Work Record* (1991). That Weston slept with his models is an unsurprising but irrelevant piece of information—the photographs are completely realized works that raise no biographical questions. Penn's nudes, in contrast, have an unresolved and unnerving character—"experimental," you could call them—and thus invite biographical speculation. To learn of Penn's lack of desire for his models causes a penny to drop in regard to the mercilessness of many of the images. The idea seems to be to make beautiful pictures of ugly bodies.

The series to which the cover picture of a standing figure belongs is the most extreme example of this tendency. The radical stylization Penn achieves with his darkroom hocus-pocus does not obscure, in fact augments, the ungainliness of the body, which is framed from the thighs to the waist and features a large belly that pours down over the pubic triangle. In other versions the framing moves up from the belly to include breasts that echo the stomach's stylized pendulousness.

Hambourg connects these radical images to a more conventional nude Penn made in 1947 (*Nude 1* in the catalog) and then connects *it* to a prehistoric sculpture of a fertility goddess, known as the Venus of Willendorf. ("Whether he had seen a reproduction of the little statuette in Vienna or not, he was in touch with the same instinct that called forth that Venus from her Neolithic sculptor—the recognition that the mysterious, procreative power of the female body is of such majesty that it has symbolized creativity since the dawn of art," she writes of the nice man in blue jeans.) But the 1947 nude, though it bears a certain resemblance to the primitive sculpture in its monumental frontality, has an entirely different character from it—and from the nudes in the 1949–50 series. *Nude 1* harks back to the nineteenth century, to the dark, painterly images of the Photo-Secession, and only accentuates the decisiveness of the move into the twentieth century that Penn made two years later.

Even the most (so to speak) conservative of the 1949–50 photographs, employing standard props of nineteenth-century photography—a black velvet robe and a velvet chair—reflect the urgency of the photographer's desire to take his place among the makers of modernist art and to distance himself from his photographic precursors. The stark whiteness and flatness of the body created by the bleaching solution is set off by the dark tactility of the velvet robe, which mysteriously withstood the insults of the darkroom and is draped around the waist and hips and thighs in such ways as to underscore their resemblance to forms that Matisse, Arp, and Schlemmer, among others, have put on the map of our associations. But Penn does not stop there. The originality of these images lies in their perversity. The desireless Penn avoids the poses developed by classical art to display the body's beauty; he is interested in poses that testify to the body's grotesquerie. In a number of the photographs with the velvet robe, for example, the model sits in such a way as to create an eccentric puckering of her stomach on one side. The sweeping curves of the white body, the abstract forms, the art references—all these recede before the anomalous bulge, which looks like a third breast and rivets the eye like a gravy stain on a white dress. Penn's gaze is not unfriendly. If the art school models do not arouse his lust, they do not invite his scorn, either. On the contrary, one can almost read a kind of gratitude into the photographs, a sort of salute to heavy bodies for the opportunity they have offered a young fashion photographer to break ranks—and to make art.

•

The show of Penn's nudes at the Whitney, called *Dancer*, is the product of four occasions in 1999 when a heavyset dancer with the Bill T. Jones/Arnie Zane Dance Company named Alexandra Beller came to Penn's studio and posed and danced for him naked. In her catalog essay, Anne Wilkes Tucker, curator at the Museum of Fine Arts in Houston, where the show is also on view, can't resist a bit of curatorial one-upmanship. Comparing the dancer to her rivals at the Met, Tucker writes, "Beller is compact and muscular where the earlier models were flaccid and overflowingly fat." But there is a more significant difference between the women at the Met and the woman at the Whitney; where the former were rendered as faceless fragments, the latter is photographed in her entirety.

For good reason, the classical works of twentieth-century nude photography—by Stieglitz, Weston, Callahan, Cunningham—are faceless. There does not seem to be any way that a naked person in front of a camera can fail to betray his or her sense of the, as the case may be, silliness or pathos of the situation. Whether the object of the exercise is art photography or pornography, the model does not know what to do with his or her face. Probably the most comic examples of facial at-a-lossness are to be found in photographs of men showing off erections, and, of course, the most pathetic in examples of child pornography. But the expressions on the faces of subjects of ambitious art photographs are no less problematic. The photographer cannot invent the expression on the face as the painter and sculptor can. The mystery of who scratched out the faces on some of E. J. Bellocq's nudes is easily solved in the light of this discussion. Bellocq himself must have made the savage marks when he saw his picture spoiled by the all-wrong expression on the face of the model. But in other cases, Bellocq made head-to-toe photographs of unclothed New Orleans prostitutes that entirely escape the problem of the face. As one scrutinizes these pictures, trying to account for Bellocq's strange success, one notices the smiles on the faces and receives a sense of the fun the photographer and the model are having. They are horsing around. The silliness of the situation, far from helplessly leaking out of the photograph, is acknowledged, is its subject. It is what gives these photographs their wonderful warmth and life.

The Penn nudes at the Whitney are another exception—face and body have no quarrel with each other—but Penn's dancer has nothing in common with Bellocq's larkily relaxed whores. With regard to this photographic encounter, it is only the viewer who has trouble keeping a straight face. As Beller, with lowered eyelids or averted gaze, strikes one absurdly theatrical attitude after another, Penn photographs her with an almost religious solemnity. In his book *Worlds in a Small Room* (1974), Penn remarks of the Moroccan village elders he has photographed, "They are simple people but their burnooses and turbans of white wool are spotless." I felt a similar condescension—an unspoken "but"—waft out of Penn's ponderous pictures of this assertive, squat woman who is as alien to him as the amazingly tidy Arabs.

The last eight photographs, taken at a final session, have a different character from the preceding nineteen. They show the dancer in motion and have a mysterious blurred painterliness. They were taken at three-second-long exposures, and thus record the model's movements as ghostly afterimages. In one example, the model has acquired wings and two heads, as if she were a mythological creature in a symbolist painting. In another, where her head is thrust back and the motion of her body is recorded by the blurred doubling of her limbs, one receives a sense of ecstatic dance. These images evoke but by no means return to the nineteenth century; they shimmer with newness and strangeness. But they cannot change the show's overall daunting impression. When Penn showed the *Earthly Body* series to Alexander Liberman in 1950, Liberman was unimpressed, and so—when Liberman brought him the work to make sure he was right—was Edward Steichen. It took thirty years for Penn to dare to prove Liberman and Steichen wrong. But the Libermans and Steichens are not always wrong. Not all experimental work works, and sometimes rejection is a form of protection. The first nineteen images of *Dancer* illustrate the perils of renown. Someone should have dared to protect Penn.

A GIRL OF THE ZEITGEIST

1986

Rosalind Krauss's loft, on Greene Street, is one of the most beautiful living places in New York. Its beauty has a dark, forceful, willful character. Each piece of furniture and every object of use or decoration has evidently had to pass a severe test before being admitted into this disdainfully interesting room—a long, mildly begloomed rectangle with tall windows at either end, a *sachlich* white kitchen area in the center, a study, and a sleeping balcony. A geometric arrangement of dark-blue armchairs around a coffee table forms the loft's sitting room, also furnished with, among other rarities, an antique armchair on splayed carved feet and upholstered in a dark William Morris fabric; an assertive all-black minimalist shaped-felt piece; a strange black-and-white photograph of ocean water; and a gold owl-shaped art deco table clock. But perhaps even stronger than the room's aura of commanding originality is its sense of absences, its evocation of all the things that have been excluded, have been found wanting, have failed to capture the interest of Rosalind Krauss—which are most of the things in the world, the things of "good taste" and fashion and consumerism, the things we see in stores and in one another's houses. No one can leave this loft without feeling a little rebuked: one's own house suddenly seems cluttered, inchoate, banal. Similarly, Rosalind Krauss's personality—she is quick, sharp, cross, tense, bracingly derisive, fearlessly uncharitable—makes one's own "niceness" seem somehow dreary and anachronistic. She infuses fresh life and meaning into the old phrase about not suffering fools gladly.

I have come to her loft to talk with her about the history of the magazine *Artforum*. I am preparing an article about the magazine's present editor, Ingrid Sischy, and have been speaking with some of the old guard—the people who were at the magazine in the early seventies, when it was such a formidable critical force in the art world as to give rise to the expression "*Artforum* Mafia." The editor then was Philip Leider, followed by John Coplans, and the editorial board included, along with Krauss, Annette Michelson, Lawrence Alloway, Max Kozloff, Barbara Rose, Peter Plagens, Robert Pincus-Witten, and Joseph Masheck. In 1975, Krauss and Michelson left *Artforum* to found *October*, a taut, Eurotropic intellectual journal, which they have coedited since then. In addition, Krauss has been a professor of art history at Hunter College since 1975 and has written vanguard art criticism since the sixties. Her writing has a hard-edged, dense opacity; it gives no quarter, it is utterly indifferent to the reader's contemptible little cries for help. (Another art critic, Carter Ratcliff, told me, "I remember one of the writers at *Artforum* in the old days—I think it was Annette Michelson—saying, with a kind of pride, that *Artforum* was the only American journal that seemed to be translated from the German.") I am therefore surprised by the plain, entertaining way in which Rosalind Krauss speaks as she sits in the Morris chair with the gold clock beside her on a little table—a Minerva with her owl. She is a handsome, dark-haired, elegant woman in her mid-forties, reminiscing, with a sort of peevish relish, about the bad feeling that existed among the con-tributing editors of *Artforum* in the seventies: "Lawrence Alloway was forever sneering at me and Annette for being formalists and elitists and not understanding the social mission of art. There was also a quite unpleasant quality emanating from Max Kozloff. He was always very busy being superior—I could never understand why. He, too, had this attitude that the rest of us were not aware of art's high social function. Neither Annette nor I would buy into this simplistic opposition that they set up between formal inven-tion and the social mission of art. Our position was that the social destiny, responsibility—whatever—of art is not necessarily at war with some kind of formal intelligence through which art might operate, and that to set up that kind of opposition is profitless. It's

dumb. I remember having all these stupid arguments with Lawrence, saying things like 'Why are you interested in art in the first
place?' and pointing out that presumably one gets involved with this
rather particular, rather esoteric form of expression because one has
had some kind of powerful experience with it—and that presumably this powerful experience then makes you want to go on and
think about it and learn about it and write about it. But you must
have at some point been ravished, been seduced, been taken in. And
it's this experience that is probably what one calls an aesthetic experience. And it probably doesn't have very much to do with the
message."

Rosalind Krauss pours tea from a clear-glass Bauhaus-design
teapot into thin white porcelain cups and asks me if I have heard
about "the Lynda Benglis thing." I have. It is a famous incident.
In the November 1974 issue of *Artforum*, an advertisement appeared—a two-page spread, in color—that caused readers to disbe-
lieve their eyes. It showed a naked young woman, the artist Lynda
Benglis, with close-cropped hair and white-rimmed harlequin sun-
glasses, standing with her breasts assertively thrust out, one arm
and hand akimbo and the other hand clutching an enormous dildo
pressed against her crotch. The ad not only caused a stir among
the *Artforum* readership but impelled five of the editors—Krauss,
Michelson, Masheck, and (for once aligned with Krauss and Michelson) Alloway and Kozloff—to write a letter, published in a subsequent issue, stating that they wished to publicly dissociate themselves
from the ad, to protest its "extreme vulgarity" and its subversion of
the aims of the women's liberation movement, and to condemn the
magazine's complicity with an act of exploitation and self-promotion.
An article about Lynda Benglis, written by Pincus-Witten, had appeared in the same issue as the notorious ad. According to the
Alloway-Kozloff-Krauss-Michelson-Masheck letter, "Ms. Benglis,
knowing that the issue was to carry an essay on her work, had submitted her photograph in color for inclusion in the editorial matter
of the magazine, proposing it as a 'centerfold' and offering to pay
for the expenses of that inclusion. John Coplans, the editor, correctly refused this solicitation on the grounds that *Artforum* does
not sell its editorial space. Its final inclusion in the magazine was

therefore as a paid advertisement, by some arrangement between the artist and her gallery."

Rosalind Krauss recrosses her handsomely shod feet, which are stretched out on the coffee table before her, and says, "We thought the position represented by that ad was so degraded. We read it as saying that art writers are whores."

I had heard that in addition to the Benglis affair there had been a struggle between Coplans and some of his editors over the issue of "decommodified" art vis-à-vis advertising. Many of the most advanced artists of the seventies—the people doing conceptual art, performance art, film and video art, multiples—were deliberately creating work that had little, if any, market value. Their work constituted a kind of protest against the fact that unique, one-of-a-kind art objects, possessed of an "aura," which could be bought and sold for huge sums of money—i.e., commodities—were still being made in our "age of mechanical reproduction" (as Walter Benjamin identified it in his classic essay). Coplans, who had become editor in 1972 and was trying to keep the magazine financially afloat (when he took over, *Artforum* could barely pay its printing bill), was felt to be selling out to advertisers by turning down articles on (unmarketable) film and performance and conceptual art in favor of articles on (marketable) painting and sculpture.

"Yes," Rosalind Krauss says. "That's how we felt. And one of the things that Annette and I have done with *October* is to free ourselves from that. We've never had a single piece of gallery advertising. But our theory about John's courting of the dealers and gallery owners, which was certainly why Annette and I thought that various projects of ours were not acceptable to John—that theory failed in the light of what John subsequently did. Because John's policies in the last years of his editorship alienated every advertiser. He accepted Max's position and carried on in a way that had to do with becoming this—I don't know—this *Novy*-left type, dumping on the art market, and writing all kinds of attacks on it, and running the magazine absolutely contrary to the interests of the dealers and the advertisers, to the point that the owner, Charlie Cowles, simply sacked him."

I ask Rosalind Krauss what she thinks of the present *Artforum*. She replies, "I just got so bored with it that I stopped subscribing.

I've just not looked at it. I'm just not interested in it. Ingrid's sensibility just doesn't interest me."

I ask her what she thought of Thomas McEvilley's critique of William Rubin and Kirk Varnedoe's primitivism show at the Museum of Modern Art—to whose two-volume catalog she had contributed an essay on Giacometti. The controversial McEvilley article appeared in the November 1984 issue of *Artforum*.

"I thought it was very stupid," she says. "I think Tom McEvilley is a very stupid writer. I think he's pretentious and awful. His piece seemed to be primarily involved in trying—as Tom McEvilley always seems to be trying—to present himself as some sort of expert while misrepresenting what the museum was doing."

"Did you read the exchange of letters that Rubin and Varnedoe had with McEvilley?"

"Yes. And I must say I found it very unpleasant, because you couldn't tell which side was the more horrible. On the one hand, you had Rubin and Varnedoe sounding like complete assholes and, on the other, you had McEvilley doing his hideousness. I have never been able to finish a piece by McEvilley. He seems to be another Donald Kuspit. He's a slightly better writer than Donald Kuspit. But his lessons on Plato and things like that—they drive me crazy. I think, God! And I just can't stand it."

John Coplans's loft, on Cedar Street, has the look of a place inhabited by a man who no longer lives with a woman. There are ill-defined living and work areas (after being fired from *Artforum*, Coplans became a photographer, and the loft serves as his studio and darkroom as well as his living quarters), punctuated by untidy mounds of things on which a gray-striped cat perches proprietorially. The furniture is spare and of simple modern character. Coplans is a man of sixty-six, with curly gray hair and with black eyebrows that give his eyes a kind of glaring gaze. He speaks with a British accent in a vigorous, incisive, almost military way. (I later learn that he was in fact a British Army officer.) At the same time, there is something ingratiating and self-depreciating in his manner. Coplans leads me to a table strewn with papers and books, brings a bottle of seltzer water and two glasses, and talks about the early history of *Artforum*, in California.

The magazine, he says, was founded in San Francisco in 1962 by John Irwin, a salesman for a printing company who had formed the desire to start an art magazine—"a sweet, naive guy, in his early thirties, who had very little idea of what he was doing." Coplans had recently come to San Francisco—he had gone to art school in London after leaving the army and was now a painter and occasional art teacher—and he was with the magazine from the start, serving as an adviser to the wide-eyed Irwin and writing reviews and articles. But Irwin's most important recruit was a brilliantly intelligent young man named Philip Leider, a law-school dropout who had briefly been the director of a San Francisco gallery that showed Coplans's paintings and was now employed as a social worker in the San Francisco welfare department. Within a few months of his joining the magazine, Leider was asked by Irwin to become the magazine's managing editor (and its only paid staff member), and then its editor—a position he held for the next seven years. But even as early as 1964 the magazine was failing financially. It was rescued the next year by the publishing magnate Gardner Cowles and his stepson, Charles Cowles, who had just left Stanford and was looking for something to do. Charles Cowles became publisher. (Irwin, when last heard from by Coplans, was running a dry-cleaning business in Cleveland.) "Gardner Cowles provided the magazine with an annual subsidy and Charlie with a job and a position in the world," Coplans says. "But Phil Leider couldn't stand Charlie, who was concerned with social position and with the prestige of being publisher, and was indifferent to the everyday minutiae of publishing. Phil was the kind of intense human being who could sit for five years in this tiny office next door to Charlie Cowles and never say a word to him. Phil came out of a quite poor, nonintellectual Jewish immigrant family—Jewish immigrant in the most traditional sense: high morality and very involved with Jewishness itself. He got through college by writing papers for other people, at five or ten dollars apiece. He got a master's degree in English and then served in the army, where he worked as a typist—he was one of the fastest typists the army had. Later, he went to law school, but he sheered off from that. Phil was always wary, alert, and skeptical. He had no personal ambition; he was not a careerist in the American sense. He wanted nothing to do with power or money. He lived with his wife and children in the simplest way. Furniture was just plain, straightforward furniture, like mine—whatever could be bought cheap, like office furniture. He loathed and hated decoration, social ambition, careerism, making money. He dressed simply but neatly, in a black suit. The whole orientation of his life was his family. I've rarely come across a man so involved with his wife—they used to read together every night—and with his children. His only aberration was that every year he and his wife would drive down to Las Vegas, and he would take maybe a hundred dollars and gamble as long as the money lasted. Then he would come home; he had purged himself of frivolity for the year. He was an enormously articulate man, and he couldn't stand inarticulateness in others. He was offended by it, by the dumbness of artists. His best friends eventually were the artist Frank Stella and the art historian Michael Fried, two of the most articulate men in the American art world. I took to the guy tremendously; I really liked him, and he saw in me someone deeply strange and felt that there could be some dialogue between us. I have to say that he didn't trust me, really, because as time went on he thought—and he may have been right—that I was too interested in power. He saw in me some aspect of worldly ambition that he backed away from.

"I am a self-educated man. I was raised in South and East Africa, in a Russian-Jewish family, and I left school when I was sixteen. I joined the British air force and then the British Army, for a total of eight years of military service. I didn't go to college, but I wanted to learn everything. I was curious. I became an art historian. I taught art history at the University of California at Irvine. I became a curator at the Pasadena art museum, a writer, an editor. When I was editor of *Artforum*, I had half a dozen editors on my board. They were always quarreling with each other. They all hated each other. They were strong people, all academically very well trained, all extremely knowledgeable, the most experienced writers and critics in America, who had all gone through the various evolutions of art since the fifties. And now here's this young lady Ingrid Sischy, who goes in at about twenty-five and has been learning everything on the job and trying to find out what to do. She has no background in American art—this moment in art is all she can deal with—and she doesn't have the range of people I had. She's got a little board. She's got Germano Celant, who's a European, hardly ever here; and this Frenchman whom I simply don't know; and Edit deAk, a young woman like herself; and Thomas McEvilley, who is first-rate, absolutely first-rate; and a books editor who is a lightweight."

As Coplans talks, my eye is drawn to a large black-and-white photograph on the opposite wall of a male torso and genitals. It is part of a series of photographs that Coplans has taken of his own naked body, which are soon to be shown at the Pace/MacGill Gallery here and have already been exhibited in Paris. Coplans gets up and shows me other pictures in the series: brutally searching examinations of an aging, sedentary, hirsute body, which refer both to ancient sculpture and to twentieth-century art and photography and have an appearance of monumentality and solemnity that almost obscures their underlying, disturbing exhibitionism. I am therefore not surprised by Coplans's subsequent unrepentant recollections of the Lynda Benglis incident:

"The ad was in response to Robert Morris's photograph of himself as a macho German, wearing a steel helmet and iron chains over bare muscles, which he used as a poster for a show of his work at Castelli/Sonnabend. This was her message to him. She wanted it to run in *Artforum*, and I said to her, 'Look, the editorial content of the magazine can't be interfered with in any way. We don't allow any artist to have a role in what is published. I'm sorry, but you just can't have this in the magazine.' So she said, 'Well, can I do an ad?,' and I said, 'There is a publisher, and you'll have to ask him. I don't interfere with him, and he doesn't interfere with me. Go to Charlie Cowles and ask him.' Then Charlie came to me and said, 'What do I do?' I said, 'Charlie, make a decision. I will not be put in the position where you don't make a decision. You have to face the art world and the artists. I'm not saying anything. Make a decision.' After about three days of heavy sweating, Cowles came to me and said, 'I can't *not* publish it. They would hate me.' I said, 'That's right, Charlie.' So he said, 'All right, we'll run it.' I made up the magazine and sent it down to the printer, and the printer refused to print the ad. So Charlie said to me, 'It's solved. I'm off the hook.' And I said, 'No, Charlie, you're not off the hook. Those printers have no right to refuse to print, and our lawyer will tell them so. They can't select what's going to appear in the magazine.' So I went down to the printer, and the head of the printing firm was a former brigadier general in the U.S. Army, and I'm a former army officer, too, and I said, 'Come on, General, you know you can't do this.' He was a nice guy, actually. I said, 'We have a contract with you. Don't let's have to go to law.' So the general said, 'All right.' I went back to Charlie, and I said, 'Charlie, it's going to be printed. I insisted that it had to be printed as a matter of principle.' Now, I was obviously interested in seeing that ad get published. My position was that every woman had the right to make her individual choice as to how she faced her womanhood. This was an artist, and she had made this choice, and I was determined to protect her choice. Annette Michelson and Ros and Max thought it was obscene, that it was too sexually explicit. They were wholly opposed to me. Whether I was right or wrong I don't know."

Robert Pincus-Witten is a short, fresh-faced man with a sleek, well-tended look about him who seems younger than his fifty-odd years and who speaks with the accent of that nonexistent aristocratic European country from which so many bookish New York boys have emigrated. Pincus-Witten is a professor of art history at Queens College and teaches at the City University Graduate School. He was one of Coplans's gang of contributing editors, and for the last ten years he has been writing a column for *Arts* in the form of a journal. I first talked to him at a gathering of artists, collectors, curators, art-magazine editors, and critics at Marian Goodman's apartment after an opening of Anselm Kiefer's work at the Goodman Gallery, and I retain an image of him slightly bent over the buffet table as he helped himself, with a serious, responsible, almost sacerdotal air, to delicious, expensive food. Later, we talk further over lunch at a Japanese restaurant near the graduate school. He speaks of Rosalind Krauss, who is a fellow member of the graduate faculty, with grumpy familiarity: "Ros is a full professor, and she tends to pout in order to get her own way. She receives extraordinary academic consideration. She teaches only two courses a semester, instead of the three that the rest of us teach. She's a very attractive person, and many of the seemingly better students—I don't know if they actually are better— are drawn to her glamour. What happens is that she tends to be condescending, though not cruel, to students she doesn't think are intellectually desirable, so those students, as it were, become the students who come to one. They are not intellectually undesirable, but they walk around with this feeling of rejection and intellectual disparagement. Rosalind tends to attract a certain kind of stylishly intellectual student. Some of them are not particularly well prepared. I myself am more interested in general cultural knowledge than in the interpretative skills of the new dispensation, under which the truth of Derrida, the truth of de Saussure—what have you—are replacing the truth of Greenberg. The kids who can do this deconstruction talk are doing the eighties' equivalent of the fifties' Greenbergian formalist talk. It disturbs me. When I examine them, they have very little general knowledge. They have methodology, but they don't know the monuments. I happen to be interested in monuments. When one supports a certain radical position, one should know the conservative position that one is rejecting. What troubles me is the unexamined adoption of a radical stance. These kids still believe in a class struggle without realizing that they have made an a priori judgment that capitalism and its fruits are evil. I'm not happy with that, so I'm considered an archconservative. And it shocks me, because these are such privileged kids."

I ask Pincus-Witten if he feels a kinship with the New Right.

He replies, "No, I feel a kinship with something much older: the aristocracy of the intellect, the aristocracy of sensibility. The others, they're just Rotarians. They're bowling teams, whether they're bowling teams of the right or the left. I know that I must always remain an outsider. I feel a fundamental alienation that is not materialistic or class oriented, and that's why I don't join anybody. Ingrid Sischy is another person who doesn't belong to any team or party, and that's why there is a thread of identification between her and me. Ingrid is very anarchic, and that's why she is resented by some sectors of the art community. Her reluctance to adopt a party line is viewed as a *retardataire* form of bourgeois privilege and opens her to a dated form of criticism that seems to come from fifty years ago. The fact that she can be interested in any style that might be regarded as involved with commodification—or what her critics imagine to be commodification—identifies her in their minds as an enemy of the class struggle. I find it quite astonishing that people who embrace such textbook theories still have no trouble being owners of co-ops or putting copyright marks at the bottom of their writings. They're stuck in a paradoxical situation that renders their absolutism ludicrous. Ingrid is odd. She can get curious idées fixes. She is very interested in popular culture. I remember one conversation I had with her and some fairly glamorous people when she was telling us about the tragedy of an extremely popular pop singer— the one who wears a glove. His tragedy was the built-in supersedence of his prestige by another extremely popular pop singer, named Prince. And it was simply impossible for me to think of that as even remotely entering the sphere of tragedy. She was reading tragedy in connection with some issues in popular culture, and I was reading it in terms of, you know, hubris, nemesis, the idle cruelty of the gods. What was nice about the conversation was that on some level Ingrid was closer to what the conversation was really about than I was with my high-flown stuff. When I first met Ingrid, I was struck by how young she was and how she wasn't conventionally pretty—she didn't look like Gloria Steinem. I've known Ingrid for six years now, and I've never seen her behave badly or coldly or curtly. I've never seen her even be short. I've never seen her behave in an ugly way—ever."

Barbara Rose's loft, on Sullivan Street, with its mirror-filled walls, soft-gray carpeting, curved black sofa, mirror-topped coffee table, abstract and Oriental art, and fur-covered bed, looks more like a Park Avenue co-op than like a downtown living space, and Barbara Rose herself—a thin, pretty, somewhat jumpy woman of around fifty, with apricot-colored hair and wearing a loose, stylish light-blue wool dress and high heels—has a decided uptown aspect. When I arrive, she is talking on the telephone, and throughout my visit the telephone (which she sets to have answered by machine) rings frequently, with a discreet, rasping electronic sound. Barbara Rose's speech puts me in mind of simultaneous translation: she speaks very rapidly and a bit remotely, as if dealing with someone else's text. Since leaving *Artforum*, she has taught art history at several universities, has been a museum curator, and has written art criticism for *Partisan Review*, *Art in America*, and *Vogue*. "The art world today is not a serious world," she says. "Art today is an aspect of decor, of entertainment. It's like gourmet food. In the sixties, I would invite people over—I was married to Frank Stella then—and there would be raging fights. Of course, people like Barnett Newman and Ad Reinhardt were alive then. They were major intellectuals. There's nobody like them today. There are a few artists who are intellectuals, but most artists have become professionals. They're like cloak-and-suiters—they make this product, it's the thing they do. It's not about the agony and the ecstasy, or whatever, anymore; it's middle-class, it's bourgeois. There used to be a sharp demarcation between the bourgeois world and the art world. The bourgeois world was Other, its values were Other. You didn't have anything to do with these people; you didn't see them socially, you certainly didn't have dinner with them. But now that's all artists want to do—be invited to fancy restaurants and discotheques. And there are all those people from the suburbs. How do they get a foothold in Manhattan? They get involved with art. They're out there in New Jersey and Long Island collecting Major Works. And all those ladies running around with—you know—the briefcases and the slides. The people who are talking about art today are the people who twenty years ago were talking about— What were those people talking about twenty years ago? They were talking about big cars. I find the art world today very much like suburbia, and I'm not interested in the values of suburbia or its lifestyle or its aspirations. I left suburbia many years ago, and I don't want to go back.

"At *Artforum* in the sixties and seventies, we were talking to each other and we were talking to a group of artists who could understand us—Robert Morris, Donald Judd, Claes Oldenburg, Jasper Johns, the remaining abstract expressionists. They were people of high intellectual caliber—I mean major intellectuals, not dodos. We had all been formed by the same educational process. We were all trained art historians, and we all had a background in philosophy and aesthetics. We knew what we were talking about. Annette and Max and I had been pupils of Meyer Schapiro at Columbia, and Michael Fried and Rosalind had been at Harvard. Frank and Michael, who were undergraduates at Princeton together, went to hear Clement Greenberg lecture, and they were converted immediately to the Greenberg doctrine because it offered a coherent way of looking at art. Nothing else did. Harold Rosenberg wrote, but nobody serious took him seriously—it was sociology; it wasn't art criticism. It had nothing to do with aesthetics, it had no background in art history, it was off the top of the head. It was fine for a general audience, but for people who had been trained in aesthetics and art history it seemed very hollow, and it had nothing whatever to do with actually looking at art. Whereas Greenberg looked at art. Now, he was a strict formalist, but he really shone in comparison with Harold, particularly at that time. We were all very impressed by Wittgenstein and by Anglo-American philosophy and by linguistic analysis and the verification principle—by that school of philosophy, which fitted perfectly with Greenberg's way of thinking—and Harold just simply didn't seem to have any philosophical underpinning to his thinking.

"After 1967, when Philip Leider moved the magazine to New York, there was a lot of hanging out together. You had a sense of not being isolated. You were talking to other people. It might be only five people, but you were talking to somebody, and you knew who you were talking to. I would write an article knowing that what I was basically doing was having a fight with Michael. We were a group of people who had had the same kind of education addressing the same topics from different points of view. The magazine had coherence, which the culture had at that point, too. There was then such a thing as a core curriculum, there was such a thing as a liberal arts, humanistic education, there was such a thing as a thorough art history education. These things don't exist anymore. The people involved in the art world don't have them. The new *Artforum* is a media magazine; it's totally media oriented. There's no real criticism in it, or almost none. McEvilley writes criticism, and John Yau writes criticism, but I haven't found anything else that I would call criticism in the new *Artforum*. It's some kind of writing—some strange kind of writing—but it's not criticism. It's Rene Ricard doing whatever it is that Rene Ricard does. I mean, it's something weird, and a lot of the people can't write. They have no background; they don't know what they're talking about, if they're talking about anything.

"We were literary people—academic literary people. We didn't watch television. If we were interested in cinema—which Annette and I were—it was on the level of avant-garde film, not Hollywood. And we didn't like junk. There wasn't this horrible leveling, where everything is as important as everything else. There was a sense of the hierarchy of values. We felt that we had to make a distinction between Mickey Mouse and Henry James. There's a generation now that feels you don't have to make that distinction. Mickey Mouse, Henry James, Marcel Duchamp, Talking Heads, Mozart, *Amadeus*— it's all going on at the same time, and it all kind of means the same thing. For that, you have Andy Warhol to thank. I also think Susan Sontag was very influential in giving permission to so-called educated people to watch trash. Her article 'Against Interpretation' said that this idea of highbrow and lowbrow didn't matter any longer— you could just love everything that was going on, you could be positive and optimistic and just love it all.

"I used to be able to earn a living as an art critic. I got paid a lot of money by *Art in America* because there was a differential, you see: if you were a very popular writer or were considered a very good writer, you got paid more money. Then, all of a sudden, the great era of democracy came to *Art in America*, and they started paying everybody the same. So I said, 'Forget it—I have too much experience, and I'm not going to write for the same amount of money you pay my students.' I don't believe in democracy in art. I think that when elitism got a bad name in this country, it was the beginning of the end for American culture. The only interest *The New Criterion* has is its pretension of being an elitist magazine. Unfortunately, it's not. What it is is just a strange kind of dinosaur. It has such a clear party line that it's just not an interesting magazine. In fact, it's extremely boring. But its goal—the reconstruction of what was once a consensus of educated people—is correct."

•

The party at Marian Goodman's apartment where I first talked to Robert Pincus-Witten began with a certain—as Pincus-Witten would say—*déconfiture*. Almost everyone there had heard about, if not actually seen, a confrontation that had taken place between two of the party guests an hour before, at the Anselm Kiefer opening. The opening had been an enormous one, with hundreds of viewers on hand drinking bad champagne, and the confrontation had taken place in an alcove off the main, museum-size room, so that not too many people actually witnessed it. Those who did—I among them—were stunned by what had suddenly erupted in their midst. At one moment, Richard Serra and Ingrid Sischy were having a normal conversation; at the next, Serra, his face contorted with fury, was jabbing a finger at Sischy's face and abusing her with a stream of invective. "I think he would have hit me if I'd been a man," Sischy said later. "I was very glad I wasn't." Sischy—a short, very young-looking person with cropped dark wavy hair, a round, clear olive-skinned face, and large glasses, who was wearing tapered stretch pants and a tailored shirt—stood facing Serra, occasionally putting in a quiet word and showing no emotion beyond a reddening of her face. Like the other bystanders, I stood transfixed, catching some of the words but not able to understand what Serra's tirade was about or what had so enraged him. This was the first time I had seen Richard Serra, and he didn't fit the image I had formed. From his massive, thrusting sculpture, his difficult, theory-laden writing, his reputation as a major artist, and the name Serra itself, I had imagined a large, dark, saturnine man—a sort of intellectual-conquistador type, emanating an air of vast, heroic indifference. The actual Serra looked like someone from a small American rural community: a short man with a craggy, surly face, receding gray hair, and pale eyes rimmed by light eyelashes. He was wearing a long black shirt over black trousers and under a black leather jacket—an artist's costume—but his aura was of rough small-town America rather than of bohemia. I have seen men like him standing beside pickup trucks in wintry landscapes, locked in slow, obdurate, implacable argument; I have heard that voice, that aggrieved intonation of flat unyieldingness and threat, that conviction of being right, and that suspicion of being put upon; I know that closed yet oddly sly expression. Sischy stood her ground, letting Serra's abuse rain down on her without flinching, and finally he stalked off and she unclenched her fingers. I shared a taxi with her to the Goodman party, and I at last learned what she had said to trigger the explosion. It had had to do with the *Tilted Arc* controversy, which was then at its most intense.

In 1979 Richard Serra received a $175,000 commission from the federal program called Art in Architecture—whereby one-half of one percent of the cost of a new building goes for public art—to create a sculpture for the circular plaza in front of the glossy and ugly forty-one-story Jacob K. Javits Federal Building, on Foley Square, and in 1981 he fulfilled the commission by sinking a seventy-three-ton curved steel wall, twelve feet high and a hundred and twenty feet long, into the paving of the plaza, positioning it so that it seemed to be arrogantly turning its back on the bland fountain that had previously been the plaza's focal point and in every other way declaring its contempt for the characterless place it had been chosen to embellish. *Tilted Arc*, as Serra called his work, brutally dominated the plaza and confirmed the worst suspicions of the building's federal employees as to the unlovable nuttiness of modern artists. The wall blocked the view of the street and bisected the plaza like a kind of Berlin Wall, and as time went on and its surface acquired a patina of rust, graffiti, and—if one witness at a public hearing held in March of 1985 was to be believed—pee, it looked less and less like a work of art to the federal workers and more and more like a forgotten piece of industrial debris that someone would eventually come and cart away. The hearing was called by William Diamond, the regional administrator of the General Services Administration, which is the Washington agency that runs Art in Architecture; it was a somewhat belated response to a petition submitted three years earlier by thirteen hundred federal workers in and around the Javits building, asking for the removal of the Serra piece. It has been said, and it has not been denied, that the hearing was a kind of Stalin trial—that a decision to recommend removal of the sculpture had already been made by Diamond and his four-man panel—and indeed, after three days of testimony such a recommendation was handed down, even though the testimony had been predominantly pro-sculpture. It has also been observed that the art world, which appeared to be solidly behind Serra at the hearing, was in fact in a state of anxious division over the paradox-fraught controversy. For this was no simple case of a philistine public's hostility to an artwork it didn't understand. The public's objection was only secondarily aesthetic. The primary objection was to the way the sculpture had moved in on the plaza and turned it from a place of benign, ordinary workaday recreation into a kind of dire sculpture garden of the Age of Orwell. "The placement of the sculpture will change the space of the plaza," Serra had told an interviewer in 1980. "After the piece is created, the space will be understood primarily as a function of the sculpture." The disconcerting thought that the public might, after all, prefer eating lunch and hanging out to interacting with a piece of minimalist sculpture evidently never crossed his mind. What troubled many people in the art world—people who ordinarily would have sprung to the defense of avant-garde art against philistine attack—was the touching *reasonableness* of the federal employees' wish to have their plaza restored to them. Although a few people at the hearing made the obligatory hysterical references to Nazi book burning, most of the pro-Serra speakers were quiet and thoughtful, well aware of the pitfalls and traps that lurk in the vicinity of any position that puts the claims of avant-garde art ahead of those of a clerk or a secretary who wants to hold a health fair outside the building where he or she works.

The coeditors of *October* and a younger colleague, Douglas Crimp, were among the most delicate treaders in the pro-Serra party. Annette Michelson pointed out Serra's working-class origin and read a statement from him saying, in part, "As a kid, I worked in steel mills . . . and my work could have something to do on the personal level with the fact that my father was a factory worker all his life." (From Michelson's testimony, one would not have suspected that Serra also went to college at the University of California, to graduate school at Yale, and then to Italy on a Fulbright.) She went on to say that Serra was concerned that working people "be confronted with an art which . . . does not necessarily confirm their beliefs or impose second-class or third-rate qualities on them" and that "the working man and the office worker be presented with that same kind of challenge that the middle-class and upper-class art patrons have found so interesting."

Rosalind Krauss, accordingly, paid all the spectators present the compliment of speaking to them almost as she might have spoken to a seminar of her students at the graduate school. In her elegant lecture on, as the transcript has it, "minibalist" sculpture (the phonetic spellings that leap off the pages of the transcript— "Grancoozi," "Saint Gordons," "DeSuveral," "DeEppilo," "Modelwell," "Manwhole"—testify to the gap that exists between the ordinary *literate* American and the tiny group of people who are the advanced art public), Krauss told the group:

> The kind of vector that Tilted Arc explores is that of vision. More specifically: what it means for vision to be invested with a purpose, so that if we look out into space, it is not just a vacant stare that we cast in front of us but an act of looking that expects to find an object, a direction, a goal. This is purposiveness of vision, or, to use another term, vision's intentionality. For the spectator of Tilted Arc, this sculpture is constantly mapping a kind of projectile of the gaze that starts at one end of Federal Plaza and, like the embodiment of the concept of visual perspective, maps the path across the plaza that the spectator will take. In this sweep, which is simultaneously visual and corporeal, Tilted Arc describes the body's relation to forward motion—to the fact that if we move ahead it is because our eyes have already reached out in order to connect us with the place to which we intend to go.

Evidently, not everyone was up to the stern challenge of Krauss's discourse; after she had spoken, Diamond had to admonish the audience, "Please, no negative comments."

As for Douglas Crimp, who lives a few blocks from the Federal Building, he said that although he considered *Tilted Arc* the "most interesting and beautiful public sculpture in my neighborhood," he had to acknowledge that "my experience evidently differs from that of many people who live and work in the area of *Tilted Arc*." However, he went on, "I believe that this hearing is a calculated manipulation of the public . . . What makes me feel manipulated is that I am forced to argue for art as against some other social function. I am asked to line up on the side of sculpture against, say, those who are on the side of concerts or maybe picnic tables."

What Sischy had said to Serra at the Kiefer opening—which took place a few weeks after the hearing—was that she was *not* lined up on his side in the *Tilted Arc* controversy. He had begun talking to her about the case, comfortably assuming that she was one of his supporters, and she had felt constrained to disabuse him. "I felt I couldn't just stand there and say, 'Yeah, yeah, it's terrible,'" she told me. "It would have been a kind of betrayal of my job to get drawn into a conversation where it was assumed that I was one of a gang of outraged people. I knew that if I didn't say anything and then commissioned an article on the thing, I would feel like a hypocrite. As an editor, I felt that it was necessary to claim not neutrality—there is no neutrality—but that this was still an open book. So I said, 'The whole thing is very complicated.' And there was like a minute of surprise on Richard's part—which there shouldn't have been—and then he flooded out with all this stuff. Calling me a capitalist, saying that I sucked up to advertisers, telling me that I was a fascist, because 'you believe in petition signing.' I guess he thought I was a fascist because I found significance in the fact that thirteen hundred people had signed the petition. He said, 'You don't know what it's like to have your work on trial'—as if those of us who are trying to do something or make something weren't on trial all the time. He said, 'You don't know what it's like to be betrayed by your country. It was my government, and I believed in it. I believed in art and government. Don't you understand that I've been betrayed?' But how can he or I or any of us be so angry about a betrayal over an object? The betrayal wasn't Vietnam. How could we dare to be so naive and personal?

"Everything in my head and body says that we can't go around undoing works of art because people have signed petitions. But what do you do when people really don't want something? There's more than one liberty involved here. And I think that if we ever get to the point of believing that avant-garde art is so sacrosanct that we can't undo a decision, then it's all over. The worst thing we could do is to feel that our decisions are so sacred, and our committees of experts are so sacred, and avant-garde art is so sacred that the very notion that something should be debated causes us to invoke all those horrifying, atrocious episodes in history."

I asked Sischy how she felt during Serra's attack.

"I felt okay," she said. "*Before* he attacked me, I felt nervous and anxious—when he thought I was part of his gang, on the side of those who were saying that this was like a book burning. I felt like a hypocrite then. But once I'd told him where I stood, I felt okay. I felt as though I'd had a job to do and I'd done it. But he wasn't able to listen to me. It just never occurred to him that I might have something to say. He was abusive in the most extraordinary way."

"It was as if he were yelling not at you, but at some fantasy figure," I said. "Who do you think you represented to him?"

"It wasn't me, in the sense that you mean, but in another sense it *was* me. You have to remember that I haven't been overly obedient to the tyranny of this particular avant-garde. I think I've been a great disappointment to people like Richard. I've turned down articles on works like Richard's. This avant-garde was the power structure that ruled the art world and was never questioned—an authoritative, massive power structure. Its rule was that painting was dead—it was just decadent picture making, the regressive act— and all one could do was produce heroic works of abstraction, accompanied by a great deal of terminology. There wasn't room for anything else. My interest in painting—particularly in European painting—as opposed to heroic structures, was offensive to them. When I ran articles on Kiefer and Clemente and Schnabel in *Artforum*, I'm told, artists like Richard felt that I'd done something devastating. There wasn't much bridge building going on between the avant-garde and the world outside, and I think my bridge building drove—and drives—people like Richard Serra mad."

•

Ingrid Sischy became editor of *Artforum* at the age of twenty-seven. She was offered the job by Anthony Korner, a forty-year-old English former banker, and Amy Baker Sandback, a thirty-eight-year-old art historian and art-book publisher. They had jointly bought the magazine from Charles Cowles in 1979 and had decided to replace the editor they had inherited, Joseph Masheck, who had succeeded Coplans. Masheck, an art historian, was probably the most scholarly and the least impossible of Coplans's gang of warring contributing editors, and under his editorship the magazine entered a period of calm enervation and dry academicism. With the troublemakers gone (Krauss, Michelson, Rose, Pincus-Witten, Alloway, and Kozloff had all left), *Artforum* seemed somehow to have lost its reason for being; it was as if all the air had slowly leaked out of it. At the time that Korner and Sandback were acquiring it, Sischy was finishing a fifteen-month curatorial internship under John Szarkowski in the photography department of the Museum of Modern Art. Before that, she had worked as the director of an organization called Printed Matter, which had been formed by a group of artists, critics, and publishers—among them Sol LeWitt, Pat Steir, Lucy Lippard, and, fatefully, Amy Baker Sandback—to publish and distribute what they called "artists' books," as distinguished from art books. Artists' books were a pleasing expression of the decommodification ideology: where art books are about art, artists' books are themselves art of a sort—art that is mindful of its social responsibility, art that refuses to be a precious commodity, art that is cheap, multiple, and without aura. "They had a great idea, but they didn't know how to do it, and they all had other jobs," Sischy has said of the board members of Printed Matter. Sischy didn't know how to do it, either—she had had no experience running a business—but she made it her job to turn Printed Matter into a proper, self-sustaining small business, which it has remained to this day. I once watched Sischy chop tomatoes. She took a small paring knife and, in the most inefficient manner imaginable, with agonizing slowness, proceeded to fill a bowl, tiny piece by tiny piece, with chopped tomatoes. Obviously, no one had ever taught her the technique of chopping vegetables, but this had in no way deterred her from doing it in whatever way she could or prevented her from arriving at her goal. She is less afraid than anyone I have ever met of expending energy unnecessarily. While at Printed Matter, in order to convince the Internal Revenue Service of the legitimacy of the organization's claim to be nonprofit, she dragged twenty cartons of records down to the IRS office. (They were records of pitifully small transactions: in Sischy's day, the average sale at Printed Matter was five dollars; today, it is ten dollars.) At *Artforum*, she will think nothing of spending a whole night in the office working with a writer whose piece is going to press the next day, ministering to him like a kind of night nurse.

When Sischy first took up her duties at *Artforum*, a few days before Christmas, 1979, the next issue of the magazine was due at the printer's in two weeks. (She had been unable to start any sooner because of two exhibitions she was committed to do for the Modern.) "Everyone was about to go off for the Christmas holidays and probably were not very thrilled at the sight of me," Sischy recalls. "I think people were shocked at the thought of working for a young woman they had never heard of, as against an established academic man. After they were gone, I sat there looking at this pile of articles that were ready to go into the issue, and I just couldn't do it. I thought to myself, If this thing isn't going to suck you up, if it's not going to kill you, the only way you can do it—even though it will irritate everyone because you go so slowly—is to take one step at a time and do only what you know and feel secure about. The minute you do something that isn't yourself, the minute you publish something you can't stand, the minute you answer somebody faster than you want to, it's all over. I'm positive it is. So I looked at those manuscripts, and I said to Amy and Tony, 'I don't think I can publish these things.' I said, 'If I'm coming in here, and I'm this new person, I've got to say right away who I am and do what I have to do, even if it's going to be crazy or stupid or two months late.' And Amy, quite rightly, said, 'Look, it can't be two months late. Because that's a part of what they'll know about you—that you're someone who can't get the magazine out. It's got to be on time.' So I said, 'Okay. That makes sense.' We went to Amy's house for lunch and talked about what to do. The only things I knew were artists' books and projects and photographs. I didn't know how to deal with eighty manuscripts by art historians, but I did know contemporary art, and I knew artists. So I said, 'Why don't we make a whole issue of new art? And let's not get famous artists, who will do a little doodle—let's get people who have a real commitment to the printed page.' So we made lists. It was pointed out to me that we had to have a finished pile of material in two weeks. I also knew it had to be pretty good. I didn't think it had to be great. I mean, I would already have been happy if I could have figured out how to get the typesetter on the phone. I didn't even know what a typesetter was. The only thing I had was this ability to relate to people. So I called people up and told them what I wanted them to do, and they said, 'Great! When do you want it?'—thinking I would say in a month—and I said, 'In a week.' And something must have happened in these phone conversations because every one of them came through."

When the issue—the issue of February 1980—arrived on the newsstands, it caused a great stir. It was utterly unlike any previous issue of *Artforum*. The contributors included the photographer William Wegman, the English conceptual artists Gilbert and George, the German conceptual artist Joseph Beuys, the performance artist Laurie Anderson, the editors of the radical-feminist magazine *Heresies*, and the editors of the art journal *Just Another Asshole*, and the whole thing had an impudent, aggressively unbuttoned, improvised yet oddly poised air.

Sischy had happened to take over the editorship of *Artforum* at exactly the start of the new decade, and the appearance of an untried, unbookish, unknown, very young woman at the helm of a magazine whose three previous editors had been older men of parts, and whose atmosphere, even in its recent, least successful manifestation, was that of a powerful and exclusive men's club (notwithstanding its women contributors, who possibly even contributed to that atmosphere), was a kind of portent of the astonishing developments in art that the eighties were to witness. In the abrupt transformation of *Artforum*'s format from a predictable high-art austerity to an unpredictable sort of underground press grunginess/flashiness may be read the changes that were to transform the quiet and stable New York art world of the seventies—with its minimalist and postminimalist stars surrounded by familiar constellations of conceptual, performance, video, and film artists—into today's unsettling, incoherent postmodern art universe. One has to remind oneself, of course, that every present is disorderly, that art history is an artifact of time, and that certain temperaments tolerate chaos better than others. Barbara Rose, for example, found the present as threatening twenty years ago as she finds it today; the following passage, from a piece by Rose entitled "How to Murder an Avant Garde," was published in *Artforum* in November 1965:

> Today, there is no "scene." Although the slick magazines have invented a fictional scene for public consumption, the experimental artist is more alone than he has been since the thirties. There are many disturbing signs: among art students, one perceives a "make-it" mentality conditioned by mass press descriptions of artistic high-life . . . There are other bad omens. As the pace becomes more frantic and distinctions are blurred, values are equally obscured . . . Pseudo-art writing in mass magazines confuses issues, imputes artists' motives while supposedly honoring them . . . Having lost their common purpose on being accepted into the Establishment, and now rapidly losing their center as galleries and museums and exhibitions proliferate, is it any wonder that avant-garde artists are experiencing a crisis of identity?

The cover of Sischy's first issue was a reproduction of the cover of the first issue of an avant-garde magazine of the forties called *VVV*, which styled itself a magazine of "poetry, plastic arts, anthropology, sociology, psychology" and numbered André Breton, Max Ernst, André Masson, William Carlos Williams, Claude Lévi-Strauss, Harold Rosenberg, Arthur Cravan, and Lionel Abel among its contributors. The *VVV* cover, by Max Ernst, was an Ernstian design of mysterious figures and diagrams from some abstruse, invented science, which surrounded the three *V*'s in black, on a green background. Sischy had borrowed the original cover from David Hare, *VVV*'s former editor. Someone who had not come from John Szarkowski's photography department might not have been as overjoyed as Sischy was by the cigarette burn and the spills that stained it, but she correctly gauged the surreal beauty that these ghostly traces of a past life would assume when photographed, and also the sense of quotation marks that they would help impart to the notion of a cover about a cover. There was in addition a special personal fittingness to the unretouched, worn, dog-eared appearance of Sischy's first cover. Among the people in positions of power in the cultural institutions of this city—book publishers, magazine editors, newspaper executives, museum directors and curators, theater producers—there has developed a style of dealing with staff that is noted for its informality, directness, simplicity, ordinariness. The pompous, self-important boss who puts a glacial distance between himself and his underlings, the petty tyrant who surrounds himself with cowed secretaries is so rarely seen today that he is almost an endearing anachronism (in the upper-middle-class establishment of which we speak, that is). In this context, Sischy's way of running her magazine as "a kind of kibbutz" (in the words of the critic Donald Kuspit) is not all that remarkable. If there are some things Sischy does that editors of other magazines don't do—such as running out of the office several times a day to the luncheonette across the street to get coffee and pastry for the staff—her relations with her employees are, in general, only slightly more egalitarian than the norm.

Where Sischy *is* outré is in her obsessive, almost fetishistic concern with questions of ethics. She sees moral dilemmas everywhere— and, of course, there are moral dilemmas everywhere, only most of us prefer not to see them as such and simply accept the little evasions, equivocations, and compromises that soften the fabric of social life, that grease the machinery of living and working, that make reality less of a constant struggle with ourselves and with others. Sischy, however, rejoices in the struggle; she is like someone walking through a minefield who has taken a course in mine detection. She positively enjoys staring into the abyss and drawing back just in time. Once, at Printed Matter, she received a telephone call from a museum curator who wanted to buy a copy of *The Xerox Book*, a collection of work by seven conceptual artists, published in 1968, that had been very successful and had become something of a collector's item. "Our last copy had just been ordered by somebody,"

Sischy told me. "So I said to the curator, 'Sorry, it's gone.' And the curator said, 'Ingrid, we'll give you a lot of money for a copy.' We were really in deep financial trouble then, and the museum was talking, I think, a minimum of a thousand dollars. But I thought, How dare they? And I told them I had just sold it for twenty-five dollars, first come, first served, and hung up."

In the presence of such shining rectitude, one cannot—worm that one is—but feel a little resentful. One can even, if one pursues this cynical train of thought far enough, summon up a bit of sympathy for Richard Serra. Who does she think she is? Why does she always have to behave better than everyone else? There are times when the heroines of Henry James's novels provoke just such coarse thoughts—moments when the thread of sympathetic attention snaps and we fretfully wonder why these girls have always to be so ridiculously fine. But if Sischy's moral imagination is of a feverishness to invoke the spirits of Fleda Vetch and Milly Theale, her atmosphere is very different from that surrounding those tense, exquisite intelligences. She has an incongruous, almost Mediterranean easiness and dailiness. The momentary irritation one feels with her when one believes she is riding her ethical hobbyhorse too hard (I remember once standing with her outside an Italian airport sulkily watching everyone else get a taxi while we, at her insistence, honorably waited our turn behind a pair of utterly baffled Japanese) is swept away by the disarming agreeableness of her company. Her capacity for enjoyment is movingly large. She is a kind of reverse Jewish princess: she goes through life gratefully accepting the pleasures and amenities that come her way, and if they are not the particular pleasures and amenities she ordered—well, so much the better. Her relationship to the world of consumer objects is almost bizarrely attenuated. (If a person could be likened to a work of de-commodified art, Sischy would be that person.) She has no credit cards, no charge accounts, no savings account (until last year, she had no checking account), no car, no driver's license; she doesn't even have a handbag, and stuffs her money and the tiny scraps of paper that serve her as an address book into a bulging wallet, which she awkwardly carries in her hand, like a kid on the way to a show. She uses no makeup and wears the plainest of clothes: the knit pants and shirt are her uniform. She has no possessions to speak of—she has never bought a painting, a sculpture, a photograph, a decorative object, or a piece of furniture or jewelry. All her belongings (mostly books and papers) fit into a trunk that she brought to the house of the woman she lives with when she moved in four years ago, and that she has yet to unpack.

The not yet unpacked trunk is a fitting metaphor for Sischy. As a child, she was twice uprooted—first from South Africa at the age of nine, and then from Scotland at the age of fifteen. She was born in 1952 in Johannesburg, the youngest of three children (she has two brothers, one a doctor and the other a lawyer) of a Jewish professional family. Her father, Benjamin Sischy, is a physician, and her mother, Claire Sischy, is a retired speech therapist. The family emigrated to Edinburgh in 1961, after the Sharpeville massacre, and again in 1967, to Rochester, New York, where Dr. Sischy took a position in oncological research at Highland Hospital. In Edinburgh, Ingrid went to a famous private school for girls, George Watson's Ladies' College; in Rochester, she went to public high school; and in 1973 she graduated from Sarah Lawrence College. In all three places she became a leader very quickly and easily. "My ability to adjust got to be a family joke: we'd move to a new country, and within six months—at most, a year—I'd be president of the class, and eventually president of the school," she told me almost ruefully.

Sischy speaks of her parents with affection and approval bordering on reverence, and she once told me how, as a child of such a socially conscious family, she was able to reconcile herself to the apparently socially useless work that she does now. "For my parents, art was something that you did after the day's work," she said. "I grew up with the assumption that I would go into a profession like theirs—one that did some social good every day. When I took this job, I realized that the only way for me to do it was as if I were going to medical school. I worked sixteen hours a day, the way I saw my father work, and the way I saw my brother work when he was a resident, and I still work that way. I'm still serving my residency." She went on, "I used to have the fantasy that I would do this work for a few years and then one day I'd stop and dedicate the rest of my life to South Africa. But more and more I have come to understand that to edit an art magazine today is to participate in all of today's social, economic, and political discourses. Nowhere was this clearer to me than in the primitivism show."

Thomas McEvilley's attack, in the November 1984 issue of *Artforum*, on the Museum of Modern Art's major exhibition *"Primitivism" in 20th Century Art: Affinity of the Tribal and the Modern* made an extraordinary impression on the art world. There was something about the piece that was instantly recognized as more deeply threatening to the status quo than it is usual for a critique of a museum show to be—and not least aware of the threat was William Rubin, the director of the show, and also the director of the museum's Department of Painting and Sculpture. The article had a sort of dangerous luster, and this quality was also present in the two replies that McEvilley, a classicist turned art historian and critic, wrote to the letters that Rubin felt impelled to address to the editor of *Artforum*. (Kirk Varnedoe, codirector of the exhibition, joined the fray for the first round of correspondence and prudently dropped out for the second.) McEvilley's article was like the knocking on the door dreaded by Ibsen's master builder—the sound of the younger generation coming to crush the older one—and drew its power as much from the urgency of its Oedipal subtext as from the cogency of its manifest argument. Other reviews just as critical and as well argued as McEvilley's—Arthur Danto's devastating one in *The Nation*, for example—didn't get under Rubin's skin as McEvilley's did. (With one exception: an earlier piece, by Michael Peppiatt, published in *Connaissance des Arts*, caused Rubin to threaten to sue the magazine—it remained calm—when it refused to publish his long riposte, which was accompanied by fourteen color illustrations.) What also may have contributed—indeed, must have contributed—to the specially charged atmosphere of the McEvilley article was the intense pressure under which it was produced. It was written, revised, and prepared for publication in just eleven days. Sischy told me how this had come about. She and McEvilley had gone to the opening of the primitivism show together, with the understanding that he would write about it if he felt moved to do so after seeing it. "As I walked through the show, I had a really creepy feeling that here, yet again, was a case of two objects looking the same but not meaning the same," Sischy told me. "As I went along, I began to feel that yet again the Other was being used to service us. Yet again. Practically a thesis had been written on the label below a Brancusi work, but it was enough to say of the primitive sculpture beside it, 'From North Africa.' All the research had gone into the Brancusi, while the other thing was being used once again simply for affirmation of our values. A supposed honor was being bestowed on primitive work—the honor of saying, 'Hey! It's as good as art! We'll even call it art.' But now we know that a different set of questions needs to be asked about how we assimilate another culture. Tom had the same feelings—maybe even stronger. So we went to the Plaza and had about five drinks, and after the drinks Tom said, 'Look, can we get the review into the next issue?' and I said, 'Tom, the issue is all designed. It's going to the printer in four days.' And he said, 'Well, what do you think?' and I said, 'It would be incredible to come out with the piece while the show is still so new. Let me think about it.' And I had another drink and said, 'I've thought about it.' I went to the office the next day and asked Amy and Tony whether it would be possible to open up the magazine and add an article a week late, which is an insane thing to do. But Tony and Amy agreed that in this case it would be a great thing to do. So Tom wrote the piece in four days, and then we sat in my office for seven days and seven nights working on it."

The article, entitled "Doctor Lawyer Indian Chief: ' "Primitivism" in 20th Century Art' at the Museum of Modern Art in 1984," not only bore down heavily on the ethnocentricity of which Sischy (among others) was so painfully conscious ("This exhibition shows Western egotism still as unbridled as in the centuries of colonialism and souvenirism") but denied that it was any longer interesting to see modernist paintings and sculptures juxtaposed with tribal objects to which they bear formal resemblances. That sort of thing, McEvilley said, was all very well in 1938, when Robert Goldwater published his classic text *Primitivism in Modern Painting*, but today such a way of thinking is a pitiful anachronism. Writing of MoMA as "the temple of formalist Modernism," McEvilley characterized the primitivism show as a sort of last-ditch stand by the museum against the incursions of advanced thought:

> Whereas the esthetics of [formalist modernism] had been seen as higher criteria by which other styles were to be judged, now, in quite respectable quarters, they began to appear as just another style. For a while, like Pre-Raphaelitism or the Ashcan School, they had served certain needs and exercised hegemony; those needs passing, their hegemony was passing also. But the collection of the Museum of Modern Art is predominantly based on the idea that formalist Modernism will never pass, will never lose its self-validating power. Not a relative, conditioned thing, subject to transient causes and effects, it is to be above the web of natural and cultural change; this is its supposed essence. After several years of sustained attack, such a credo needs a defender and a new defense. How brilliant to attempt to revalidate classical Modernist esthetics by stepping outside their usual realm of discourse and bringing to bear upon them a vast, foreign sector of the world. By demonstrating that the "innocent" creativity of primitives naturally expresses a Modernist esthetic feeling, one may seem to have demonstrated once again that Modernism itself is both innocent and universal.

Rubin, he went on to say, made "highly inappropriate claims about the intentions of tribal cultures without letting them have their say, except through the mute presence of their unexplained religious objects, which are misleadingly presented as art objects." And he continued:

> In their native contexts these objects were invested with feelings of awe and dread, not of esthetic ennoblement. They were seen usually in motion, at night, in closed dark spaces, by flickering torchlight. Their viewers were under the influence of ritual, communal identification feelings, and often alcohol or drugs; above all, they were activated by the pres-

ence within or among the objects themselves of the shaman, acting out the usually terrifying power represented by the mask or icon. What was at stake for the viewer was not esthetic appreciation but loss of self in identification with and support of the shamanic performance. The Modernist works in the show serve completely different functions, and were made to be perceived from a completely different stance. If you or I were a native tribal artisan or spectator walking through the halls of MoMA, we would see an entirely different show from the one we see as 20th-century New Yorkers. We would see primarily not form but content, and not art but religion or magic.

The gauntlet flung down by McEvilley was picked up by Rubin in a long reply that *Artforum* published in its issue of February 1985, together with a shorter reply from Varnedoe. Rubin started out by complimenting McEvilley for being "fair-minded" and for maintaining "a high level of discourse" but quickly went on to say that "notwithstanding his evidently good intentions, his review is interwoven with sufficient misconceptions, internal inconsistencies, and simple errors of fact that—given its seriousness—it should not go unchallenged." The chief factual error of which Rubin accused McEvilley—an accusation that developed into one of the most excruciatingly particularized squabbles about a matter of doubtful significance ever published—concerned the number of objects in a pair of vitrines at the Centre Pompidou, in Paris. McEvilley, to illustrate his dismissal of the idea of the primitivism show as "not new or startling in the least," cited (among other examples) an exhibition of "about one hundred tribal objects" from the Musée de l'Homme which the Centre Pompidou had placed in meaningful proximity to its modern art collection shortly after it opened, in 1977, and left up for about five years. Rubin challenged the figure one hundred. He said that "a rapid check reveals that . . . the two vitrines at the Centre Pompidou together never contained more than twenty or so objects." I will spare the readers of this essay what the readers of *Artforum* had to endure in order to finally learn that neither contestant's figure was strictly accurate: in one of the sixteen footnotes that Rubin appended to his second reply, he confessed that according to a list he had just received from the Musée de l'Homme, there had been as many as fifty-two objects in the vitrines. As one of the readers who did not fall by the wayside in the battle of the vitrines, I can report that, despite my boredom with the particulars of the debate, I was kept going by the passionate intensity with which it was conducted. Clearly, each man had more at stake than being right or wrong about a number. The number had become a kind of objective correlative for the anxiety each man felt about his position. Rubin frankly told me later, "McEvilley was at great pains to show that the exhibition was old hat, and since I had spent five years and a pile of money on it, I took it ill. Some of our trustees are readers of *Artforum*. I didn't want them to think that I had gone to all this trouble and expense just to do a rerun of something that had already been done." McEvilley, for his part, felt that his position as challenger of the Establishment was threatened by the insinuation that he couldn't get his facts straight, and he displayed a kind of young man's anger over being corrected by an elder. (Actually, McEvilley isn't so young—he is forty-seven, to Rubin's fifty-nine—but in the psychodrama of his encounter with Rubin he fell easily into the role of the impetuous young Jack the Giant Killer, just as Rubin, by position and temperament, was a natural for the role of the giant.)

In his reply to Rubin and Varnedoe, McEvilley adopted a provocatively folksy tone. "I'm the one who barked these grouchy bears out of the woods, so I guess I have to listen to their howling and gnashing of teeth," he wrote. "In a sense, it's a chance in a lifetime. We rarely see these bears out in the open—especially the big one." McEvilley quickly dispatched the little bear, as he maddeningly called Varnedoe:

> The whole-cloth 19th-centuryism of Varnedoe's thought is revealed in a display of comedic ignorance. He quotes me as using the term "intentionalities" and notes parenthetically that this is "a word [McEvilley] favors as a substitute for the simpler 'intentions.'" He evidently doesn't recognize that "intentionality" is a technical term in the philosophy of Edmund Husserl and in the whole phenomenological movement.

Rubin, in his second letter, saw an opportunity to avenge Varnedoe's honor, and he gleefully pounced on it:

I can only envy McEvilley's authority in art history, anthropology, linguistics, phenomenology, and literary theory, and sympathize with his need to mock the comedic ignorance of those less accomplished than he. Alas, as but a poor art historian, I can only hope that after a professional lifetime in this field I know something about *it*, at least . . . McEvilley asks us to consider that "the charioteer of Delphi, ca. 470 B.C., for example, was seen totally [*sic*] differently in classical Greece from the way we see him now. He was not alone in that noble, self-sufficient serenity of transcendental, angelic whiteness that we see." Perhaps I should take it less amiss to find my own ideas being transformed beyond recognition by McEvilley when I discover that he can also somehow transform this familiar monument of introductory art history from a bronze into a marble.

I am afraid that almost all of McEvilley's art-historical assertions come from the same quarry as the marble charioteer.

But Rubin's triumph was short-lived. McEvilley retorted:

Hibernation can be a productive method—one can go into solitude and come back with understanding—or it can cloud the mind with dreams of scrambled facts, of fabricated evidence and marble charioteers. "The charioteer of Delphi," I wrote, "ca. 470 B.C., for example, was seen totally differently in classical Greece from the way we now see him. He was not alone in that noble, self-sufficient serenity of transcendental, angelic whiteness that we see." The word "marble" is Rubin's, not mine, and comes up in his claim that I misreported the classical bronze as a marble work—after which he exercises his wit against me by referring to "the marble charioteer." Rubin never deals with the question of why I brought the charioteer up in the first place. My point was about the manipulation of the object through its context; we now see the work alone on a pedestal in a white room in the Delphi archaeological museum, in the typical kind of installation with which we relate to works from other cultures or times by isolating them so that they are available to receive our projections. The charioteer is decontextualized in this artificial white atmosphere and made meaningless in terms of his native context, function, and intention. I drew the analogy in my initial article as a criticism of the installation of the primitive works at MoMA, where, similarly, fragments of complex pieces were isolated in such a way as to render them meaningless in their own terms, as if indeed they had no terms of their own. Rubin chose to ignore this issue, as well as others that related to the example of the charioteer, and instead to argue a point of physical detail that would not have affected the argument in any way even if he had gotten it right.

If Rubin did himself no good by engaging in these scholastic skirmishes, his greatest disservice to himself was his writing to *Artforum* at all, thus giving McEvilley a second, and then a third, chance to score off the primitivism show. McEvilley's original critique was probably not as airtight as it might have been if he had had more than four days in which to write it. Now Rubin had afforded him more time, and perhaps even more motivation, to shine. Taking his argument against a universal aesthetic to another level, McEvilley listed three periods in the history of the West's relationship to tribal art. In the first period, primitive objects were "denied the status of art, as if it was an honor that they did not deserve." In the second, primitive objects were thought "formally and intellectually 'good enough' to be called art." And in the third, which is the present period, "one may begin to look at the tribal objects from the point of view of their own culture and to realize that, whatever they are, they fall in between the categories on our grid." McEvilley chastised Rubin for being stuck in the second period: He accused him of presenting "a value system that had been firmly in place for sixty years as if it were a terrific new discovery," and of treating the primitive objects in the show "as if they had nothing to do with any living societies except ours, as if they were pretty objects and no more, there for us to do with as we like." In his first letter, Rubin complained that McEvilley had missed the point of the show, which was to study tribal works from the point of view of the pioneer modernists. "Of course the tribal objects in our show are decontextualized," Rubin snapped, adding, "In fact, they are more than that; they are *recontextualized*, within the framework of Western art and culture. *And that is what our particular story is all about.* McEvilley simply refuses to accept the fact that our story is not about 'the Other,' but about ourselves." But McEvilley stubbornly insisted that "to really be about *us*, the show would have to be about the evolution in our relationship to the Other." He wrote:

> We no longer live in a separate world. Our tribal view of art history as primarily or exclusively European or Eurocentric will become increasingly harmful as it cuts us off from the emerging Third World and isolates us from the global culture which already is in its early stages. We must have values that can include the rest of the world when the moment comes—and the moment is upon us. Civilization transcends geography, and if history holds one person in this global village, it holds another. In fact, if one of us is privileged over the other in art-historical terms it is the so-called primitive object-makers, through whose legacy we got our last big ride outside our own point of view, and called it Modern art.

A few months after the publication of the final round of the McEvilley-Rubin exchange, I pay a call on Rubin at his office in the Museum of Modern Art. In his embodiment of all the clichés about men in positions of power, Rubin is an almost allegorical figure. To make an appointment with him requires prolonged conversation with a secretary ("Mr. Rubin has asked me to get as much information about his calls as possible so that he may judge the urgency of returning them"), and to enter his office is to immediately experience a feeling of diminishment, in the same strange way that entering a Gothic cathedral gives one a feeling of exaltation. Rubin is extremely well dressed and well groomed, with a dark, assertive, attractive face; he sits behind an enormous, immaculate desk in a large white room that commands a spectacular view of the museum's sculpture garden and a panorama of New York buildings, and is fitted out with spare, expensive modern furniture, abstract paintings, and an African sculpture. In spite of the dossier of information I have left with the secretary, he does not know who I am and why I have come. Once my identity and purpose have been reestablished, I ask him the two questions I have come to ask: Was he satisfied with the treatment he received from *Artforum*, and was he satisfied with his performance in his two letters to the editor?

Rubin replies yes to both questions. "The people at *Artforum* were at great pains to be fair, though I think they were reluctant when we said we wanted to write a second letter," he says. "Ingrid would have liked to say no, but we made certain points about misstatements, and then she realized that the matter couldn't just be left there. I feel very secure in thinking that students and other people reading this exchange ten years from now are going to come down on our side. If I didn't feel that way, I would have to accept criticism that would put five years of work into question. Not that there aren't things in my exhibition which I wouldn't have done differently. Sure there are. And not that I'm saying that all the criticisms of the exhibition were wrong. I think there was good criticism even in McEvilley's article. But McEvilley wanted a different exhibition altogether. Someone in the department here said to me, 'McEvilley would have liked to be invited to do the exhibition.' That's the sort of thing you run into in this work. Since we invited people from all over to participate in the exhibition, to write articles for the catalog, McEvilley may have felt that the museum overlooked him. There may have been personal offense taken. Frankly, Kirk and I found McEvilley's replies to the letters much worse than his original article. We deeply felt the absence of *politesse* in the thing about the bears."

A few days after this meeting, to my surprise, Rubin telephones me and says he would like to speak to me again. Evidently under some compulsion to do everything twice, he says that he has had some further thoughts over the weekend about the McEvilley exchange and wishes to share them with me. When I arrive in his office, he hands me a three-by-five file card on which the following list has been typed:

Bears
Shoddy arguers
Poverty of intellect
19th-century
minds
Childish tactics
Arrogance
Cheapest . . .
tactics

Rubin has spent the weekend reviewing his exchanges with McEvilley and evidently no longer feels satisfied with himself. He tells me he feels that McEvilley has bested him through "rhetorical devices," examples of which he has typed out on the card. "McEvilley went down claiming that he never did or said a single thing that was wrong," Rubin says. "At least I admitted that I was wrong about the number of objects in the vitrines, though I don't think I was as wrong as McEvilley believes. The point is, these rhetorical devices that he has obviously studied somewhere are for winning arguments, not for getting to the truth. I never studied rhetoric, so I'm disadvantaged to that extent. It may be that McEvilley is emotionally so offended by the very conception of the show that he can't see straight. And I think it kind of shocked him, and hurt him, that he was being questioned at all. The tone of his reaction seems to me to contain not a little anger at being called on to defend himself. His interest only in winning an argument is how I explain his unwillingness to see if there is a common ground. I'm only human. If someone uses invective on me, and slithery techniques to prove he's always right, I'm going to come straight back—I'm not going to try and find common ground either. But I think there *is* common ground. I don't think McEvilley really believes half these extreme things he says."

Like a teacher handing out reading material to a class, Rubin hands me a pack of xeroxes he has made of McEvilley's article, of his letters and Varnedoe's, of McEvilley's replies to them, of various other reviews of the primitivism show, and of an exchange in *Artforum* in 1967 between him and Harold Rosenberg over a piece

Rubin wrote on Jackson Pollock, which McEvilley cited in his second reply. Referring to a set of xeroxes of his own, which I notice are extensively underlined, Rubin proceeds, like one of Borges's obsessed men, to go over the entire exchange, point by point. He continues this rite of self-justification for the next two hours, touching yet again on the dread vitrines, and also on the other exhibition that McEvilley cited—that of the Menil Collection in the Grand Palais in 1984. "McEvilley dismisses our show as old hat because it was done before, in the Menil show," he tells me. "Then I write in to say that in the Menil show there were only two juxtaposed examples of primitive art and modern art, and that all the rest of the tribal art was shown separately, in its own area. And how does McEvilley respond to this? He responds by *blinding the reader,* in effect: 'The fact that Rubin can neither growl away nor live with is that the tribal objects were not shown *entirely* in their own separate area,' he writes. By the time you get to this, your head is dizzy. You would have to be much more clearheaded than anyone is likely to be at this point to see that what he's saying is just ridiculous. It's so tricky and slimy."

The telephone rings, and the secretary announces Rubin's next appointment. Rubin looks at his watch and says to me, "I'll just race through this." Then, in a moment of apparent uncertainty, he lets the pack of xeroxes fall from his hand. He takes off his glasses, rubs his eyes, and seems to be hovering on the edge of seeing the absurdity and futility of the proceedings. Then he puts his glasses back on and resolutely picks up the xeroxes.

One afternoon in April 1985, I deliberately arrive late at the Upper West Side apartment of the artist Lucas Samaras, where I am meeting Sischy and Amy Baker Sandback, the president of *Artforum*. I want to make sure that I am not the first to arrive: I have never met Samaras, but his mysterious, aggressive work—menacing black boxes lined with pins, strange objects made of bright-colored yarns, fantastic pieces of painted furniture, photographs of his own leering face and contorted naked body—though it has a sort of creepy fascination, has made me instinctively feel that this is not a man I want to be alone with. I am late, but the others are even later, and I am met at the door by a tall, thin, dour man in his forties with a graying beard, who ushers me into the apartment with a resigned air and motions for me to sit on a sofa whose cushion is a tangle of colored yarns encased in a plastic cover. The place is like an enchanter's workshop, filled with rolls of sparkling metallic fabrics, collections of broken wineglasses, jars of rhinestones, long sticks to which plastic brides and grooms are affixed, sinister clay figures, a wall of necklaces, a weirdly shaped handmade table and chairs, all bearing the Samaras signature. But the place is also like one of those shabby, harshly orderly apartments inhabited by old women from Balkan countries; it lacks only the embroidered cloths and the religious kitsch to complete its authoritative dissociation from middle-class taste and fashion. When Samaras tells me that he is from Macedonia—he came here as a boy of eleven—I think, Of course, where else? He stares at me expressionlessly but not unkindly, and we fall into talk. I almost immediately realize that the dire persona that emerges from his work and the actual person who is Lucas Samaras bear the sort of relationship to each other that a lion bears to a house cat. Where the work glints with menace, irony, and disdain, the man is merely acerbic, willful, and a little needling. He says of Sischy that she is unique among editors he has known. "All the others are interested in power—they play power games. If they are women, they use their femininity to gain power. Ingrid is not interested in power."

Sischy and Sandback arrive with a vague, unrepentant story about a distrait taxi driver. Sandback is in her forties—a calm, soft-spoken, somewhat mysterious woman, with the air of a natural consoler about her, though at present she herself is in need of consolation because of a new, profoundly regretted punk haircut. Both women are very animated with Samaras. I am struck by the change in Sischy's demeanor—how much lighter she is here. With me, she has always been rather serious and subdued. Now there is a lot of banter and laughter and kidding. The purpose of the visit is to make a selection from among Samaras's new acrylic paintings for an eight-page spread in the summer issue of *Artforum*. The new paintings are a large collective portrait of the art world—a taxonomy of the dealers, curators, collectors, critics, artists, artists' wives, and failed artists who inhabit it. The paintings are all on thirty-six-by-twenty-four-inch canvas boards, and all are horribly grinning skulls. The groups are distinguished from one another largely by color and style of brushstrokes, so that each is unpleasant in a slightly different way. The dealer skulls, for example, are done in slashing, sketchy bright colors on a black background, the critics are done in a bleary gray and white, and the collectors are in thick, vividly colored strokes and have been given *two* mouths. During the two hours it takes to make the selection and agree on how to lay out the spread, Samaras serves tea and coffee and offers expensive chocolates; when Sischy says no to the chocolates because she is on a diet, he brings out three grapefruits, deftly peels them, cuts them into artful slices, and serves them in bowls with spoons, all with the sad, ironic air of one doing an avant-garde performance piece that may be beyond the grasp of the audience. The joshing and kidding continue as Samaras, Sischy, and Sandback regard the paintings that Samaras has spread out, though there is a tension beneath the surface. Sischy and Sandback will do everything to please the artist, up to a point, and Samaras, for whom it is extremely advantageous to be shown in *Artforum*, knows he must gauge where that point is and not push beyond it. However, as the afternoon wears on, the sense of cautious negotiation gives way to a rhythm of work, to a tide of interest in the task at hand into which all three are drawn—and into which even I, who have no vested interest in the project whatever and was initially rather repelled by the paintings, now find myself drawn.

At Samaras's, Sischy behaves as if she had all the time in the world to spend on the project, but in fact she is almost calamitously behind schedule. There are only eight days left before the summer issue of the magazine goes to the printer, and some of the writing that is going to appear in it has yet to be committed to paper. Thomas McEvilley has not yet finished a piece on conceptual art, and Rene Ricard, a poet and a regular contributor, is still working on an article about an unknown figurative painter named Bill Rice, whose chief subject is homosexual black men. The unconventional art criticism of Ricard has been the cause of much of the grumbling among the older art-world intelligentsia about the new *Artforum*'s lack of seriousness. Here is an example of it, from Ricard's first contribution to the magazine—entitled "Not About Julian Schnabel"—in the summer 1981 issue:

> When I wrote about Julian Schnabel's last show at the Mary Boone Gallery for *Art in America*, I became so embroiled in a distasteful episode with the gallery concerning my request for an exclusive on the picture I wanted to use as an illustration that I vowed never to cover any painter represented by that gallery. I ignored Stephen Mueller's last show there and I really wanted to write about it. Now Julian has ascended to Leo Castelli—though he's splitting the bill with Boone—and I can leave personal feelings out of the picture, where they belong. Anyway, my responsibility is not to the painter, the dealer, or myself; it is to the pictures.
>
> Nor was this the only treachery perpetrated by a dealer. I wanted to know how much a drawing Brice Marden had given me was worth. That very day, the person I'd asked (not at his current gallery) told Brice's best friend that I was selling his drawing. Next time I saw Brice the first thing he said was, "I hear you're selling my drawing!" As a point of fact I'd never part with it. I just wanted to know how much it was worth. For someone of my generation the possession of a Marden drawing is a big thing. I call it my de Kooning, and I *have* a de Kooning.

Ricard is thirty-nine years old, has published a book of poems that inevitably bring the verse of Frank O'Hara to mind in their emotional immediacy (though their descriptions of very rough homosexual sex are beyond anything O'Hara dared or cared to render), and at an early age was a member of Andy Warhol's Factory. He lives in a very bad, brutish tenement on East Twelfth Street, in an apartment that he keeps in a condition of aggressive squalor and disorder. He has no telephone, and it is unclear what he does to support himself. It is not his writing. Sischy has spoken to me about the gross financial inequalities of today's art world between the artists who have made it and the ones who haven't. "As for those of us who work in a reporting or critical way, our lives are a sort of joke in comparison to what we're dealing with," she added. "I'm lucky. I happen to live with someone who owns her own house. I'm in comfortable circumstances. But I know that most of our writers have nothing, and when I took this job I made it clear that I hoped to reach a point where writing about art would be taken seriously enough so that maybe we could provide some income for the writer. Our fee is now up to eight hundred dollars for a piece—and a writer may work for a year or more to earn it. So whenever I'm out with a writer the least I can do is make sure that there's a decent meal. It's crazy, but that's the level it's on."

For the past three days, Sischy has been going to Ricard's place in the evenings to work with him on his piece about Bill Rice, staying until two or three in the morning and somehow getting it out of him. On the day it is finished, I join her and Ricard for dinner at an East Village restaurant called Evelyne's. Ricard has brought along a friend named George Condo, an agreeable and short young artist who is wearing a white shirt and a red crewneck sweater under a dark suit that is two or three sizes too big for him, to indicate that he is not an Ivy League college student but an artist. Condo does luridly expressionistic paintings of heads on long necks, which are enjoying a vogue in Europe. Ricard is dressed in a gray sweatshirt over jeans; he is thin and wiry, his brow is deeply lined, his eyes are frightened, and his mouth is petulant. His voice is high-pitched, and in it there is spite, self-pity, self-parody, seduction, false innocence, anxiety. As he talks, he gesticulates wildly and reaches out to touch and stroke you. He dominates the conversation, but unlike most people who are nakedly interested in themselves, he is also aware of what is going on with others, though in a specialized way. Certain things capture his interest: he comments on people's looks and clothes and mannerisms. When a woman at the next table takes out a compact and puts on lipstick, he says, "That's my favorite gesture in the world. I love it. It's so twenties. Isn't it the twenties?" A beautiful and elegant young woman wearing a pristine white linen suit, whom Ricard knows (and, bafflingly, introduces as "someone I was engaged to eight years ago"), joins our table, as does, when he arrives, the good-looking man—a curator of a small museum in Colorado—she has been waiting for at the bar. After introductions are made, the curator asks Sischy what she does. She replies, "I work in the editorial department of *Artforum* magazine." After the curator and the young woman have left for the Danceteria discotheque, Ricard turns exasperatedly on Sischy and says, "Why did you say that to him?" He does a mincing parody of Sischy saying "I work in the editorial department of *Artforum* magazine," and goes on, "Why didn't you say, 'I am Ingrid Sischy, *the editor of Artforum* magazine. I'm this big deal. I'm this powerful person. I'm the whole thing'? Telling him 'I work in the editorial department'! Come *on!*" Sischy quietly glares at Ricard, like the older sister of a child who is doing something embarrassing.

The dinner arrives, and Ricard eats it hungrily. He tells, as if for the first time, the story he told in "Not About Julian Schnabel" concerning the "exclusive" he lost at the hands of Mary Boone. He says that everyone he has ever written about has become a millionaire. "That's why everybody wants a Rene Ricard write-up," he explains. "It's like magic." Sischy looks pained. Condo politely suppresses a yawn. Ricard goes on to tell about an auction in New Jersey the previous day where two Picabias went for two hundred and three hundred dollars, respectively. "You made me miss that auction," he says to Sischy accusingly, and then, to me, "She made me stay here and work on my piece." I ask Sischy if it is true about the Picabias. She replies, "Whatever Rene says is true." But I remember a poem of his about malevolence—a litany of such acts of bad faith as

> I've advised people to get haircuts that made them
> Look a mess, and poked fun behind their backs.
> I've convinced writers to destroy their best work.
> I've thrown people out of their own apartments
> I've sublet, and never paid the rent.
> I've conned young girls into giving me heirlooms to pawn.
> I tease people who stutter. I like to talk dirty in front
> Of old women.

> I've talked nouveau-riches people into letting me throw
> A party and then invited derelicts into their home,
> Leaving it in shambles.

The last line is "I made a lot of this up, but a lot of it is true."

During coffee, the conversation turns to Henry James, because Ricard has paraphrased a line from *The Portrait of a Lady* in the Bill Rice piece but cannot remember where in the novel it appears. Nor does he care. But Sischy is adamant about finding the line so the paraphrase can be checked, and though I don't recognize the allusion, I offer to look for it in my copy of the novel at home. Condo politely yawns again. Ricard says that he admires James but feels constrained to add, "*I* would never write fiction. It's lying." Sischy listens but does not join in the conversation. She once told me that she wasn't bookish. "Everyone I've ever been close to and loved and lived with has been a person who reads all the time," she said. "It would be very nice if I could say the same about myself. But the truth is I've never in my life been a reader." Among the things that she had not read, she astonishingly confessed, was the old *Artforum* itself. Until she became editor, seven years ago, she would buy the magazine but not read it. "Even now, if I wasn't forced to edit them, I probably wouldn't read some of the things we publish," she said. This confession followed a confession of my own about finding much of the magazine unreadable. Sischy was sympathetic. "It's always been a problem, this troublesome writing we print," she said. "The bigger question is: How does one write about art? That's what the magazine has been struggling with—probably quite disastrously, in the end—for twenty-two years. How does one write about something that is basically mute? Any cliché about *Artforum* is always about its problem with writing. That is probably why I was brought in as editor—because I found much of *Artforum* unreadable myself. I never used to read the magazine, and when I look back I must have been mad to take on the job of editing this thing I couldn't read. It was like a penance for all those years of not reading it. And I still have the problem, which may be why the magazine is so damn nervous inside itself. That's why you see so many different kinds of writing in it. An object lesson I keep before me all the time is that of my mother, who picks up *Artforum*, who is completely brilliant, sophisticated, and complex, who wants to understand—and then *closes* it."

There is one contributor to the summer issue about whom Sischy can feel easy, whose article will come in exactly on time, will not require all-night editing, and will never be anything less than a piece of workmanlike prose. This is Carter Ratcliff, who, like Ricard, is identified as a poet at the end of his articles in *Artforum* but is as far from the flamboyant Ricard as one can get. Ratcliff is cool, detached, impassive, reserved, rational, elliptical, grudgingly kind, pale—a sort of Alan Ladd of art criticism. He has written about art for more than fifteen years, has published five book-length critical studies, five monographs, and two books of verse, and has taught modern art and criticism at Pratt, the School of Visual Arts, and Hunter. He is forty-five years old. His loft, on Beaver Street, is as clear and clean and uncluttered as the man. When I visit it, a few days after the dinner with Ricard, it has the appearance of a place that someone has just moved into and hasn't furnished yet, but Ratcliff mentions that he and his wife have lived there for a year. There is a new, highly polished light wood floor, two off-white sofas facing each other across a pale wood coffee table, a dining table and chairs at a remove, and nothing else. Ratcliff's study, filled with books and papers, looks more inhabited. Ratcliff offers no refreshment, and we sit and talk, facing each other on the two sofas.

Ratcliff writes for *Art in America* as well as for *Artforum*, and I ask him whether there is any difference in the way he writes for each. He says, "Yes. My tone for *Artforum* is less formal. At *Art in America*, there is an ideal of responsible, properly organized, moderately political writing with a moderate tone—a kind of standard essay style that has survived into the present and that Ingrid simply isn't interested in. I find it annoying sometimes, but its influence isn't all that bad. I think, for example, that the Frank Stella piece I wrote for *Art in America* was far more convincing than the piece I did on Andy Warhol for *Artforum*, because I took more care to argue points in the Stella piece, whereas in the Warhol piece I felt freer to simply make assertions, or argue from an attitude, or have prejudices—as opposed to substantiating everything in a responsi-ble manner. I'm not sure that in a collection of my pieces one could tell which article was written for which magazine. Maybe one could. But when I'm writing for *Artforum* I feel free to write in a way that is more direct and more responsible to what I feel and less respon-sible to some standard of rationality."

I ask, "Does this sense of permission to write more freely and less responsibly come from Ingrid directly, or do you get it from reading people like Ricard in the magazine and feeling, Well, if they can write like that so can I?"

"Both are true," Ratcliff says. "Just from reading the magazine, one gets the sense that Ingrid is encouraging individual voices. But, also, when Ingrid is talking over a project with you or going over a text, often what she wants you to leave out is art-historical substan-tiation of a point, or an extended description. I'm fascinated by that absurdity—trying to describe what a painting is like. Both the de-scription of art and the invocation of historical evidence are a kind of striving for proof: not direct proof, but an attempt to impart an air of scientific rationality to one's writing—you know, all the apparatus of sounding as though you knew what you were talking about. But Ingrid is not interested in that. She's interested in an as-sertion of a point of view and in a tone of voice and in one's feeling about things. When we were going over the Warhol piece, I remem-ber her saying it was too smooth. She was afraid that people wouldn't get the point. What she wanted to do in the editing was to leave things out and have it be a little choppier—to sort of wake up the reader, to have him make more leaps. I think she sees art writing as something declamatory and gestural; her ideal is not that of the well-wrought essay. She has a feeling that art-world readers need to be jolted, that they're not literary readers. I don't think she sees this as a fault on the part of art-world readers or writers. It's just that that's the way it is—it's basically a visual world, with visual con-cerns. Her own orientation is visual, and that strongly affects her idea of what is acceptable as a piece of writing. In a certain way, I think that Rene Ricard is the writer closest to Ingrid's vision of the magazine. I think she feels that *Artforum*'s function is to be on the spot when something newly pertinent pops up, and I think she feels that you can't, on the spot, come up with a considered argument about anything new. You can only say things that point in interesting ways. You can only strike illuminating postures in the vicinity of things. The sorts of things that she's interested in are not yet subjects for the responsible treatment they will eventually get in other magazines. She feels that *Art in America* is the magazine that stands off a little to the side and tries to get a rational view of things, while *Artforum* is more on the spot. She feels that it's not a problem if something sounds silly—that *Artforum* is a place where this kind of risk can be taken, where this kind of irresponsibility is possible. When everything is new and in flux, the writing should reflect that. It's not that she cultivates irrationality for its own sake; it's that she tries to deal with things very intensely and fully, still leaving them in their immediate state.

"I don't do that myself, so it's presumably not the only thing she's interested in. But it's what is at the center of the magazine. Rene Ricard and Edit deAk really keep track of the art world. They really know what's going on. There are other people who keep obsessive track of that world, but only within the framework of that tiny world itself, and they're very boring. Rene Ricard and Edit deAk, in their strange ways, are connected to many other worlds as well—a bewildering variety of them, especially in Ricard's case—and that's where their criticality comes in: from being outside. Ricard lives in a very strange world, with all kinds of very strange people. He is an ex-Warhol person, and his world is one I don't know very much about. He seems to have a strong art-historical background. And also—it's all very eccentric—he is involved with the side of the art world that has to do with collecting. All his personalities are available at once, so you get this strange refraction. What holds it all together, it seems, is the sort of ecstatic, fanlike involvement he has with one thing or another from moment to moment, so that his obsessions kind of recapitulate the whole art world. He's impossible, he's hopeless. He is someone who is always connected to someone else. There used to be Warhol; now there's Ingrid."

"He's supposed to be an important figure in the art world," I say. "But I find his significance elusive."

"Yes, very. Because you can't ever find the center of a Rene Ricard article. I'm not sure I know what he's talking about a lot of the time. He's this kind of gestural presence—the spirit of the new painting. And it's not just a question of someone coming along and saying that the new painting is great, because others have done that, and they don't occupy Ricard's position. These gestures he makes in the vicinity of the new painting seem to reflect something about it, seem to illuminate it in some way. He's a kind of messenger figure: he's bringing us news about the new painting, assuring us of its significance, or at least making a very strong claim for it. I think he's important, because if there hadn't been this irrational love that he, and maybe deAk, expressed for the new painting—and by 'irrational' I mean a love based not on argument and sober judgment, but just on this really flamboyant embrace—then people's suspicions that the new painting is empty and calculating and manipulative might be stronger. I am almost swayed by Rene Ricard. I don't know him, and I don't pay all that much attention to him. But I do pause at the spectacle of his mad love for this new painting. I don't quite see it—I mean, I think that in many ways Schnabel's painting is banal and predictable—but the presence of Rene Ricard calls my judgment into question in some way.

"The other thing I think is important about Ricard is that he represents a kind of sordidness that it's important for the art world to believe it is still capable of. The art world is supposed to be alienated, to be on the periphery—and it's not. In fact, it's very much integrated into the mainstream of culture. It's not that most people like art; rather, it's that the art world has found a secure place in ordinary life—which goes against all the avant-garde's claims to being adventurous and in opposition. At a time when artists bring in architects to design their lofts, a flaky character like Ricard is very important. He makes it more believable that art is odd and weird and challenging."

Thomas Lawson is another of Sischy's more dependable and quiet writers—personally quiet, that is. His writing is tough, sharp, hard-hitting, very cold-eyed. In the November 1984 issue of *Artforum*,

Lawson published a short article ironically entitled "Hilton Kramer: An Appreciation," which had nothing good to say about Kramer. In one of its milder passages, Lawson wrote: "Kramer and the *Times* were a formidable combination. There, on a regular basis, he could press the authority of his opinions on those who were unable or unwilling to think for themselves; there his forceful mediocrity found its most congenial home." Earlier, in a piece published in the October 1981 issue of *Artforum* entitled "Last Exit: Painting," Lawson had not scrupled to attack a fellow contributor to *Artforum*:

> Rene Ricard, writing in these pages on Julian Schnabel, has offered petulant self-advertisement in the name of a reactionary expressionism, an endless celebration of the author's importance as a champion of the debasement of art to kitsch, fearful that anything more demanding might be no fun. The writing was mostly frivolous, but noisy, and must be considered a serious apologia for a certain anti-intellectual elite.

Lawson is a calm, fresh-faced, somewhat burly thirty-five-year-old Scotsman with a very level gaze, who came to New York in 1975 to pursue a career as an artist. During a conversation with him, I ask how he got into art criticism, and he replies, "Desperation. When I first arrived here, there was apparently no space for younger artists. There was a real doctrinaire thing going on. Every gallery was selling and every magazine was covering something called postminimalism. Postminimalism was very systematic and black and low performance, which was fine, but it was the only game in town. I began to meet other younger artists who had also just arrived and were also dissatisfied; the connective tissue between us was an interest in mass media. We felt that TV and the movies and advertising presented a problem and a challenge to visual artists that these postminimalists were avoiding. What we did, first of all, was to perversely deny ourselves originality of any kind—and this denial runs the gamut of all young artists working today. Even artists who are not directly involved in appropriating mass-media imagery—Julian Schnabel, for instance—refuse to accept the idea that you have to invent. There is something melancholy about our work. If pop art represented a kind of optimistic acceptance of mass culture, ours is a kind of melancholic acceptance. We never had coherence as a movement. For some reason, this generation has a particularly high incidence of extreme individualism and of paranoia about one's peers. So there has never been much of a group. This all took place after 'the death of painting.' We had all been schooled in the idea that painting was finished, and the second perverse thing we did was to decide to paint. Since there's a deadness to mass-media imagery, there was a fittingness to our decision to work in a medium that we didn't have all that much conviction about. But, interestingly, once you start working in it you become more and more convinced by it. All these years later, painting actually seems interesting in itself, rather than a mere perverse challenge.

"Anyway, I started writing reviews for *Art in America* because I was so irritated with the situation. And soon I got a little name for myself as someone who could write quite acerbically about older art, who would throw a negative light on what was being shown, and who was something of a participant-champion of the new art. But then I had a falling-out with *Art in America*, though not to the point of exchanging words. David Salle and Cindy Sherman had shows that I desperately wanted to write about but wasn't allowed to, and I began to feel used, I began to feel like a hired gun. I'm really quite good at cutting away the pretensions that accrue around a body of work, and I had done this to some established artists, which was obviously what they liked at *Art in America*. But it wasn't exactly what I wanted to base a career on. My whole intention had been to be more constructive, and suddenly, with these two shows I wanted to do, I found myself being denied the opportunity. There had been a misperception at *Art in America* of my relations with Sherman and Salle—with whom I was neither friendly nor unfriendly. I do have sympathy for their work—I don't see anything wrong with that. I'm an advocate of partisan criticism. Most art writing is from an insider point of view; there is very little that has an Olympian distance. I remember once reading something about Harold Schonberg, the music critic of the *Times*—about a deadly, life-denying thing he did. He forbade himself any personal contact with musicians, on the ground that it might influence his judgment. He wouldn't even let his wife, who was a musician, have anything to do with them. Apart from the horror of that on the human level, I think it's just crazy. You learn so much by knowing what in fact musicians and artists are actually thinking about and talking about, instead of pretending to drop in from the sky."

Of his work with Sischy, Lawson says, "She's almost chameleon-like. When I talk to her, we appear to be in complete agreement. But then an issue of *Artforum* comes out and—" Lawson gestures his feeling of betrayal. He goes on to describe a strange evening he once spent at the old *Artforum* office, on Mulberry Street (it recently moved to Bleecker Street), working with Sischy late into the night on an article about to go to press, and being acutely conscious of the presence of Rene Ricard in another room. Sischy was like a doctor going back and forth between patients in cubicles. "She would spend half an hour with me, and be extremely helpful and sympathetic, and then she'd get up and say, 'I have to go and see how Rene is doing,' and presumably she'd be equally helpful and sympathetic to him," Lawson says. "There was no communication between Rene and me. We can barely talk to each other anyway, we're so opposed in our opinions and our lifestyles. But Ingrid could move back and forth between us all night with ease. The Feast of San Gennaro was going on that night, and all that fairground noise outside—the firecrackers and the hawkers and the vendors—only accentuated the feeling of unreality which that night with Rene had for me."

For the past seven years Lawson has been publishing a small art magazine of his own, called *Real Life*, with grants from the National Endowment for the Arts and the New York State Council on the Arts, which reflects, in its unpretentious format and its radical critical content, the no-frills avant-gardism of its editor. The following excerpt from an interview by Rex Reason with Peter Nagy and Alan Belcher, the directors of the Nature Morte Gallery, in the East Village, gives some sense of *Real Life*'s tone:

RR: You guys are so modern. What do you look for in an object? What qualities?

AB: Right now we like either black, white, or gray, or generic color.

PN: We're pretty anti-color.

RR: By generic you mean red as "red" rather than modulations of it?

AB: Yeah.

PN: So many people bring us slides that are just like Salle, Basquiat, or Roberto Juarez. These poor kids are out there going to the galleries and they say, "This is what I have to do to have a show." So they run home and paint them. We don't want that—we want stuff we've never seen in a gallery before.

RR: And what do you think is the best art? What influenced the shaping of your taste?

AB: Right now, we like pretty classic late modern stuff: Pop Art, Paolozzi, Indiana for logos, Duchamp, Manzoni, Beuys, Klein. Scarpitta's a favorite of mine.

PN: We think Op Art is highly underrated. Bridget Riley. That's corporate psychedelia, the orgasm of modernism.

AB: We started the gallery because we really just wanted to get our voices in.

PN: And chose the name "Nature Morte" for its Fifties-jazz, pseudo-continental appeal. Ersatz European. Franco-American Chef Boy-ar-dee.

AB: We wanted to be the Leper Gallery.

PN: But then I thought of the Wallet Gallery.

After her three nights of ministering to Ricard at his place on Twelfth Street, Sischy begins a similar series of vigils with Thomas McEvilley at his place, on Clinton Street near Houston. I attend one of these sessions, which begins in the late afternoon and goes on until two or three in the morning. (I do not last the course.) McEvilley is a thin, bearded man, harried-looking but cheerful, who wears old corduroys during the day and in the evening often appears in a dashing white suit that he bought in a secondhand-clothing store. As I look around his place, I am struck by its peculiar combination of poverty and electronics, which speaks of our coming predicament with a kind of satiric authority. The apartment is a former ground-floor shop, and McEvilley has painted over the show window jutting out into the street, both for privacy and in order to have more wall space for books: the tiny room is entirely lined with books in cheap commercial cases. It has a lairlike aspect. There is an orange shag rug on the floor, and the furniture is four chairs of the sort you see thrown out on the street. But on a huge desk near the ex-window is a word processor; classical music is playing from an advanced stereo system; and there is an electric coffeemaker on a rickety side table, in which McEvilley's girlfriend, Maura Sheehan, prepared an odd herbal drink before leaving for her studio—an identical space across the hall—where she is painting classical Greek-vase motifs on cracked automobile windshields.

McEvilley, as he once told me, sort of drifted into art criticism. He is a classicist by training (he has a Ph.D. in Greek and Latin) and some years ago shifted from the Classics Department of the University of St. Thomas to the Art and Art History Department of Rice University, in Houston, to which he actually commutes from New York during part of the school year. Before his critique of the primitivism show, he had done pieces on the conceptual artists Yves Klein, Marina Abramović and Ulay, and James Lee Byars, as well as an article called "Art in the Dark," about extreme types of performance artists, among them people who subject themselves to very unpleasant ordeals, such as spending five days and nights in a two-by-three-foot locker without food, or sitting on a shelf in a gallery for twenty-two days. McEvilley said that he had dabbled in the genre himself, "but strictly as ordeal, not in an art context." He told me that he had spent a year sleeping only four hours a night—a notion he had got from Buddhist monks—and that he had also experimented with fasting, vegetarianism, and meditation. However, one day he had caught himself feeling superior to other people because of these activities and had decided to curb them.

McEvilley began writing for Sischy's *Artforum* in 1981. "In the seventies, I couldn't stand the magazine," McEvilley said. "It was promoting minimal art in overwhelming doses, and it had forced reductionist art modes on everybody with its aggressive ideological stance. Its power was undeniable—everyone knew the term *Artforum*

Mafia, and used it." (A disaffected member of the Family—Max Kozloff, the critic and editor, now turned photographer—once spoke to me in a similar vein about the old *Artforum*. "The magazine was looked upon with a kind of delirious bitterness," he said. "It solaced the readership to know that there were people of such self-confidence and commitment at the helm, rendering such zippy and righteous judgments right and left. But if you were an artist they were not interested in—and they were interested in a very few artists, about whom they wrote repeatedly—then you found this a repellent phenomenon. You were put off by this *camarilla* of king-makers and bully boys—or, as the case may be, bully women— who wrote in a hermetic language that they were partially inventing and who took themselves with ultra-seriousness. They used to say that *Artforum* was like Listerine: it tasted terrible, but it was good for you.")

McEvilley went on to speak of Sischy's ideological suppleness. "She's very sensitive to the Frankfurt school's perspective on the social function of art, and she wants to maintain that perspective in the magazine. But she has gone far beyond what I see as the naive hostility of the old regime to the art market—a hostility that I myself used to share, I should add. I came to the magazine with a poet's or a scholar's or a philosopher's antagonism to the market process. But Ingrid has pointed out to me very intelligently that in the past fifteen years, as the major New York museums have withdrawn from what is happening in art, serious dealers have become terribly important. They are the people who nurture contemporary art and bring it to us."

Now I sit in a corner of McEvilley's living room diligently jotting down snatches of the inscrutable dialogue going on between him and Sischy at the desk, punctuated by long silences while McEvilley works at the word processor.

"Is the idea that selfsameness is the only reality? I don't think so."

"Can I get rid of it?"

"Let's see. Later it becomes clear that . . . Okay, let's take the sentence out."

"Okay."

" 'Preemptively.' What do you mean, 'preemptively'?"

McEvilley goes to the word processor and unknots a sentence. Sischy looks it over. "It now reads as if Beuys is mad because Duchamp got there first."

The telephone rings. McEvilley picks it up and hands it to Sischy. It is Ricard. Sischy speaks to him in a motherly way. She explains, as if speaking to a child, that she is busy at the moment. "Rene, you *knew* I was going to be working with Tom." She listens to him talk at length, occasionally interjecting a "Great!" or a "Beautiful!" As soon as she can, she ends the conversation and returns to the manuscript.

"Is Rene okay?" McEvilley asks.

"Yes."

"I thought he looked a little freaked the other day."

"Maybe he didn't have enough sleep," Sischy says, with the dryness that I have come to recognize as her characteristic response to an invitation to be indiscreet.

A few days later I run into Ricard himself at the recently opened Palladium discotheque. The place is the creation of the former owners of Studio 54, Steve Rubell and Ian Schrager, who, after finishing jail sentences for tax evasion, hired the eminent advanced Japanese architect Arata Isozaki to turn the old Academy of Music, on Fourteenth Street, into a state-of-the-art discotheque, and the result is now being hailed as an improbable triumph of architecture, art, and chic by the city's architecture critics, art critics, and arbiters of chic. The young artists who have done paintings on the walls and ceilings of the Palladium's various rooms and corridors—Francesco Clemente, Keith Haring, Kenny Scharf, and Jean-Michel Basquiat—are receiving renewed, wondering notice as nouveau riche media stars from a press apparently still haunted by the idea of a revolutionary, marginal avant-garde; and the Palladium itself is being viewed as a kind of metaphor for the current state of art—the implosion of high and low culture into ever more grungily demotic and sleekly marketable forms. On this night, the Palladium has been turned over to a party for Keith Haring, and it is filled with beautifully and/or weirdly dressed people from the art world and its periphery. I come upon Ricard in a room that is apart from the discotheque proper, called the Mike Todd Room, which has a large bar, small marble-topped tables, and wire-back chairs, and is where the celebrities of the art world like to congregate. Ricard, resplendent in a white sharkskin suit, is sitting at one of the tables in a state of high, almost incandescent excitement. As I glimpse him, I recall a passage, in a recent *Art in America* article on Watteau by the art historian Linda Nochlin, about the painting of the clown Gilles in the Louvre:

> You can see *Gilles* as a small, vague, white glow shining in the distance. As you draw nearer, the glow assumes a shape, a significance, and, finally, a vast authority. Grand in scale, looming in its frontal pose, half-sacred in its silky whiteness, it becomes the famous *Gilles*, Christ-like in his innocent exposure to the gibes of the crowd, the very prototype of the tragic clown, the clown with the broken heart, avatar of Pierrot Lunaire, *He Who Gets Slapped*, and Prince Myshkin—that whole galaxy of more or less holy fools whose existence has marked the art, literature, and film of the modern period.

Ricard beckons me to sit with him, gives orders for drinks to a passing waiter, and points out celebrities as they go by. "Isn't she *pretty*," he says of Marisol. Of another well-known artist he says, "He's a closet queen," adding, "*I'm* no closet queen." The poet Allen Ginsberg pauses at the table to chat with Ricard, and after he leaves, Ricard grumbles about what he took to be a piece of prospective *schnorring* on Ginsberg's part when he looked longingly at our drinks. Several times, I get up to leave, and each time Ricard clamps a hand on my arm. "So, what I was about to say," he begins, and I am obliged to stay. I ask him whether he has been writing poetry, and he replies, "The manuscript of my new poems is in Julian Schnabel's safe. If you want to read them, go to Julian's house, get the manuscript, strap it to your person, and have it xeroxed." As Ricard speaks, he keeps scanning the crowd for people he knows. I counterpropose that Ricard himself go to Schnabel's house and get the poems out of the safe. "Or are you too busy?" "I have too much to do, and I have nothing to do," he replies. I laugh and once again get up to leave, and once again I am prevented from doing so by Ricard's desperate clutch. I don't know why he wants me to stay—and I don't know why I do stay. I only know that I am drawn to this Factory-made Myshkin; he is an oddly familiar, possibly anachronistic figure. In his "Not About Julian Schnabel," Ricard wrote about a kind of line that "just gets tuckered out after a while," adding, "The beautiful charcoal smudges and style we can follow from Matisse through de Kooning to Rivers, Serra, and, in its ultimate decadence, to Susan Rothenberg are perfect illustrations." He went on, "Judy Rifka told me that when she was in art school all her teachers drew that way. That was the way you were taught, and no matter how lousy the drawing was, it always looked pretty good, like 'art.' " The conventional bohemianism that Ricard embodies may be going the way of the art line he so tellingly describes.

I receive an acute sense of the newer bohemianism during two visits I pay to the artist Sherrie Levine—first to her studio, in Little Italy, and then to her apartment, a few blocks away. The studio, on the second floor of a small, run-down commercial building, is a twelve-by-seven-foot room that has nothing in it but a table, four chairs, and a fan. If you know Levine's work, the studio is not a surprise, but a kind of inevitability. She is a conceptual artist, and the conception for which she first became known, in the early eighties, is a series of twenty-one photographs entitled *After Walker Evans.* The photographs bear an uncanny likeness to the famous Farm Security Administration photographs that Evans took of tenant-farmer families in Hale County, Alabama; in fact, they *are* those photographs. Levine wrote away for copies of the Evans photographs to the Library of Congress, which owns the negatives; had them recopied at a commercial lab; and then—following Duchamp—made them her own work simply by signing them. If Duchamp's signed urinals and snow shovels and bicycle wheels redefined art as whatever somebody designates as art, Levine absurdly extended the world of objects that are potential ready-mades to include already designated works of art. *After Walker Evans* was succeeded by an *After J.M.W. Turner* series, which was exhibited in London in 1984; it consisted of twenty color reproductions of paintings by Turner that Levine had cut out of an art book, signed, and had matted and framed. When I visit Levine in her studio, she is engaged in a third technique of appropriation: she is tracing reproductions of drawings and paintings by Matisse, Schiele, Léger, and Morandi and then adding washes of watercolor.

Levine is a pleasant, unmannered woman in her late thirties, with dark, wavy hair, wearing a denim shirt and a gathered skirt, who delivers difficult explanations of her work with such an air of directness and naturalness as to almost cause one to feel that what she is saying is self-evident. Distinguishing between the rephotographed works and the cutout works, she says, "I used to think that the cutout things were the more extreme, but now I think that the rephotographed things are more transgressional. They're more mine. Ultimately, though, all my work is a feminist statement. It deals with the difficulty of being a woman who is trying to create images that are not a product of the expectations of male desire, in a culture that is primarily a celebration of male desire. What I do is to come at the problem through the back door; I appropriate images of male desire as a way of not being co-opted by that desire. I appropriate only the great modern male masters, and I choose only works that I love and value."

We are talking in Levine's apartment, on the fifth floor of an untended tenement—a single long room of bare-boned plainness, where she lives alone, with her cat. There is a bathtub in the kitchen area, and the sparse furniture has a bleak, cast-off character. We sit at the far end of the room, near the windows, in an area of incongruous conventional decorativeness—at a pale wood table on which a vase of flowers and a spread of bread and cheese and Granny Smith apples has been pleasingly set out. The walls of the room are painted a dull gold. "When I moved in, I painted the walls this way, under the mistaken idea that it would make the place less depressing," Levine says. "It looks more depressing."

"I have heard your work described as melancholy, as a sort of depressed expression of the feeling that there is nothing left to do," I say.

"I wouldn't deny that there is a sadness in the work," Levine says, "though I don't think that's all there is."

"Do you feel that at another time you might have been doing work of your own instead of appropriating the work of others?"

"Or not working at all. I might have been raising babies. I don't have any feeling of destiny about doing this, but it's a choice I've made. I've been an artist since I was a very young child. My mother gave me crayons to keep me quiet. It was an activity that has always emotionally sustained me. I enjoy the solitude of it. There was a period in which I considered becoming a filmmaker—I was very tempted because in some ways movies are my first love—but then I realized that the communal activity of filmmaking was very different from the solitary activity of making a painting."

"With the tracing and painting you're doing now, you seem to be working your way back into conventional art making."

"Well, I never thought that what I was doing was anything *but* that. That's the irony. I have always regarded my work as conventional art objects. They are always presented that way—matted and framed. I have never considered myself anything but a gallery artist. Several years ago, some friends of mine were in Holland, and they were really excited because they saw this show and thought it was my show, and then realized that it was a Walker Evans show. Or sometimes I'm looking through a magazine, and I think, Oh, great, they've reproduced an image of mine, only to see that it's a real Matisse, not one of my appropriations. When I first started doing the appropriative work, a lot of the criticism written about it—much of it in *October*—was based on ideas of the Frankfurt school of philosophy, but somehow I felt that these sociological explanations coming out of Marx were insufficient. I had the intuition that if I started reading psychoanalytic theory I might find more satisfying explanations. Appropriating art is not all that different from wanting to appropriate your father's wife or your mother's husband. It's the same psychological mechanism: the Freudian idea that desire is triangular—you desire what the other desires."

"Are you able to support yourself from your work?"

"For the past few years, I have been. But it's been a long time coming. I'm thirty-nine years old. Previously, I did waitressing, commercial art, some teaching. At that time, my support systems were critical rather than financial. *October* was the earliest of these systems." Levine goes to a ramshackle metal cabinet and brings out some xeroxes of writings about her work that appeared in *October* and elsewhere, along with some statements that she wrote herself to accompany exhibitions of her work. The statements are stiff and portentous. When, later in the conversation, Levine remarks that she is attracted to the painters of the sublime but can't conceive of herself doing such work, because "I just can't take myself that seriously," I tell her of my sense of the discrepancy between herself and the forbidding writer of the statements, who seems able to take herself *very* seriously.

Levine says, "I know. Many people have said they were surprised when they met me—how different I was from the writer of those statements. The tone of those things isn't right. I guess I get intimidated when I'm faced with writing."

One of Levine's early statements—quoted in part by Douglas Crimp in a 1980 article in *October*—has an arrestingly different character:

Since the door was only half closed, I got a jumbled view of my mother and father on the bed, one on top of the other. Mortified, hurt, horror-struck, I had the hateful sensation of having placed myself blindly and completely in unworthy hands. Instinctively and without effort, I divided myself, so to speak, into two persons, of whom one, the real, the genuine one, continued on her own account, while the other, a successful imitation of the first, was delegated to have relations with the world. My first self remains at a distance, impassive, ironical, and watching.

The surprise of this passage is followed by an even more astonishing revelation by Crimp: "Not only do we recognize this as a description of something we already know—the primal scene—but our recognition might extend even further, to the Moravia novel from which it has been lifted. For Levine's autobiographical statement is only a string of quotations pilfered from others."

Sherrie Levine's bleak little conceits have stirred the imaginations of some of the art world's most advanced thinkers. Rosalind Krauss, at the end of the extraordinary title essay of her book *The Originality of the Avant-Garde and Other Modernist Myths*, in which she magisterially makes her way (with a few French litter-bearers) through the thicket of the discourse on originality set in motion by Walter Benjamin's essay "The Work of Art in the Age of Mechanical Reproduction," holds up Levine's purloined photographs as a kind of master trope of postmodernism. Another theorist—the critic Benjamin H. D. Buchloh—in an *Artforum* article entitled "Allegorical Procedures: Appropriation and Montage in Contemporary Art," compliments Levine on being "the strongest negation within the gallery framework of the re-emergent dominance of the art commodity," adding, "Her work, melancholic and complacent in defeat, threatens within its very structure, mode of operation, and status the current reaffirmation of individual expressive creativity and its implicit reaffirmation of private property and enterprise." Buchloh goes on to say, "Baudelaire was wrong when he argued that the poetical was necessarily alien to female nature since melancholy was outside the female emotional experience. Enter the female dandy, whose disdain has been sharpened by the experience of phallocratic oppression, and whose sense of resistance to domination is therefore more acute than that of her male colleagues, if they still exist."

Julian Schnabel is believed to be the richest artist working in New York today (there are waiting lists for his paintings), so I am not surprised to learn—when Sischy takes me on a visit to his studio on White Street—that this is only an auxiliary studio to the main one, on Twentieth Street. (There is a third studio at Schnabel's country place, on Long Island.) Schnabel is a large, broad-shouldered man of thirty-five, with a fresh, clear, ruddy face, a direct gaze, and a natural, simple, friendly manner that inclines toward good-natured kidding. A pretty blond assistant meets us at the door and ushers us into a vast two-story loft, where Schnabel, who is wearing dark baggy trousers and a dark turtleneck sweater, awaits us. He leads us to one of two enormous paintings that are hanging loosely from beams high up and explains that it is painted on a tarpaulin from a truck that he came across on a trip to Mexico the previous year; the truck had broken down on the highway, and Schnabel bought the tarp from the driver for seventy dollars. "That's all I had on me—I would have given him more if I'd had it. I want you to look at those creases and folds, and at those patches." Schnabel adjusts lights to bring out the textures of the weatherworn brown tarp, on which he has painted, in broad strokes of white paint, a monstrous sort of primitive beast-man, with a leering face, an exposed rib cage, and a pair of clawlike extremities; at the top left, the letters "AZ" have been painted twice in red. In the late seventies, Schnabel began to attract notice with his "plate" paintings—he would affix a thick encrustation of crockery to the canvas before starting to paint—and the creased and patched tarpaulin is evidently another expression of his disinclination to start with a blank canvas (or, in Lawson's terms, to be original). An even more striking example of this refusal, which Schnabel shows us later at the main studio, is a series of paintings done on the stage sets of a Kabuki drama, which a friend sent him from Japan. These are six panels bearing delicately colored, stylized scenes of trees and flowers, over which, like a vandal, Schnabel has done brutish expressionist drawings in thick, dark strokes. If Sherrie Levine's reverent little thefts are "transgressional," what are we to call Schnabel's rude violations? As Schnabel directs a strong young assistant to turn the heavy Kabuki sets this way and that, he keeps up a line of easy, agreeable, anecdotal patter about his work. What he says doesn't make too much sense; it isn't "hard," it's just talk— one has to say something to people who come to one's studio. Schnabel shows us an enormous amount of work—his output of the year—with the modestly pleased air of a successful entrepreneur. His energy and enterprise seem boundless; he tries all kinds of things in all kinds of figurative and abstract styles, and everything has a look of bigness and boldness and confidence. One work has a discrepant look of insignificance: it is a white shag rug on which a black-and-brown cross has been painted. I ask him about it, and he says something cheerfully vague about how the rug had been in a summerhouse he had rented and had got stained, so he bought it from the owner.

I recall the first time I met Schnabel, at the opening of the Museum of Modern Art's show of international contemporary painting, to which I had gone with Sischy: she and I were standing before a Schnabel abstraction—done on cowhide, with a pair of antlers sticking out of it—when Schnabel himself appeared. Positioning himself behind Sischy, with his hands on her shoulders, he gazed fondly at his work and said, "I bet you're the only person at this opening who is having her back rubbed by the artist whose picture she is standing in front of." Now, in the studio, he talks about the "objectness" of his work. I ask him if he is using the word in the sense in which Michael Fried used it in his famous essay "Art and Objecthood," first published in *Artforum* in 1967. Fried's difficult, profound meditation on the threat to art posed by what he called literalism (more commonly called minimalism) is a sort of culminating aria, sung from the ground with the knife in the chest, of the enterprise known as formalist art criticism. It is an extraordinary performance—written in the driest, densest, most disdainful language, and yet permeated by an almost hysterical emotionality. As Fried's argument develops, it becomes a kind of allegory of good and evil—good being modernist painting and sculpture, which seek to transcend or "defeat" their "objecthood" (the canvas and paint, or the stone, metal, or wood they are made of) and thus achieve the "presentness" of true art; and evil being literalist painting and sculpture, which embrace their objecthood and thus degenerate into the inartistic condition of "theater." Schnabel says he doesn't know Fried's essay and asks me what it is about. After I tell him, he nods, and says with devastating carelessness, "All that is the language of another generation. We don't use language like that today. We're a different generation. We're interested in different things."

Edit deAk lives on Wooster Street in a loft (clearly not designed by an architect) with a shabby, functional, and only slightly—and rather haphazardly—funky appearance. She herself is a striking, good-looking woman of thirty-eight, with shoulder-length bright-red hair worn in bangs, who dresses in vivid, interesting clothes that have a sense of quotation marks around them. She speaks with an

East European accent in a low, melodious voice, and as she speaks she has a trick of moving her stiffened right hand up and down in a tender chopping gesture. She likes to play Nabokovian games with language (her speech and writing are filled with terms like "ego beaver" and "tour de farce"), though when she did gallery reviewing for *Artforum* in the seventies, she curbed her Pninisms and confined herself to straight, opaque Artspeak. But now, under Sischy's permissive reign, she denies herself very little and writes pieces entirely composed of epigrammatic, near-scrutable paragraphs such as the following, which appeared in an article entitled "The Critic Sees Through the Cabbage Patch":

> In the contrast of scale, small imagery in large surroundings becomes all powerful when it is happening and speedily traversible when it is not. Tiny gland-sized figures, capable of being fondled, emphasize their secret porno charm as tiny emblems of hidden desires. Like makers of Oriental porn, the Italian telescopes, allures, and funnels with a sense of security in codes which give comfort like the reliable conventions of the geisha. The German closes up; shoved in your face is a violent eruption reflecting our Judeo-Christian body guilt. They just can't mix. Sandro Chia has spread his work too thick. Dial *Q* and *A* (like in Questions and Answers) for Quotation and Appropriation. Dial *T* for Terminal Terminology. Again the terms engender a limitation on thinking about the issues. "Quotation" is anchored as a quicky, and Appropriation as mere antics. These terms are not comprehensive enough to deal with the realm involved: it makes it all seem like a klatch of bourgeois plagiarisms. We should be contending with counterfeit gestalt (Gesamtkunstpatch, in cabbage-patch terms). Asking, where has the original of the whole world disappeared to? Has Rammellzee taken it to the Van Allen Belt?

During the seventies, deAk and Walter Robinson, an artist, coedited a magazine named *Art-Rite*, a messy, impudent sort of in-house organ of the New York avant-garde. Printed on newsprint, published irregularly, and run with a kind of ironic amateurism ("Unsolicited manuscripts are welcome, and you don't even have to enclose a self-addressed and stamped envelope to get them back," an editorial notice read), it observed the large and small movements of the advanced art scene of the seventies at a very close, somewhat blurring range. Although Sischy's *Artforum* is more formal, more professional, more like a real magazine than *Art-Rite* ever approached being, it has never entirely abjured the samizdat quality of *Art-Rite* and the other rakish little magazines of the period, such as *Heresies* and *Just Another Asshole*, whose spirit Sischy immediately recognized as her own. Attempting to characterize this spirit, and not doing too badly, Rene Ricard once remarked, "Ingrid put cheapness into *Artforum*." My own point of reference for the special demotic strain that runs through Sischy's magazine is the cover of the summer 1981 issue, which she herself conceived. Other Sischy covers have made a bigger stir—for example, a famous cover featuring a sulky model wearing a remarkable long black evening dress (by the Japanese designer Issey Miyake) whose bodice was a kind of rattan cage—but this one shows Sischy putting the cheapness into *Artforum* in a particularly artful way. At first sight, it looks like a work by a postmodern conceptualist; in fact, it is an arrangement of twelve blue-and-white paper take-out coffee containers. Eleven of them show a lumpish discus thrower posed beside a Doric column that supports a bowl containing the Olympic Flame; the twelfth container, centrally placed, is turned to show its other side, which bears the message IT'S OUR PLEASURE TO SERVE YOU. Ricard's piece "Not About Julian Schnabel" appeared in that issue, and while Sischy was selecting the illustrations for it, she was suddenly struck by the preposterous similarity between a Schnabel painting called *Blue Nude with Sword* and the picture on the coffee container she was drinking from; the cover was the result.

When I visit deAk in her loft, she brings out a bottle of wine and two glasses and says, "I always thought I did *Art-Rite* to defy the idea of art magazines. I spent the best years of my life doing it, for free. In my mind, it was a project to undermine art. Mine is an anarchistic, negative feeling. I don't believe in anything until it is proven—and I don't like proving. *Artforum* is a magazine that comes out every month. My mentality is not used to that. I spent my entire life not being anybody, defying schedules, not having a job. At a moment when you are what job you do, people are constantly saying to me 'Who are you?' and it's a question I can't answer."

Another of deAk's nonremunerative activities was serving on the board of Printed Matter, which is where she met Sischy. "Ingrid sort of stabilized everything at Printed Matter," deAk recalls. "She got it out of chaos, out of the bowels of the board. There's no 'no' to her. When she was at Printed Matter, the two of us used to go and see if we could get corporate support for certain projects. I'll never forget the time when we went to the Xerox Corporation, in Rochester. I got up that morning to dress, and I was scared to death. I didn't know how you go in to see a corporation, so I put on the best dress I thought I had—all frills and shiny—and I looked like some kind of overdressed person who hadn't gone home the night before. As for Ingrid, she was wearing this badly cut three-piece man's blue suit. We were staying with Ingrid's parents, and when Ingrid's mother saw us coming down the stairs in the morning, ready to go on our executive trip, she just broke down laughing.

"Ingrid's father is one of the three doctors I've met whom I actually think of as a human being. He considers the totality of a person. The mother is brilliant, kind of filigreed, and fast, but with a soft edge, never stabbing. They're radical thinkers. Their ideology is really complex. They know so much. Their way of thinking is so much more contemporary than mine that I would have expected them to be weirdos, but they're not. They're completely regular people; they completely fit into society. They're exquisitely civilized.

"I had written for *Artforum* for four or five years before Ingrid came, so I knew the other regimes, and they were very different. Ingrid centered the whole operation on herself. The previous editor didn't. He was a very quiet person who sat at his desk, and the office was very quiet, and the manuscripts came in. He regarded the job as, sort of, 'Okay, here is my desk, and here comes a manuscript, and I'll take care of it.' When Ingrid got into the office, there was no desk left unturned. She checked everything. The smallest note didn't leave that office without her checking it. She was even friends with the night cleaner. But when I say that she centered the whole operation on herself I don't mean that she was building herself up. If you look at the jobs that Ingrid has had, they were always concerned with the projects of others. She's just the opposite of a hustler. She's not going to hold up a cue card and say, 'This is what I am.' She will not guide you to her. She will show you the irrigated areas of the Nile. Her achievement is like that of the Nile—the fertilization of a certain area of culture."

A week after the summer issue has gone to press, Sischy takes me to the fifth-floor studio—in a commercial walk-up on Canal Street—of a pair of Russian-Jewish émigré artists named Alexander Melamid and Vitaly Komar, who collaborate on satiric paintings done in the style and employing the iconography of socialist realism. Melamid, a slight, thin, dark, quick man of around forty, wearing horn-rimmed glasses and jeans and running shoes, looks like any number of boyish New York Jewish or New York Italian men. Komar is fat, looks much older than Melamid but isn't, has a dark beard and small, cunning green eyes and red lips—a minor character out of Gogol, probably a horse trader.

The studio is bright, noisy from the traffic on Canal Street, and bare. Several large canvases are propped against a wall, their faces inward. (A year later, at a large SoHo gallery, I see them unveiled: brilliantly sharp-sighted pastiches of old, modernist, and last week's postmodernist paintings, with an occasional Stalin or Hitler thrown in as a kind of signature.) Komar and Melamid lead Sischy and me to a group of wooden chairs near the Canal Street window and bring a bottle of seltzer water and white plastic cups, and a basket of red apples that immediately evoke Mother Russia. After a minimal amount of desultory small talk, the two men abruptly plunge into a philosophical argument about the nature of time. Do we live in a space between past and future or are we perpetually in the past? Melamid argues that the present exists. No, Komar says, the present does not exist; there is only the past and the future. They argue back and forth, speaking very rapidly in accented English and gesticulating vehemently. Then, like a pair of house cats aimlessly walking away from a fight, they simply stop arguing. Melamid shrugs and says, "We always argue like this." Komar smiles benignly. He speaks worse English than Melamid, who often corrects his pronunciation in a brotherly way.

Melamid tells us of the great discovery that he and Komar made in Russia before emigrating here, in 1978. While other Russian artists publicly did socialist realism and secretly worked in advanced modernist styles, he says, "it dawned on us that socialist realism could itself be a vehicle for avant-garde art." Komar tells of an American friend in Russia who brought them a can of Campbell's soup as a work of conceptual art. "One day, there was nothing in the studio for a snack, so we ate the soup," he says. "It was not a bad snack." "It was bad," Melamid says. "It was not bad," Komar says. They start another animated debate, one that soon gets into art theory, the condition of art today, the situation of art in New York. As this argument, too, begins to peter out, Melamid sighs and says, "We sit here, and we talk, and I think, Where is *life* in all this? Life! Life! We go at things obliquely, to the side," making a gesture of ineffectuality with his hand, "instead of straight, like this," pounding his fist into his palm. He continues, emotionally, "Last year, I woke up in a hotel room in Amsterdam. There was a woman in my bed. I looked in the mirror and saw that my eyebrows were gray. I saw that I was forty."

You got that from Chekhov, I say to myself. I am no longer charmed by this pair. I find their performance tiresome, calculated. I look over at Sischy, who is enjoying herself, who thinks they are "great," and I ponder anew the question of authenticity that has been reverberating through the art world of the eighties. The feeling of mistrust that Komar and Melamid now arouse in me is the feeling that has been repeatedly expressed, within and without the art world, about the work of Julian Schnabel, David Salle, Francesco Clemente, Jean-Michel Basquiat, Keith Haring, Robert Longo, Cindy Sherman, and the other new stars who have emerged into prominence during the past five years. In a long poem, published in *The New York Review of Books* in March 1984, that was modeled on Pope's *Dunciad* and entitled "The Sohoiad: or, The Masque of Art, A Satire in Heroic Couplets Drawn from Life," Robert Hughes, the art critic of *Time*, brought this feeling to a brilliant, splenetic apogee. Lashing out at artists, dealers, critics, curators, and collectors alike, he offered a vision of the contemporary art world as a Bosch-like inferno of greed, fraud, hype, and vacuity. After dispatching "Julian Snorkel," "Jean-Michel Basketcase," "David Silly," and "Keith Boring," among others (and treating Snorkel—"Poor SoHo's cynosure, the dealer's dream, / Much wind, slight talent, and vast self-esteem"—with special savagery), Hughes went on to mordantly inquire:

> Who are the patrons whose indulgent glance
> The painter craves, for whom the dealers dance?
> Expunge, young Tyro, the excessive hope
> Of gathering crumbs from *Humanist* or *Pope*:
> No *condottiere* holds his exigent sway
> Like MONTEFELTRO upon West Broadway—
> Instead, mild stockbrokers with blow-dried hair
> Stroll through the *soukh*, and passive snuff the air.
> Who are the men for whom this culture burgeons?
> Tanned regiments of well-shrunk *Dental*
>   Surgeons . . .

When I showed the poem to Sischy, she was not amused. "Forgive my lack of a sense of humor," she said, "but what I see in that poem is just another reinforcement of stereotypes about the art world. It's like a Tom Stoppard play, where you have an entire Broadway audience snickering about things they haven't understood. It makes outsiders feel clever about things they know nothing about. *The New York Review* is a magazine I really respect—I respect its editors and I respect its audience—but this poem reflects the gap that exists between the serious literary audience and the serious art audience. Hughes's overwhelming message is that all of today's art is worthless, that the whole art world is a bunch of frauds and grotesques. I would agree with him that about half of what is being produced today is worthless, but I get worried when everything and everyone are lumped together and jeered at. That's too easy."

Sischy's fascination with what's difficult sometimes leads her into incoherence and opacity, as in a recent special issue of *Artforum* called "the light issue." It was conceived (according to an editorial by Sischy and Edit deAk) as a response to "the failure of the recent spate of big international shows to intelligently meet the development of contemporary art, and . . . their tendency instead to carelessly throw all 'the names' together in an expensive but cheap hanging spectacle of so-called international pluralism." The alternative it offered its readers was a survey of international art (the issue had no articles and was made up entirely of reproductions of paintings and photographs, some of them created specially for the issue) based on the common denominator of light. The issue left its readers utterly mystified. Since light, perforce, is the common denominator of *all* visual art, something other than the mere statement of this truism must have been intended—something less obvious and more particular to contemporary art—but to this day no one knows what it was. The light issue included, among other works, photographs by Joel Meyerowitz of moonlit water; ink-and-watercolor drawings by Agnes Martin of horizontal bands and lines; a neo-Expressionist painting by Enzo Cucchi of a piano playing itself on a vast white plain; a cryptic five-panel figurative work by Komar and Melamid; a foldout four-page spread by Francesco Clemente showing a pair of monstrous creatures emitting a sort of white gas from their posteriors; a photograph by Weegee of lightning in Manhattan; photographs of a set from Paul Schrader's film *Mishima*; a photograph of a starving African child vomiting. These were followed by a page of "shadow captions," whose explanatory texts only deepened the enigma of what all these works were doing together and what they were saying about light. The caption for Clemente's contribution, for example, read:

> The pink raybow of light dawns on you as the ribbon of the wrapping unfolds the tales of light about never being able to see all light at once. You can only get the heads and tails of this if you reshuffle the wrapping to cover the adjoining body of the riddle getting an ellipse of the senses; you have to have blindness to have insight.

The light issue has become a famous, interesting failure of Sischy's—people in the art community talk about it indulgently, as if speaking of the endearing foibles of a beloved, brilliant child. Sischy herself has no regrets about it, and of all the issues she has produced, it may be the one that most tellingly elucidates the character of her editorship. Its mysterious amorphousness is akin to her own boundless and restless energy. She is the Ariel of the art world, darting hither and yon, seeming to alight everywhere at once, causing peculiar things to happen, seeing connections that others cannot see, and working as if under orders from some Prospero of postmodernism, for whose Gesamtkunstpatchwork of end-of-the-century consciousness she is diligently gathering material from every corner of the globe as well as from every cranny of the East Village. Sischy not only travels to the big international art expositions, such as the Venice Biennale and the Kassel Documenta, but will impulsively get on a plane to check out a show in London or Paris that she thinks the magazine might want to review. She will spend a week in Spain or Italy recruiting reviewers and writers; she will fly out of town to give a talk at a museum or a university; she will journey to Japan on an exploratory mission for some possible future inscrutable special issue. While in New York, she tries to see as many as possible of the fifty or sixty gallery and museum shows that open every month, to attend as many openings and after-opening parties as possible, and to pay as many studio visits as she can.

During this ceaseless activity Sischy remains unhurried, relaxed, and strangely detached. "In a world where all kinds of people—from editors to curators to collectors to dealers—want control, where control is of the essence, she doesn't seem to want it," the critic Donald Kuspit observes to me over a drink at a bar near Gramercy Park. Kuspit is a fifty-one-year-old professor of art history at Stony Brook who has been writing art criticism of a dense prolixity for *Art in America*, *Arts*, and *Art Criticism*, as well as for *Artforum*, for the past dozen years. He goes on, "She's not looking to be the Archimedes of the art world, with a lever that can move it. I think one of the things she realizes is that that whole way of thinking is obsolete. She's smart. There's a kind of canniness to her, what Hegel calls 'the cunning of reason'—insofar as there *is* reason in the art world. Frankly, I think the art world would be a terrible place without her. It would be a macabre place. Even as it is, it's a dreadful place. The megalomania that is rampant among artists is unbelievable, and so is the self-importance. Bankers must be the same, but the cry for attention from artists—the ruthlessness of their sense of what is due them—is extraordinary. When I first moved to art criticism, which was a natural extension of my work with Adorno in critical philosophy, I had a great need to concretize the importance of art. Now I go through bouts of wondering whether art isn't just a matter of fashion and glamour. The artists are getting younger by the minute, and, increasingly, anything with a little flip to it gets visibility. It used to be that when art was made, people would be unsure of its value until—slowly, through all kinds of critical discourse and debate—the art would acquire cultural significance. And *only then* would people arrive with money and say, 'I want that.' Now—and I think this started with pop art—there's money waiting like a big blotter to blot up art, so that the slightest bit of inkiness is sponged up. That's a very hard thing to keep a distance from. In-grid walks around it. She doesn't let her magazine serve as a little subservient blotter for whatever powers there may be. She is fear-less. Nobody owns her, yet she doesn't give offense because of that. I'm not saying that the editors of the other art magazines are owned, but somehow this free-spiritedness seems a more vivid part of Ingrid—almost as if she doesn't want to be owned even by herself."

During the year that Sischy and I have been meeting for interviews, she has been unsparingly frank about herself. She has confessed to me her feelings of self-doubt and inadequacy, she has told me stories of rejection and mortification, she has consistently judged herself severely. At the same time, she has not been altogether uncritical of me. I have not lived up to her expectations as an interlocutor. She fears that I do not understand her. As I ponder this tension between us, a story that she told me early in our acquaintance comes back to me with special weight. It was an account of a small humiliation—one of those social slights that few of us have not in our time endured—that she had suffered the previous day at a public lunch honoring a sculptor who had done a work for the city. Sischy had sat down at a table next to a stranger, a sleek, youngish man who, as soon as they had exchanged names, turned away from her and began talking to the person on his other side. The guests at the lunch were from both the art world and the city government, and this man was a city politician. "He was clearly disappointed that someone who looked like me should have sat down next to him," Sischy told me. "I could see him thinking, What a waste of a lunch! I considered getting up and going to sit with some people I knew at another table, but then I thought, No, I'll stay here. A little later, a woman who had sat down on my other side asked me my name, and when I told her, she figured out who I was, and she was very interested. And then two people across from me figured me out, and they started talking to me. And eventually this guy, taking it all in, said, 'I'm terribly sorry—I didn't get your name.' So I told him again, and the woman beside me told him what I did, and his whole manner changed. He suddenly became very interested. But he'd lost me by then." Sischy told me this story with no special emphasis—she offered it as an example of the sexism that women still regularly encounter—but I obscurely felt it to have another dimension besides its overt one. Now, a year later, the latent meaning of the story becomes clear to me: it is a covert commentary on Sischy and me. I had formed the idea of writing about her after seeing *Artforum* change from a journal of lifeless opacity into a magazine of such wild and assertive contemporaneity that one could only imagine its editor to be some sort of strikingly modern type, some astonishing new female sensibility loosed in the world. And into my house had walked a pleasant, intelligent, unassuming, responsible, ethical young woman who had not a trace of the theatrical qualities I had confidently expected and from whom, like the politician at the lunch, I had evidently turned away in disappointment.

In a charming and artful essay of 1908 entitled "A Piece of Chalk," G. K. Chesterton writes about taking some brown paper and colored chalks to the Sussex downs on a fine summer day to do Chestertonian drawings of "devils and seraphim, and blind old gods that men worshipped before the dawn of right, and saints in robes of angry crimson, and seas of strange green, and all the sacred or monstrous symbols that look so well in bright colours on brown paper." But as he begins drawing, Chesterton realizes that he has

left behind "a most exquisite and essential" chalk—his white chalk.
He goes on:

> One of the wise and awful truths which this brown-paper art
> reveals is that . . . white is a colour. It is not a mere absence of
> colour; it is a shining and affirmative thing, as fierce as red, as
> definite as black . . . Virtue is not the absence of vices or the
> avoidance of moral dangers; virtue is a vivid and separate thing,
> like pain or a particular smell. Mercy does not mean not be-
> ing cruel or sparing people revenge or punishment; it means a
> plain and positive thing like the sun, which one has either
> seen or not seen. Chastity does not mean abstention from
> sexual wrong; it means something flaming, like Joan of Arc.
> In a word, God paints in many colours; but He never paints
> so gorgeously, I had almost said so gaudily, as when He paints
> in white.

Since Chesterton wrote these buoyant words, the world has seen
two world wars and a holocaust, and God seems to have switched to
gray as the color of virtue—or decency, as we are now content to
call it. The heroes and heroines of our time are the quiet, serious,
obsessively hardworking people whose cumbersome abstentions
from wrongdoing and sober avoidances of personal display have
a seemliness that is like the wearing of drab colors to a funeral. In
"Why I Write," George Orwell said, "In a peaceful age I might have
written ornate or merely descriptive books, and might have remained almost unaware of my political loyalties. As it is, I have been
forced into becoming a sort of pamphleteer." One feels about Sischy
that at another time she, too, might have been less grave, less morally weighted down, and more vivid. She told me that as a child she
had been extremely naughty and wild. What remains of this naugh-
tiness and wildness finds expression in the astonishing covers, the
assertive graphics, and the provocative special issues of *Artforum*.
Just as Sischy's personal muteness is the by-product of an Orwel-
lian sense of cultural crisis, so her vision of contemporary art is
shaped first by societal concerns and only secondarily by aesthetic
concerns. Her interest in the neo-Expressionist painting that is

coming out of Germany today, for example, is bound up less with the painting's aesthetic claims than with its reflection of the anguished attempt of young German artists and intellectuals to come to terms with the Nazi past. Sischy once said to me, "My greatest love is conceptual art. I may be even more interested in thinking than in art." She added, "Rene and I used to have an argument. He'd say something like, 'Well, that work is really beautiful,' and I'd say, 'So?' and he'd say, 'Well, you hate art if you say "So?" about something being beautiful,' and I'd say—and I've come to realize that it's more complicated than this—'Well, maybe I just hate art when the only thing going for it is that it's beautiful.'"

ADVANCED PLACEMENT

2008

As Lolita and Humbert drive past a horrible accident, which has left a shoe lying in the ditch beside a blood-spattered car, the nymphet remarks, "That was the exact type of moccasin I was trying to describe to that jerk in the store." This is the exact type of black comedy that Cecily von Ziegesar, the author of the bestselling Gossip Girl novels for teenage girls, excels in. Von Ziegesar writes in the language of contemporary youth—things are cool or hot or they so totally suck. But the language is a decoy. The heartlessness of youth is von Ziegesar's double-edged theme, the object of her mockery—and sympathy. She understands that children are a pleasure-seeking species, and that adolescence is a delicious last gasp (the light is most golden just before the shadows fall) of rightful selfishness and cluelessness. She also knows—as the authors of the best children's books have known—that children like to read what they don't entirely understand. Von Ziegesar pulls off the tour de force of wickedly satirizing the young while amusing them. Her designated reader is an adolescent girl, but the reader she seems to have firmly in mind as she writes is a literate, even literary, adult.

As the first book opens, Blair Waldorf—who is almost seventeen and lives in a penthouse at Fifth Avenue and Seventy-second Street with her divorcée mother, Eleanor, her younger brother, Tyler, and

---

The Gossip Girl novels by Cecily von Ziegesar

her cat, Kitty Minky—is sulking in her room. Blair, in the description of a classmate, is "the bitchiest, vainest girl in the entire senior class, or maybe the entire world" and an antiheroine of the first rank: bad-tempered, mean-spirited, bulimic, acquisitive, endlessly scheming, and, of course, dark-haired. The blond heroine, Serena van der Woodsen (who lives at an even better Fifth Avenue address, right across from the Metropolitan Museum), is incandescently beautiful, exceptionally kind, and, in the end, it has to be said, somewhat boring. The series belongs to awful Blair, who inspires von Ziegesar's highest flights of comic fancy.

Blair is sulking because her mother's new boyfriend, a Jewish real-estate developer named Cyrus Rose, "a completely annoying, fat loser," and her mother are in the kitchen eating breakfast in matching red silk robes. When dressed, Rose "looked like someone who might help you pick out shoes at Saks—bald, except for a small, bushy mustache, his fat stomach barely hidden in a shiny blue double-breasted suit. He jingled the change in his pocket incessantly . . . He had a loud laugh." *What?* We're only on page 6 and already reading about a fat, vulgar Jew! Doesn't von Ziegesar know that anti-Semitic stereotypes are no longer tolerated in children's literature? Of course she does. Cyrus Rose is only one among many tokens of her gleeful political incorrectness. An elderly guest speaker at Blair's high school graduation is another:

> "Auntie Lynn," some old lady who'd basically founded the Girl Scouts or something, was supposed to talk. Auntie Lynn was already leaning on her metal walker in the front row, wearing a poo-brown pantsuit and hearing aids in both ears, looking sleepy and bored. After she spoke—or keeled over and died, whichever came first—Mrs. McLean would hand out the diplomas.

Only someone very hard-hearted wouldn't laugh at this. The way von Ziegesar implicates us in her empathic examination of youth's callousness is the Waughish achievement of these strange, complicated books. And in Blair she has found a powerful pivot for her feat.

She has equipped this girl with an excess of the most unattractive but also perhaps most necessary impulses of human nature—the impulses that give us such up and go as we have. Unlike her forerunners Becky Sharp and Lizzie Eustace, who ruthlessly elbowed their way into wealthy aristocratic society, Blair already has all the money and position anyone could want. She is pure naked striving, restlessly seeking an object, any object, and never knowing when enough is enough. However—and, again, unlike her prototypes—Blair never harms anyone but herself. She thinks malevolent thoughts about everyone, but she does not act on them. It is her own foot that she invariably shoots. Her goals of the moment—to lose her virginity to her boyfriend, Nate Archibald, and to get into Yale University—elude her. Something always gets in the way of her doing it with Nate, and her Yale interview is a catastrophe beyond imagination.

Nate is a kind of Vronsky manqué, with a grande dame mother, like Vronsky's, and a navy-captain father who is "a master sailor and extremely handsome, but a little lacking in the hugs department." (Too bad Tolstoy didn't think of a father like that for V.) Nate "might look like a stud, but he was actually pretty weak." This is because he is stoned most of the time. He lives in a town house in the East Eighties and is a senior at St. Jude's, a private school that appears to be modeled on the Collegiate School, as Blair and Serena's school, Constance Billard, is modeled on von Ziegesar's old school, Nightingale-Bamford.

Unlike the actual private schools of New York, however, which give a fair number of scholarships to low-income minority students, von Ziegesar's private schools are almost a hundred percent minority-free. (I say almost because of Carmen Fortier, a scholarship girl from the Bronx, who appears—chewing gum—on page 86 of the first book of the series and is never seen again.) Of course, this glaring absence is necessary to von Ziegesar's program of provocation. She does not compromise it. There are no brussels sprouts hidden in her Rice Krispie marshmallow treats. She is writing a transgressive fairy tale, not a worthy book for a school reading list. "Welcome to New York's Upper East Side, where my friends and I live and go to school and play and sleep—sometimes with each other" is von Ziegesar's opening volley, delivered in the voice of an anonymous figure called Gossip Girl, who continues: "We all live in huge apartments with our own bedrooms and bathrooms and phone lines. We have unlimited access to money and booze and whatever else we want, and our parents are rarely home, so we have tons of privacy. We're smart, we've inherited classic good looks, we wear fantastic clothes, and we know how to party."

Von Ziegesar understands that the princes and princesses of fairy tales require the foil of beggars and commoners, and so, of her six main characters, only three—Blair, Serena, and Nate—belong to the world of the disgustingly rich. Of the others, two live on the wrong side of the Park, and one lives in Williamsburg. Dan and Jenny Humphrey share a decaying West End Avenue apartment with their father, Rufus, "the infamous retired editor of lesser-known beat poets," whatever that means, who goes around the house in his underwear and a three-day-old gray beard and cooks inedible tagines from Paul Bowles recipes. But he lacks nothing in the hugs department and, indeed, turns out to be the only attentive parent in the series. (He is also a single parent—his wife ran off to the Czech Republic "with some balding, horny count" a few years earlier.) He "hated the Upper East Side and all its pretensions," but he sends Jenny to Constance Billard and Dan to a private school called Riverside Prep because "the way he saw it, you had two choices in this city":

> Either you spent an arm and a leg to send your kids to private school, where they learned to shop for insanely expensive clothes and to be snobbish to their father, but also to converse in Latin, memorize Keats, and do algorithms in their heads; or, you sent them to public school, where they might not learn to read, might not graduate, and risked getting shot.

The question of where Rufus gets the money for the private school fees—and for the designer clothes that Dan and Jenny buy on his credit card as their lives intersect with those of the East Side kids—is left unanswered. Von Ziegesar has other concerns than writing books that make a lot of sense. Along with the pieties of political correctness, she has taken on the indecencies of consumer culture. Insanely expensive clothes are the engine of her send-up of our time of ceaseless shopping. There is scarcely a page on which the name of a fashion designer doesn't appear. The kids don't wear dresses and coats and pants and shoes; they wear Diane von Furstenberg dresses, Stephane Kélian shoes, Hugo Boss coats, Marc Jacobs shirts. If the book has any redeeming social value, it is as an education in label recognition. After reading the Gossip Girl books, you will never walk into a department store again without feeling a little surge of pride as you recognize Christian Louboutin and John Fluevog and Michael Kors—who are to their world what Marcel Proust and Henry James and Theodore Dreiser are to the bookish audience for whom von Ziegesar writes in the guise of writing for the pre-SAT young. The books are full of literary allusions: there are quotes from Wilde, Hemingway, Shakespeare, references to Goethe and Tolstoy, and chapters entitled "The Red or the Black" and "What We Talk About When We're Not Talking About Love."

Dan Humphrey is a caricature of the angst-ridden nerd who writes poetry. Dan's friend Vanessa Abrams is so taken with a poem of his, called "Sluts," that, behind his back, she sends it to *The New Yorker*, where it is immediately accepted by the magazine's revered (if imaginary) submissions editor, Jani Price. After the poem is published, Dan, who previously spent his after-school time in his room "reading morbid, existentialist poetry about the bitter fate of being human," becomes a star. He is courted by an agent. A rock band hires him to write lyrics. He starts shopping at Agnès B.

His sister, Jenny, is a shy ninth grader who "preferred to be invisible" and might have succeeded "if her boobs weren't so incredibly huge." She is a kind of stand-in for the eighth and ninth graders who read the Gossip Girl books, and who will identify with her innocent worship of the cool senior girls. But except for her boobs, she is not very interesting.

Vanessa is "an anomaly at Constance, the only girl in the school who had a nearly shaved head, wore black turtlenecks every day, read Tolstoy's *War and Peace* over and over like it was the Bible [and] had no friends at all at Constance." Her hippie parents, Arlo and Gabriela, who live in Vermont in a house made of recycled automobile tires, have allowed Vanessa to live in Williamsburg with her older sister Ruby, who plays bass in a rock band, on the condition that she get "a good, safe, high-school education." Writing of a visit the hippie parents make to New York, von Ziegesar fulfills her pact with youth to lose no opportunity to express the disgust it feels for the old and unbeautiful and deviant. She dresses the "gaunt and alarmed" Arlo in a Peruvian poncho and ankle-length hemp skirt ("Yes, that's right, a skirt") and the gray-braided Gabriela in a garish African schmatte and sends them off to an exclusive New York benefit. When Vanessa asks where the benefit is being held, Gabriela replies, "Somewhere called the Frick. It's on Fifth Street, I think . . . I've got the address written down somewhere." Weightless little in-jokes like this are scattered throughout the books, like the optional confectioner's sugar on tea cake. Von Ziegesar's hands are never idle.

Of course, the cake itself is of Hostess Twinkie immateriality—the Gossip Girl books are the lightest of light reading. They revolve around the twin desires of von Ziegesar's high school seniors: to have a good time and to get into college. The conflict that might exist between these desires in the real world does not exist in the world of the Gossip Girls. No one ever cracks a book (they are too busy shopping at the three "B's"—Bendel's, Bergdorf's, and Barneys—or working in soup kitchens so that they can say they did on their college applications), and (with one exception, a vicious boy named Chuck Bass, who "could barely spell, had never read a book in its entirety, and thought Beowulf was a type of fur used for lining coats") everyone gets into college. This is not much of a plot, admittedly, but von Ziegesar's impudence invests the dopey activities of her characters with true page-turning interest.

Von Ziegesar uses the technique of narration through interior voice with all her major characters, but when she gets into the id-shaped mind of Blair Waldorf she crosses a kind of boundary. Blair is both a broader caricature and a more real person than the others. Her over-the-top selfishness and hatefulness has the ring of behind-our-masks-we're-all-like-that truth. And among her malevolent internal mutterings lurk some of the series's funniest lines. When her mother marries Cyrus Rose, for example, and proposes that Blair reconsider her refusal to take his name, Blair's inner voice growls back, "*Blair Rose?* No thank you. It sounded like the name of a perfume made especially for Kmart." Her refusal is a rare gesture of defiance. In almost every other respect she is an obedient, even rather docile, child. She is angered and embarrassed by her mother's marriage to the oily Cyrus (and by her pregnancy at forty-seven), but she confines her fury to her thoughts. She is always perfectly civil to Cyrus, who is a perfectly amiable goof. Nor does she kick and scream when her pretty bedroom is requisitioned as a nursery for the baby and she has to move into her stepbrother Aaron's ugly, ecologically correct room (it has a cruelty-free mahogany dresser), which smells so strongly of his dog, Mooky, that Kitty Minky urinates all over the bed in protest. She merely packs a bag and moves into a suite at the Plaza. Have the powerlessness of children and the power of money ever been so nicely fused? The gesture also gives rise to one of the series' best set pieces.

Ensconced at the Plaza, Blair calls Nate and tells him to "get your ass over here right now." Nate agrees, but because he is with friends getting stoned, he quickly forgets about the call. Blair waits and waits. She calls Nate and gets no reply. (He has wandered off to the Battery to sail his father's boat to Bermuda and left his cell phone behind.) Blair is wearing black silk La Perla underwear and has ordered champagne and caviar on toast points. She eats a toast point, then another, and calls her father, Harold Waldorf, in the South of France, "where he'd been living since he and Eleanor split up over his gayness almost two years ago." It is late at night in France, and "Blair could picture him perfectly, naked except for a pair of royal blue silk boxer shorts, his sleeping lover—François or Eduard or whatever his name was—snoring softly beside him."

" 'Bear? Is everything okay? Did you hear from those fuckheads at Yale yet? Are you in?' her father demanded as soon as he heard her voice."

Blair reflects that "talking to her dad was exactly like talking to one of her girlfriends." As she finishes the toast points and begins drinking the champagne, Harold inanely tells her, "You deserve to have it all." She is moved to ask, "If I deserve to have it all, then how come stupid Yale hasn't let me in yet?"

" 'Oh, Bear,' her dad sighed in his manly-but-motherly voice that made both men *and* women fall in love with him instantly. 'They will, dammit. They *will* let you in.' "

I will not give away whether Blair does or doesn't get into Yale. I would like to go on telling Blair stories until they are gone, like the toast points. The platter has barely been touched. But I think I have given enough of an idea of what she and her creator are about. The television series based on the Gossip Girl books was reviewed in *The New Yorker* by Nancy Franklin (November 26, 2007). I completely share Nancy's (or should I say Nanci's?) dim view of the adaptation. It is related to the original only in the names and outlines of the characters. " 'I don't know what I'd do without Barneys.' Serena sighed, as if the store had saved her life." Without von Ziegesar's fast, mocking commentary to propel them, the TV episodes are sluggish and crass—a move from Barneys to Kmart.

Among the many errors that the TV series makes, perhaps the most glaring is its promotion of the books' parents from their status as emblems of parental inadequacy to that of characters in their own right. In the TV version, we are asked to follow the stories of the parents in tandem with the stories of their children: Lillian van der Woodsen and Rufus Humphrey, for one particularly unfortunate example, are thrust into a trite romance. What makes classic children's literature so appealing (to all ages) is its undeviating loyalty to the world of the child. In the best children's books, parents never share the limelight with their children; if they are not killed off on page 1, they are cast in the pitifully minor roles that actual parents play in their children's imaginative lives. That von Ziegesar's parent characters are ridiculous as well as insignificant in the eyes of their children only adds to the sly truthfulness of her comic fairy tale.

THE NOT RETURNING PART OF IT

2007

Maxim Gorky wrote of Chekhov that "in the presence of Anton Pavlovich, everyone felt an unconscious desire to be simpler, more truthful, more himself." The persona that emerges from *Wish I Could Be There: Notes from a Phobic Life,* Allen Shawn's book about his life as a phobic, produces a similar effect. Shawn's writing generates an atmosphere of almost palpable authenticity; one reads the book in a kind of trance of trust, certain that the writer is incapable of pretense and falseness. To learn that he grew up in a household ruled by pretense and falseness is to hear the shoe drop. Yes, of course. Those who have been lied to are especially prone to compulsive truth telling.

Allen Shawn was born into one of those postwar upper-middle-class families where nothing is what it seems. The parents were Jewish—but not really Jewish. The mother was depressed—but always cheerful. A daughter (Allen's twin) was autistic—but not acknowledged to be, and then sent away. The marriage was troubled (the husband had a mistress)—but appearances were kept up. If the family habit of lying gave Allen Shawn his taste for truth, it had less desirable consequences as well. "The secrecy itself and the atmosphere it created are surely relevant to the evolution of my phobias," Shawn writes in a passage about his father's double life (of which he

Wish I Could Be There: Notes from a Phobic Life by Allen Shawn didn't learn until he was almost thirty) and its sometimes comical complexities: "It wasn't uncommon for him to eat, or at least, *attend* four or even five meals a day to accommodate all the important people in his life."

The father, as the reader must know, was William Shawn, the late legendary editor of *The New Yorker*, whose own phobias are part of the legend. When Allen Shawn writes of what he calls his father's "additional partner," he is letting out no family secret. The secret was let out by the partner herself, Lillian Ross, in 1998, when she published a memoir, *Here But Not Here*. The book came as a shock to many people who had known William Shawn. Shawn guarded his privacy as if it were his most precious possession, and Ross's heedless chronicle of their forty-year-long affair (with photographs to buttress her words in case anyone doubted them) seemed an especially brutal violation of trust. Today, fourteen years after Shawn's death, the book reads differently. The waters have closed and Shawn has entered the ranks of the illustrious, unmortifiable dead. Ross's revelations about Shawn's intimate life that seemed distasteful when he was freshly dead now seem merely—interesting. They will be gathered by Shawn's biographers and pasted into some corner of the collage of found scraps that constitutes biographical portraiture. Most important, perhaps, they freed Allen Shawn to speak of the family secret that gave his childhood its phobia-inviting unease. Here is his problem:

> I don't like heights. I don't like being on the water. I am upset by walking across parking lots or open parks or fields where there are no buildings. I tend to avoid bridges, unless they are on a small scale. I respond poorly to stretches of vastness but do equally badly when I am closed in, as I am severely claustrophobic. When I go to a theater, I sit on the aisle. I am petrified of tunnels, making most train travel as well as many drives difficult. I don't take subways. I avoid elevators as much as possible. I experience glassed-in spaces as toxic, and I find it very difficult to adjust to being in buildings in which the windows don't open . . . When I am invited to a new house or apartment or to an event of any kind, my

first reaction is to worry about its location . . . The degree of my self-preoccupation is appalling.

The last sentence underscores Allen Shawn's capacity for detachment. Indeed, his whole book reads as if it were written by a gifted and humane doctor studying a patient who happens to be himself. "What precisely is the matter?" he asks. Shawn suffers from agoraphobia, which is a "more global" condition than simple phobia. (Among the examples he uses to illustrate simple phobia is a woman who was afraid of chicken legs. "Every time she was asked to a party she had to call up and ask, 'You're not serving chicken legs, are you?' The one time she went to a party and there were chicken parts for dinner, she had a huge reaction. She had to be taken to the emergency room.") Agoraphobia is "a restriction of activities brought about by a fear of having panic symptoms in situations in which one is far from help or escape is perceived to be difficult." Allen Shawn's agoraphobia has kept him from going to many places he wanted to go, some of which he even started out for but was unable to reach before panic set in. However, it has not set him back in his career as a composer, pianist, and college professor and may even have been—as it was for his father—a kind of gift.

People who suffer from phobias seem to suffer from a disorder of the imagination. They are afraid when there is nothing to be afraid of. Or is there? As Allen Shawn points out, the world *is* a dangerous place, disaster *may* strike at any moment. The phobic isn't crazy to think that a stretch of lonely road makes him vulnerable to attack. When the horror of death sweeps over a phobic and overwhelms him, he is surely only facing what the rest of us irrationally deny. The almost uncanny rapport that William Shawn was able to establish with his writers derived from his agoraphobia, Allen Shawn believes: "Had he been an inveterate traveler, a doer, or a true extrovert, he would have become too jaded and worldly to maintain the striking innocence and almost infinite receptivity that made him capable of listening so raptly and carefully to what writers had to say."

In its affectionate perspicacity, Allen Shawn's portrait of his father brings to mind Edmund Gosse's portrait of Philip Gosse in *Father and Son*. It will give enormous pleasure to those who knew

William Shawn and felt that Ross's memoir failed to do justice to his sensibility. Writing of the double life, Allen pauses to quietly remark, "It was only double viewed from the outside, of course. To him it was just his life." This capacity for entering into the subjectivity of another (the word "empathy" doesn't convey the difficulty and generosity) separates *Wish I Could Be There* from the usual accusatory memoir of troubled childhood. Allen Shawn writes of his father not as the callous agent of his sufferings, but as a fellow sufferer, to be no less tenderly treated by the attending narrator-physician than he treats himself. He writes of his father's adultery not as a transgression, but as an attempt to cure a loneliness so extreme that no one woman could fill it.

It is known that William Shawn had a troubled relationship with the physical world—that he couldn't stand the sight of blood or to hear about diseases and operations; that he wore warm clothes when the weather was in the nineties; that he was afraid of germs (he "wasn't someone who would taste something from someone else's plate"); that he had many of the phobias his son was to acquire. Allen Shawn doesn't so much add to this picture as render it without the usual subtle contempt.

Shawn writes about his mother with similar affection and compassion. Cecille Shawn had been a reporter at the *Chicago Daily News*, a lively, "ripely attractive girl," when she and William Shawn met, in the 1920s. "They were intellectual equals, with my mother being the tougher, more practical, and more experienced of the two," he writes. But after marriage Cecille abandoned her career and, over time, succumbed to an unacknowledged depression. The death of her first baby and a later miscarriage, the husband's affair, and the daughter's mental impairment all contributed to a gradual sad diminishment. In a passage about his mother's face, Allen's metaphoric point is almost too obvious:

> Like many women of her day, I suppose, she considered putting on makeup before seeing anyone to be practically a religious commandment. She called this colorful mask her face, as in "I need to put my face on." When I was small, I was fascinated by the sophisticated and wonderfully hard-boiled

look her features had when unadorned. To me, this highly intelligent, older-looking, more complex face was her real one, and I used to try to encourage her to leave off the makeup once in a while. She wouldn't.

She couldn't. The Shawns needed to deny harsh realities and paper over unpleasant ones. It was evidently not pleasant to be Jewish. "Being Jewish was also a matter for some distant uneasiness, at least enough for it to be fun for my brother to begin a dining table discussion, 'Well, we Jews . . .'" (The mischievous brother is Wallace Shawn, the playwright and actor, who is five years older than Allen and was a kindly, protective presence throughout Allen's childhood.) On the matter of the family's Jewphobia, Allen Shawn cannot resist a dig at his father: "When a minister friend of my brother's visited the house and said a prayer at Thanksgiving dinner, he was deeply moved, but it is hard to picture him being as moved if the friend had been a rabbi."

Sex was another difficult subject. Shawn is very funny about his father's attempt to provide sex education:

Before I left for music camp at thirteen, my father told me that I might encounter an activity called masturbation while I was there, but he looked as if he might be about to commit suicide after our conversation . . . I know now that he must have been afraid of handling it the wrong way and scarring me for life. He was incapable of saying, "I have done this myself"; it had to be "we" or "it" or "one" ("It's perfectly normal . . ."). In an effort to be tactful, he managed to imply that the concept of masturbation was sure to be new to me. This reinforced my shame about pleasures already taken.

Wish I Could Be There is an oddly structured book. The autobiographical writing is interspersed with chapters—that have some of the flavor of school reports—on the clues that evolutionary biology, brain anatomy, and Freudian psychology, among other disciplines, might offer to the enigma of phobia. But the clues remain clues, the enigma remains an enigma, and as we read, we notice that the book is circling back on itself rather than moving forward. Allen Shawn acknowledges his nonlinear approach with his subtitle *Notes from a Phobic Life*. But the subtitle may be more than a disclaimer—the double meaning of the word "notes" (fittingly enough) may point to a musical model for the book's organization. Like the recapitulations of themes in music, Shawn's obsessive returns to already dealt with subjects have a quality of intentionality, even of inevitability.

The subject that he returns to most often and that comes closer than anything else to answering the question "What precisely is the matter?" is Mary, his autistic twin, whose strange nature and disruptive behavior became too painful for the parents, and who was put in a home at the age of eight. "I often wonder what would have happened to her if she had been born into the—then rare—type of family that could have more resourcefully incorporated her into their routine," Shawn writes. But, more to the point of his book, what would have happened to *him*? "Mary's 'exile' demonstrated that one could be turned out of the house for being too difficult to handle or understand, for being too inefficient mentally, or for being too wild. This added yet another layer of mystification to an already fairly mystifying atmosphere."

To avoid Mary's "punishment," Allen cultivated the role of the preternaturally "good" child, who never gave trouble and was always reasonable and agreeable—a role that he has carried into adult life, and into his literary persona. But he believes that there is "something false" about this persona and that "my better, darker music represents something truer about me; it is way ahead of the rest of me," he writes. "In music I could be wild, aggressive, irreverent, and unpredictable; in life I shunned behavior that would remind me of the chaos of Mary's mind."

It is as his twin that Mary casts her deepest shadow on Allen's life. He records his memory of being in a crib parallel to hers, rocking in time to her rocking. He knows how unlikely such an early memory is, but cannot shake its force. He writes of Mary as his first love, and associates the experience of sleeping next to her in infancy with adult sexual happiness. He writes of the "grief, loneliness, guilt, bewilderment, rage, disillusionment, shock, the sense of having been betrayed by my parents, and, perhaps, also relief" he felt when Mary disappeared. Finally, in a stunning tour de force of interpretation, he draws a parallel between her autism and his agoraphobia:

> I can't help noticing that she, like me, is subject to "attacks," lives within a fixed routine, resists even minute changes from what she expects, is extremely limited in her ability to travel. She is institutionalized, I am out here, "free" and "functioning"; yet I have managed to build some invisible walls around myself. I have remained her "twin," finding ways to make my life parallel to hers.

Shawn writes of a recent journey he forced himself to make to Mary's institution in Delaware. He started out once and had to turn back. When he tried again a week later, he woke up dizzy and nauseated, and did his laundry. Finally he got on the road and repeatedly felt an impulse, "coming with the force of the cargo in the hold of a ship lurching to the opposite side of the boat," to turn back. He managed to reach the motel where he had booked a room to break up the trip—and where something extraordinary happened to him: "I had an unexpected mental image, like a waking dream. I saw Mary before me, and I slapped her. 'How could you put me through this?' I was yelling. 'How could you?' In my imagination she burst into tears, baffled, and said my name, and said, 'What are you doing, Allen? That's not nice, Allen,' and I cried, and she cried . . ."

The author of the waking dream was clearly Allen's wild, aggressive, irreverent, unpredictable self—and this self is not absent from the book that the nice self is writing. The "good" self set out to write a book about his phobias and phobia in general, but the "bad" self ensured that the book would defy the conventions of its genre and become a "better, darker" thing. As Allen Shawn circles his mysterious putative subject, he is drawn to the mysteries that everyone who thinks bumps up against. When he writes about the death anxiety he experienced as a child—lying terrified in the dark at the thought that "there was no help, that my parents could not help me, and that there was no escape from the fact of it, not even some special hint of a way out that might just apply to me"—he is hardly describing thinking exclusive to phobics. Many—perhaps most—normal children and adolescents are terrified, if not traumatized, by the idea of mortality. Shawn returns to the subject in a poetic passage that suddenly and for no apparent reason floats into a late chapter and takes on the weight of a vatic message:

> Life's unknowns are often knowable; many can be rehearsed or at least imagined. But death is surrounded by an infinite fog on an ocean without end. It is perhaps simplistic to say it, but one can understand death only in terms of its opposite, life. For me, it was always the not returning part of it that made me start up in the dark, suffocating. Yet after my father, who had never even ridden on an airplane, disappeared into that fog, it began to take on other meanings, and I began to dimly see that the not returning part of it is there with us all along, inside us, from the moment we appear into the bewildering new stimuli of the world, even from the moment we start to form out of the fertilized ovum. Now that my mother is gone, it is clearer still. There is only forward motion, and there always was only forward motion. There was never any turning back.

When Allen finally reaches his sister at her institution, he feels "an indefinable emotion, essential, yet as colorless as water" and "a sense of wholeness, a kind of relaxation response." Mary no longer has "the almost porcelain prettiness and look of utter normality" she had as a child. She is a middle-aged woman who has been medicated for a long time and has an atmosphere of abnormality. But "being with her locates the source of a strange feeling I carry around with me everywhere. I wouldn't be myself without her." Moreover, "she exudes an essence of personality uncannily reminiscent of my father's and brother's." Allen's own essence, as it wafts out of his book, has a similar uncanny evocativeness. The editor, the playwright, and the essayist are bound by a thread of—what? Is the word "innocence"? Allen uses it to describe his father's capacity for listening to writers, in opposition to the word "jaded." The writing of both Wallace and Allen Shawn has, as the conversation of William Shawn had, a rare quality of cleanness—as if it came from a spring rather than from the stale pool of received ideas that most talk and writing comes from. Such purity would be chastening were it not accompanied by a playfulness that takes away the sting and puts in a kind of good word for us all.

WILLIAM SHAWN

1992

Every encounter with William Shawn was a somewhat mystifyingly intense experience. You left his presence as you leave a play or a film that has taken you out of your own life and plunged you into a world that is more vivid, coherent, and *interesting* than the real world. Shawn was a great teacher, and the lesson he taught—the lesson every great teacher teaches—was the lesson of himself. He was the model and emblem of the uncorrupted intellect. T. S. Eliot's famous description of Henry James—"He had a mind so fine that no idea could violate it"—could be a description of William Shawn. He never said anything that wasn't profoundly intelligent and utterly intelligible. We, his students, without ever presuming to imitate him, tried to be like him in our work. We sought to eliminate from our writing the pretentiousness, intellectual shallowness, moral murkiness, and aesthetic limpness that come naturally to the pen. He was our beacon in a treacherous terrain. The thought of him ultimately reading what we had written both slowed us down and gave us courage to continue. The slowing down was the important thing. Shawn knew—and we knew he knew—that writing is a process that can't be hurried, and that each piece has its natural, sometimes preposterously long term. He taught us to be patient, and to trust our material. He had the gaiety and the playfulness that all deeply serious people have. He was an enchanting person and an Enchanter. He was our Mr. Chips and our Prospero. We have missed him and we will always miss him.

JOSEPH MITCHELL

1996

There is a remarkable passage in *Huckleberry Finn* about a circus act in which twenty bareback riders, "resting their hands on their thighs, easy and comfortable," as Huck reports, enter the ring, then rise to standing positions on the horses' backs and, as the horses go faster and faster around the ring, execute a series of effortless dance steps. I thought of this scene (an account of true, as opposed to sham, aesthetic experience) while trying to think of some way to describe the effect Joe Mitchell's writing produced on his students—as my generation of nonfiction writers at *The New Yorker* have always thought of ourselves. Joe's feat—which looked so effortless that some reviews of his books actually condescended to him—was so far beyond what anyone could do that it inspired no envy; it simply inspired. As listening to Mozart is widely known to be a cure for flagging creativity, so reading Mitchell has been famous among writers as a remedy for stuckness. After reading a few of Joe's easy and comfortable sentences (about matters of life and death), one would blush for the flaccidity and pretentiousness of one's own efforts; Joe's work forced one to take more risks and put on fewer airs.

Joe himself progressively risked more and more. As his pieces got more complex and profound, they took longer to write. In 1964, after writing his masterpiece, *Joe Gould's Secret*, he undertook a work so labyrinthine and deep that at his death it was still not finished. Much has been made of the fact that Joe didn't publish anything for thirty years. To his friends this was not remarkable; it was simply another sign of Joe's seriousness about writing. During his period of patient struggle with unimaginably daunting artistic problems, Joe retained the gaiety, charm, and lovableness of his days on the lower slopes of literature. If there was an unkind word ever spoken about Joe, the person who uttered it must have been mad or thinking of someone else.

THOUGHTS ON
AUTOBIOGRAPHY FROM
AN ABANDONED AUTOBIOGRAPHY

2010

I have been aware, as I write this autobiography, of a feeling of boredom with the project. My efforts to make what I write interesting seem pitiful. My hands are tied, I feel. I cannot write about myself as I write about the people I have written about as a journalist. To these people I have been a kind of amanuensis: they have dictated their stories to me and I have retold them. They have posed for me and I have drawn their portraits. No one is dictating to me or posing for me now.

Memory is not a journalist's tool. Memory glimmers and hints, but shows nothing sharply or clearly. Memory does not narrate or render character. Memory has no regard for the reader. If an autobiography is to be even minimally readable, the autobiographer must step in and subdue what you could call memory's autism, its passion for the tedious. He must not be afraid to invent. Above all, he must invent himself. Like Rousseau, who wrote (at the beginning of his novelistic *Confessions*) that "I am not made like anyone I have ever been acquainted with, perhaps like no one in existence," he must sustain, in spite of all evidence to the contrary, the illusion of his preternatural extraordinariness.

Since one of the occupational hazards of journalism is the atrophying (from disuse) of the journalist's powers of invention, the journalist who sets out to write an autobiography has more of an uphill fight than other practitioners of the genre. When one's work has been all but done—as mine has been for more than a quarter of a century—by one brilliant self-inventive collaborator after another, it isn't easy to suddenly find oneself alone in the room. It is particularly hard for someone who probably became a journalist precisely because she didn't want to find herself alone in the room.

Another obstacle in the way of the journalist turned autobiographer is the pose of objectivity into which journalists habitually, almost mechanically, fall when they write. The "I" of journalism is a kind of ultra-reliable narrator and impossibly rational and disinterested person, whose relationship to the subject more often than not resembles the relationship of a judge pronouncing sentence on a guilty defendant. This "I" is unsuited to autobiography. Autobiography is an exercise in self-forgiveness. The observing "I" of autobiography tells the story of the observed "I" not as a journalist tells the story of his subject, but as a mother might. The older narrator looks back at his younger self with tenderness and pity, empathizing with its sorrows and allowing for its sins. I see that my journalist's habits have inhibited my self-love. Not only have I failed to make my young self as interesting as the strangers I have written about, but I have withheld my affection. In what follows I will try to see myself less coldly, be less fearful of writing a puff piece. But it may be too late to change my spots.

CPSIA information can be obtained
at www.ICGtesting.com
Printed in the USA
LVHW042030090523
746524LV00004B/116

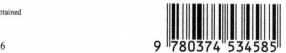